THE JEWISH DESIGN FOR LIVING

THE JEWISH DESIGN FOR LIVING

by

S. M. LEHRMAN

M.A. (Cantab.), Ph.D. (Lond.)
Tyrwhitt Scholar, Cambridge
Formerly Lecturer in Homiletics, Jews' College
Rabbi, New Synagogue, London

והודעת להם את־הדרך ילכו בה ואת־המעשה אשר יעשון

*"And thou shalt show them the way wherein they must walk, and
the work that they must do"* (Ex. xviii. 20).

LONDON
BACHAD FELLOWSHIP
1951

Printed by Page & Thomas Ltd., Chesham
and bound by Novello & Co. Ltd., London, W.1

ERRATA

Page 11. The Hebrew in note 16, at the foot of the page should read

כל־המרחם על־הבריות בידוע שהוא מזרעו של אברהם אבינו

Page 66. Read דבר שהוא שׁוֹעַ טָוּוּי וְגוֹז

Page 130. The No. 43 should be in word *Turim*, not in *Asher*.

Page 213. The No. 81 should accompany the reference to the N.T. in *last* line of the page.

Page 237. The year should be 1950 in last line of note 60.

Page 240. Note 83 should read

טוב למיתה תך דו מלמיתה ארמלתה

Page 273. Note 116 should read

אין אדם נוקף אצבעו מלמטה אלא א״כ מכריזין עליו מלמעלה

Page 280. Note 143 should read

מעשיך יקרבוך ומעשיך ירחקוך

Page 291. The last words of note 50 should read thus:
(Rashi *ad locum*).

Page 335. The quotation at the head of Appendix I should read " Know then thyself," etc.

CONTENTS

PREFACE BY THE AUTHOR vii

INTRODUCTION BY THE REV. DR. A. COHEN,
M.A., PH.D., D.H.L. xi

BOOK ONE: AN HISTORICAL PERSPECTIVE

I.   JUDAISM ETHICALLY PRESENTED 3
II. ETHICAL JUDAISM COMPARED WITH OTHER
     BELIEFS 17
III. ETHICAL TEACHINGS IN THE BIBLE .. 32
IV. ETHICS IN THE TALMUD 52
V.   ETHICS IN MEDIEVAL TIMES 83
VI. ETHICS IN MODERN TIMES 111

BOOK TWO: APPLIED ETHICS

VII. OUR APPROACH TO GOD 143
VIII. WHAT HIS FAITH MEANS TO THE JEW .. 168
IX.   OUR SOCIAL ETHICS 195
X.   ETHICS OF EVERY DAY 225
XI.   ETHICAL INSTRUMENTS IN CHARACTER
      BUILDING 255
XII. PHYSICAL AND SPIRITUAL WELFARE .. 285
XIII. A RETROSPECTIVE SURVEY 315

APPENDICES

I. THE JEWISH CONCEPTION OF MAN .. 335
II. WHAT IS JUDAISM ? 349

INDEX 367

CONTENTS

PREFACE vii

INTRODUCTION xi

PART ONE: INCEPTION AL EXPERIENCE

I. 1

II. . . . .

III. . . . .

IV. . . . .

V. . . . .

VI. 111

PART TWO: SPIRITUAL LIFE

VII. . . . .

VIII. 195

IX. . . . .

X. . . . .

XI. . . . .

XII. . . . .

XIII. . . . .

APPENDICES

I. . . . .

II. . . . .

INDEX . . . .

PREFACE

IT is common knowledge that the *last* thing an author does when his book is finished is to write the Preface which appears *first*. In a book on Ethics, this thought is significant. Those who occupy the exalted places in our midst are not always those who merit them most. Rank cannot therefore always be a measure of inherent value. One Talmudic Rabbi, who was said to have been afforded during a serious illness a glimpse of Heaven, reported to his father that there he had seen the very reverse of what was the usual spectacle on earth. For those who were at the bottom rung of the ladder here, were on top there; and *vice versa*. This should cheer many a foot-sore pilgrim chafing at the unfairness rampant around him on this earth.

The object of this Preface, however, is not to moralize, but to recall the concluding words of Dr. Samuel Johnson to his Introduction to the English dictionary he compiled. Here they are: "*In this work, when it shall be found that much is omitted, let it not be forgotten that much is likewise performed. It may repress the triumph of malignant criticism to observe that, if our language is not here fully displayed, I have only failed in an attempt which no human powers have hitherto completed.*" Some of these words can be equally applied to the work now before the reader, a work which craves judgment not so much on what it has failed to achieve, but on that which it has, I hope, performed; namely, to present a popular, if not a scholarly, digest of Jewish moral teachings and to weave a colourful picture of the Jewish design for living.

Jewish ethics present before us a life that is real and a world that is full of *living* things. With this presentation is issued a challenge: either to serve mankind, or destroy it; either to be bent only on getting as much out of life as possible, or on putting more into life than we found therein. The ideal Jew realizes that there is only one choice—the latter. He cannot, from an ethical standpoint, live for himself alone. He must prove his affinity with the rest of humanity by his spiritual relationship to it.

In the pages of this book, I have tried to show that man testifies to what he *is* by what he *does;* showing by his readiness to serve others the vigour of his own religious faith. That part in him, the soul—where Heaven meets earth—will teach him that Judaism is translated into life only when it has inspired him to be thoughtful in word, and responsible in action. Not to have achieved this state of perfection is to have missed the essential purpose of the Torah-true life.

*   *   *

This prefatory note must conclude with feelings of deep-felt gratitude to my life-long friend, Dr. Geo. J. Webber, LL.D., for once again trying to purge these pages from some floridness of style—a failing to which the author readily admits. His help in all my literary effort is a debt which I can never hope adequately to repay; but his reward is shared with mine in helping to spread a knowledge of Judaism. I must also thank Dr. A. Cohen for his stimulating introduction to this work. To my friend, David Hudaly, of Liverpool, my thanks are due for reading the proofs so carefully. Finally, in appreciation of the Bachad Fellowship which has invited me to write this book and which is responsible for its publication, I have decided to dedicate these pages to its noble work in preparing Anglo-Jewish youth to take its proper share in the upbuilding of Israel.

S. M. LEHRMAN.

London, 1951.

INTRODUCTION

THE author of this volume has previously enriched Anglo-Jewish literature with several works which aimed at a presentation in attractive form of the rites and practices which distinguish traditional Judaism. The present work may be regarded as a desirable and necessary supplement. The history of religion amply illustrates how the performance of ceremonies not infrequently degenerates into an automatic act and comes to be considered an end in itself. Worse still, as the denunciations of the Hebrew prophets so forcefully reveal, religion may be debased into nothing more than a punctilious observance of rites to the exclusion of the morality which they are intended to teach.

After describing and expounding the numerous religious practices enjoined by Judaism, Dr. Lehrman logically proceeds in this volume to lay bare the ethical foundations upon which the Jewish Faith rests. With an abundance of quotations from the classical sources—Bible and Talmud—he demonstrates how prominent is the place occupied by moral principles in Jewish doctrine which has as its purpose the regulation of "the good life".

Incidentally, the volume is a refutation of the appraisal of Judaism as a religion of the letter and the Halachah as deadening the spirit. Such a misconception, to be expected of those who understand Torah merely as "law", has unfortunately spread within the Jewish ranks. The picture of the Talmudic Rabbis as hair-splitting casuists whose minds were concentrated upon the elaboration of laws is here shown to be a caricature. By a host of illustrations the author proves that these teachers were, at least in equal measure, ardent exponents of the ethical and spiritual aspects of religion.

True to tradition, Dr. Lehrman argues that Judaism is "a design for living". Such has always been its aim. It offers its adherents direction how to conduct their life in all its phases. One of its finest features is the insistence that Torah must govern the whole field of human activity, declining to draw a sharp line of demarcation between what comes under the auspices of religion and what may be excluded therefrom. In this sense it refuses to attach the label "secular" to any department of life, whether individual or corporate. On the contrary, it demands that what is commonly regarded as "secular" must be hallowed by the spirit of religion; then only can the varied interests of man be directed to his own and the common good.

These are some of the main thoughts which stand out boldly in the author's exposition of his subject. In the matter of presentation, this volume has the same characteristics as its predecessors. Dr. Lehrman avoids the formal style of the secluded scholar who writes for the eye of the reader, substituting for it the more animated and rhetorical diction of the lecturer or preacher. He thinks of his readers as an audience of men and women to whom he addresses himself in a heart-to-heart talk. His method imparts to his writing a liveliness and warmth which will make his new book, like his others, acceptable to a wide circle.

A. COHEN.

BOOK ONE:
AN HISTORICAL PERSPECTIVE

CHAPTER ONE

JUDAISM ETHICALLY PRESENTED

I. MAN NOT CREATED PERFECT

WHEN God created man, He left the task of moral perfection to man himself. That is why the divine refrain *"And He saw that it was good"* that accompanies the other acts of Creation which sprang into life at the *fiat* of God, is significantly omitted when man was shaped in the likeness of his Creator. For though the first chapter of Genesis concludes the six days of Creation with *"And God saw everything that He had made, and behold it was very good"*, this approval seems to be of the work in general, and not specifically of man. In fact, man is described a few chapters later (viii. 21) as possessing *"from his youth, an evil inclination"*. In this steep climb towards nobility, the ethics of Judaism, as presented in belief and action, will serve as competent guides. To help man in his aim of becoming spiritually perfect, the Torah has outlined the unique design for living which we call Judaism.

The purpose of this book is to show that, provided the effort is conscientious and unflagging, man *can* accomplish this perfection. No miracle, no sacrament, no vicarious saviour can achieve for him only what his own efforts in this direction can. It all depends on the manner of his translation of his affirmation into action, a power of which he usually is the master. *"For the word is very nigh unto thee: it is in thy mouth and heart to do it"* (Deut. xxx. 14). What singles out the Jewish way of life as unique is its sane, balanced approach and outlook on life. Both the Bible and the Talmud—not to mention our medieval and modern writers on Judaism—lay greater stress on purity of motive and ethical conduct than upon ceremonial practice and ritual observance, essential as these are as aids to and reminders of the higher life upon which they flash a beacon of light. Zechariah, long ago, announced to mankind the supremacy of the spirit over force and the cataclysm of war: "*Not by might, nor by power, but My spirit, saith the Lord of Hosts*" (Zech. iv. 6). Two wars in the space of two decades have corroborated this prophetic utterance. These tragic lapses of a civilization that had been boastfully heralded as the solution of most of human ills, have shown that the categorical moral law of the universe is as ineluctable as its physical laws. To ignore either set of rules is to court disaster. It would seem that the best commentary on the Bible is that written by Time itself.

In this search for security of existence and peace of mind, man will find the Jewish design for living invaluable. Fighter-planes and battleships, guns and bombs, atomic warfare and diplomatic statecraft may have their part to play in the political and economic sphere in the comity of nations; but they will not help man in his quest for holiness and happiness. On the contrary, the placing of complete trust in these weapons of war becomes eventually a decisive menace to the peace of the world— a boomerang which wounds the victors no less than the vanquished, leaving both panting for breath when the struggle is over. Through one way only can the individual or nation enter the realm of peace and plenty: that is, through ethical conduct illumined by a vision of truth and justice, as revealed by Judaism in its Biblical and post-Biblical sources. The Rabbis conveyed this warning graphically: "The Book and the Sword descended into the world together". Judaism advises us to cast away the sword and meditate in the Book day and night.

Colourful as is the spectacle of divergent opinion within our communal ranks in its interpretation of Judaism and its mission to mankind, general agreement exists on one point. This is: that true faith is grounded on ethical conduct; that the *real* Jew is he who models his earthly life after the heavenly pattern revealed on Sinai. To *do* good is not so important as to *be* good. For whereas the performance of a noble act may not necessarily reflect the motive behind it, the fact that one is, by nature, good means that he is not capable of any mean act. Motive is a vital factor in Jewish ethics.

II. HOW TO BECOME PERFECT

The mainspring of ethical Judaism is its insistence upon man to carve out his life on the lines delineated for him in the Torah. Prefacing that succinct summary of Jewish teachings and responsibilities outlined in the nineteenth chapter of Leviticus, is the divine declaration: "*Ye shall be holy, for I, the Lord, your God, am holy*". This idea of imitative holiness (*Imitatio Dei*) has provided the Jew with the loftiest motives for perfection, and has supplied him with a powerful incentive towards a sublime conception of life and its purpose. It was to help man in this laudable effort at perfection that the six hundred and thirteen precepts were given; precepts which will help him to steer clear of the temptations to slide from the path of virtue that strew life's road. Ethical Judaism helps man to retain the impress of divinity in his bearing. Its application to life is measured by the compliance with its behests.

In Judaism, God is regarded as transcendental: "*The heavens belong to God: it is the earth that He has given to the children of men*" (Ps. cxv. 16). He is, however, also immanent in that He has prescribed guidance on every aspect of life, intimate and public, holy and secular. All those qualities that should be most pronounced in human conduct are made to appear conspicuously in our description of the heavenly attributes. Here is a typical presentation of ethical Judaism in the Talmud.[1] "Rabbi Hama, son of Rabbi Hanina, said "What means the text *'Ye shall walk after the Lord your God'?*[2] Is it, then, possible for a human being to walk after the *Shechinah*? Has it not been said: *'For the Lord thy God is a devouring fire'?*[3] But (the meaning is) to walk after the attributes of the Holy One, blessed be He." As He clothes the naked, for it is written: "*And the Lord God made for Adam and for his wife garments of skin, and clothed them*",[4] so do thou also clothe the naked. God visited the sick, for it is written: "*And the Lord appeared unto him by the oaks of Mamre*",[5] so do thou also visit the sick. He comforted the mourners, for it is written: "*And it came to pass after the death of Abraham, that God blessed Isaac his son*";[6] so do thou also comfort the mourners. The Holy One, blessed be He, buried the dead, for it is written: "*And He buried him in the valley*";[7] so do thou also bury the dead.

III. THE IMPORTANCE OF MOTIVE

Throughout the ages, this conscious effort to imitate God and walk in His ways has proved a spur to righteous-

[1] Sotah 14ᵃ.
[2] Deut. xiii. 5.
[3] Ibid. iv. 24.
[4] Gen. iii. 21.
[5] Ibid. xviii. 1.   Since the preceding verses deal with Abraham's circumcision, it is deduced that the occasion was when he was recovering.
[6] Gen. xxv. 11.
[7] Deut. xxxiv. 6.

ness. The Rabbinic conception of the Messianic era is not so much of a World to Come, but of a Moral Order in which Truth, Justice and Holiness may reign supreme and undisturbed among the comity of nations. The blue-prints for this ideal era are to be found in our ethical teachings, whose objective is not to uproot or stifle instincts which are, in their essence, natural and human, but to guide these instincts aright so that they become the means of preserving and promoting the welfare of man-kind. Far from being regarded as an intrusion into our inner life, or as an imposition on our public activity, the ethical teachings of Judaism seek to regulate our motives and deeds, to help us to acquire a truer standard of values which will make life more purposeful and contentful.

It is the thoughts we think daily—from the moment we awake from refreshing sleep until labour's task has been done and we are ready to retire for the night—that shape our lives and control our health and happiness. Our thoughts are the one thing we cannot escape; they accom-pany us everywhere. As a tree is known by the fruit it bears, so shall we be judged by the opinions to which we give expression, especially in our unguarded moments. That is why the integrity of motive and sincerity of thought (*Kavanah*) play such a great part in Judaism, when it is ethically presented. Let our thoughts be happy, our actions constructive, our motives *"in the name of heaven"*,[8] and they will enrich the heart, elevate the mind, and sweep away lust and unworthy feelings, as the wind chases from the tree or the ground the fallen, sere leaf. Angry thoughts rush through the soul like a storm through a city; pleasant thoughts warm the soul as the sun warms the earth, kissing into loveliness the sleeping beauties of nature like some Prince Charming.

Complete control of our all-pervasive thoughts will be

[8] *Leshem Shamayim:* see Abot ii. 17.

possible, says Judaism, if life be spent in the consciousness that an "*all-seeing Eye*" watches all action, private as well as public.[9] This omnipresent consciousness of the Presence of God (*Shechinah*) moved our ancestors to piety and spurred them on to an heroism which was often sealed by martyrdom (*Kiddush Ha'shem*). The mystic it excited to emotional exhilaration, the medieval philosopher to unbounded admiration. Its effect on the ordinary man was to make him transmute the commonplace and the humdrum into the eternal and the imponderable. No belief this, cold and aloof, but one which has, in ways most glorious, manifested itself throughout our history.

This knowledge of the immanence of God, in all His affairs, exhorted the ideal Jew to strive for unity and for friendship with those around him. His heavenly Father he regarded as a Unity, brooking no outside interference with his monotheistic belief. To remind him of this Unity, the Jew is asked to recite the *Shema* solemnly at least twice daily. Not until one is singled out for his genial disposition and generous nature; not until one acts as feet to the lame and eyes to the blind; not until one succeeds in lessening human suffering and kindling the star of hope in darkening skies, can one be said to have woven the moral demands of his faith into everyday life. Only then will he emerge from the process as the perfect Jew, bearing on his face the image of the divine likeness.

IV. THE LETTER AND THE SPIRIT

Jewish Ethics brook no cleavage between the form and the content of a divine command. Both are essential to

---

[9] Abot ii. 1. "*Reflect upon three things, and thou wilt not come within the power of sin: Know what is above thee—a seeing eye, and a hearing ear, and that all thy deeds are written in a book.*"

each other as the body is to the soul. A verse in Proverbs[10] may serve as an illustration: *"For the precept is a lamp; but the Torah is a light"*. The purpose of our ceremonial observance could not have been expressed more convincingly or more graphically. The lamp is the receptacle which holds the oil; the light is diffused by the flaming wick. Just as there can be no light if it be unfed by oil, so can there be no spiritual faith unless the mechanics of Judaism—its ceremonies—are meticulously regarded. All men need these reminders and sign-posts if they are not occasionally to lose their way in their quest of the holy life;[11] for *"There is no man so righteous on earth that he doeth good and sinneth not"*.[12] True to this belief, our great figures in the Torah are depicted not as unapproachable paragons of immaculate virtue, whom to emulate would be idle, but as frail mortals who used their occasional lapses as stepping-stones to a nobler existence. In this frank admission, Jewish ethics are seen at their finest. The Jew is taught to be not *"all things to all men"*, but to be loyal to his religion and devoted to the cause of humanity.

An interesting episode in the life of Rabbi Israel Lipkin (Salanter), the founder of the *Musar* (ethical) school in the *Yeshivot*, that were once the glory of Russian and Polish Jewry, comes to our mind in this connection. When he was criticized for diverting students from their Talmudic studies by the introduction of these seemingly extraneous subjects, the reply he gave deserves to be better known. "When a man has before him two loaves of bread, one larger than the other, but already broken into; the other smaller, but whole, the prescription of the Law (*Din*) is

---

[10] vi. 23.
[11] See the writer's "Jewish Folklore and Customs", 1950.
[12] See the Memorial Prayer recited in the House of Mourning, Singer's Prayer Book, pp. 323-324.

that Grace before Meals be recited over the complete loaf (see Ber. 39[b]). Similarly, Judaism prefers perfection of character, even if the Talmudic learning be of a smaller compass, rather than the parading of much knowledge without a corresponding, far-sighted attitude towards life." This view-point reminds one of the claim made by a teacher of English literature for his subject:[13]"Literature is a nurse of noble natures, and right reading maketh a full man, in a sense even better than Bacon's, not *replete* but *complete*, rather to the pattern for which Heaven designed him." Both the letter and spirit of Jewish observances are necessary for the carving of the ideal Jewish character. "*And see that thou make them after their pattern, which is being shown thee on the mount.*"[14]

V. OUR ANSWER TO DETRACTORS

The implementation of our ethical system into the life of the nation has made a decisive contribution towards the survival of Israel. Moreover, the fact that, persecuted for its idealism, the Jewish people barred feelings of hatred from colouring its prayers or souring its outlook on life, is evidence of its potency. Judaism not only ceaselessly *preached* that "God is Love",[15] but has unwaveringly *practised* its corollary in dispensing kindness towards all, within and without its ranks. To the Jew, God is the creative and the moral force of the universe, the power that makes for righteousness. The Torah is the reservoir for his spiritual invincibility, with its eternal message of love for all and malice towards none. According

[13]Sir Arthur Quiller Couch in his inaugural lecture "On the Art of Writing" (Cambridge University Press).
[14]Ex. xxv. 40.
[15]Sanhed 106[b]: "The Holy One, blessed be He, requires the service of the heart."

to a Talmudic sage:[16] "He who has no compassion on
those whom God has created, forfeits his claim of being
a descendant of Abraham".

It has just been mentioned that the suffering inflicted
on the Jew by a hostile world did not warp his relationship with his fellow-men. This is true, on the whole; but
it would be expecting too much of human nature to find
no vestige at all in our literature of the demoralizing
effects produced by prolonged torture. Only angels do
not retaliate; and Jews are not angels. These traces are,
however, limited. When they do occur, they can easily
be accounted for. On the whole, however, it would be
true to say that the tempestuous waves of hatred have
lashed their fury in vain against the Jewish plan for
living. The mud flung at our teachings has contaminated
only those who flung it. The Jew has always purified
himself at the water of the Torah. Just as the caravan rolls
on, though the dogs bark after it, so has Judaism marched
on towards the light which shone for him out of the
pages of his holy heritage. *"When thou passest through the
waters, I will be with thee, and through the rivers, they shall
not overflow thee; when thou walkest through the fire, thou
shalt not be burned, neither shall the flame kindle upon thee.
For I am the Lord thy God, the Holy One of Israel, thy
Saviour."*[17]

Judaism has so often been depicted as a tribal faith,
over which a *jealous* God held cruel sway, that to come
across a study in which our religion will be ethically
presented in all its beauty and power, will possess the
same exhilarating effect for the reader as that felt by the
visitor to an over-heated sick-room when he emerges into
the bracing air of the heath. This aim has spurred the

[16]Bez. 32[b], Sabb. 151[b].
א״א של כל־המרחם על־הבריות בידוע שהוא מזרעו
[17]Isa. xliii. 2-3.

writer of this book. Far from being parochial in its outlook, Judaism is universal in its sweep. Which other faith can boast of a prophet who advised his people in exile to pray for the peace of the nation in whose midst they dwell,[18] though they were still smarting from the crucible of persecution and the baptism of fire from which they had but recently emerged? In the words of a Jewish scholar:[19] "While the Christian oppressed the Jew, because he deemed the act pleasing to his God, the Jew was deterred by the fear of the disapproval of God from revenging himself upon the Christian. To wrong the Gentile, in the smallest particular, was to be distinctly guilty of *Hillul Ha'shem*. All medieval moralists enforce this lesson upon their readers time and again." All thoughts of retaliation are alien to the Torah-true Jew who is advised by his faith not to be elated when another is dejected, or dejected when another is praised. "*When thine enemy falleth, rejoice not: neither let thy heart be glad, when he stumbleth.*"[20]

"What happened to their ancestors", says a Midrash, "will also happen to their descendants."[21] Just as Jacob, at Peniel, wrested a blessing from his unknown assailant after prevailing over him,[22] so did his descendants emerge from their chequered history ennobled and hopeful, without the iron of cruelty having entered their own attitude towards life. Tirelessly, did Jewish ethical precepts inculcate gentleness and humility, a love of peace and a passion for justice, so that the temporary resentment on the part of the Jew towards those who hated and baited him gave way to a co-operative relationship at the slightest display of tolerance towards him.

[18]Jer. xxix. 7.
[19]Dr. Guedemann, "Culturgeschichte", Vol. 1, p. 150.
[20]Prov. xxiv. 17.
[21]מה שאירע לאבות אירע לבנים
[22]Gen. xxxii. 32.

He was obedient to his codes of honour, because these bore the impress of divinity on their surface and in their content, and because these were regarded as the direct communications of a heavenly Father to His children on earth. To be disobedient to them, would be interpreted as an insult to Him who had declared that the sole purpose of human existence is to hallow every aspect of life. It is this sanctification of life, this consciousness that goodness in thought and deed links man with heaven and is worthy of sacrifice, great and small, that made the ideal Jewish ethical life the *summum bonum*, the target, of Judaism. The ideal Jew became "*a partner with God in the work of Creation*",[23] by implementing his beliefs in the world of action.

VI. THE IDEAL JEW

The ideal Jew must be neither a cynic nor a sycophant; but one happy and triumphant in his faith, pursuing virtue and peace, shrinking from doing anything in private of which he would be ashamed in public. Insincerity, dishonesty, corruption, will all be *taboo* to him —so many guises of *Hillul Ha'shem* to be shunned at all costs. Accordingly, he will be modest and sincere in all his dealings, avoiding, even in thought, all dalliance with sin and eschewing the breath of suspicion. How can he harbour lewd or dishonest thoughts if God sees the heart? He will, therefore, avoid such acts or thoughts that are, in themselves, not criminal and for which no human tribunal would punish, that he may the better be equipped to fight the temptation of perpetrating practices that are injurious to the individual and to society. Such a man, even when reviled, will not lose his sense of proportion.

[23]Shabb. 9b—(שותף במעשה בראשית)

His greatness will not be minimized by the revilings of others. He will think of the star which, spacious though it be, appears tiny to those who pace the earth.

In this introductory chapter, only the general aspects of our subject have been lightly touched upon. Individual aspects of this theme will become manifest in the course of the book. It has, however, become apparent that Jewish Ethics penetrate the *letter* of the Law by asking its faithful followers to be undeterred by corrupt example, and to regard the whole of life as an attempt to bring earth nearer heaven.[24] As in the acquisition of genius, the gift of holiness can be acquired only by an infinite capacity for taking pains. To assist man in this holy quest, the sages of Judaism widened *"the fence round the Law"*,[25] so that it confined the entire moral domain.

Our codes cast their net wide, catching in their haul every aspect and angle of life. Human restrictions, voluntary and self-imposed, were advised in order to safeguard from violation those precepts whose Author was the Master of Life Himself. These restrictions were not to make for bitterness, for asceticism, or for a negation of the legitimate pleasures of life. *"If there be grief in thy heart"*, writes a saintly, medieval Rabbi (the *Rokeah*),[26] *"put it away from thee at prayer-time: for when thou standest before the great King, it is of thy love for Him, and not of thy troubles, that thou hast to think: for God only dwells with the joyful heart."*[27]

Judaism looks askance both at the renunciation and at the gratification of desires. The *"golden mean"*—equidistant from the realm of too much and of too little—is the bridge between them both. The *Rokeah* exhorts his

[24]Deut. xi. 21.
[25]Abot i. 1.
[26]His work will be cited in Chapter Five.
[27]Shabb. 31[a]

readers not to desire greatness, but to love holiness instead. So deep must be their faith, as to be prepared, if needs be, to die for Him joyfully. The dominating thought of the Jew should be, he continues in his heart-to-heart talk with his reader—"*How can I give back my soul to God as pure and as unsullied as when He first gave it to me?*" This is Jewish ethical teaching *in excelsis*, preached and practised by a gentle soul whose cup of suffering was filled to overflowing; who saw his family butchered before his eyes and all his worldly possessions stolen from him by the Crusaders, men who had religion on their lips but who practised evil and harboured hatred in their hearts. The advice of Cardinal Wolsey to Lord Cromwell was anticipated centuries before by this great and humble teacher in Israel. "*Still in thy right hand carry gentle peace, to silence envious tongues. Be just and fear not.*"

We shall conclude this fleeting survey of our subject with a digest of the teachings of Judaism.[28] Our faith teaches that the Brotherhood of Man is a corollary of the Fatherhood of God, who created all and loveth all, both great and small. It teaches man to love his neighbour; to be considerate towards a pupil, and obedient towards a teacher;[29] to respect the opinions of others, and to exercise tolerance towards all; to eschew the life of a parasite and choose a profession or trade;[30] to speak the truth and practise humility towards God and man;[31] to arm himself with patience, and to dispense charity and kindness unto all around him.

Ethical Judaism urges the Jew, true to his ethical code, to be moral in all actions, holy and pure in his domestic life and in his family relationships; to be patriotic to the

[28]See Appendix II at the end of the book.
[29]Abot iv. 15.
[30]Ibid. ii. 2.
[31]Micah, vi. 8.

State in which he lives, and obedient to all its civil laws. The care of all must be his concern; for *"If everybody cared enough, and everybody shared enough, then everybody would have enough."* His system of ethical conduct urges the Jew to make his life a continuous sanctification of the Name of God (*Kiddush Ha'shem*).

As a famous Anglo-Jewish preacher has expressed:[32] "To be a Jew is to be a faithful and fearful witness for God, and to feel oneself a member of a great brotherhood, in which the safety, welfare and honour of *all* is in the keeping of *each*. To be a Jew, means to make sacrifices of time, toil, treasure and comfort for our faith, and to answer all detractors by a blameless life. It is to be in sympathy with, and bear a part in, all the endeavours for the betterment of the world. It is to cherish our inheritance in the Word of God, and diligently and lovingly to study it; to unite with all who are willing to help to roll away the reproach of religious apathy from a people against whom such a reproach is least pardonable. To realize these truths, and to translate them into life and action, this is what is meant by being *"an ideal Jew"*.

The answer to the question often asked *"What is Ethical Judaism?"* is the way of life whereby man, of purpose created morally imperfect, can achieve the ideal of being godly and thus become a partner in the Creation with God. Man will, gradually, reach perfection when he finds the answer to this question in our teachings and when he conscientiously resolves to weave them into the warp and woof and the entire fabric of his life. Like the parson in Chaucer's "Canterbury Tales", the Jew must show the world, not so much by his *preaching*, as by his *practice—* *"a living sample of the truths he taught"*. For study is important in Judaism only when it leads to action.[33]

[32]S. Singer, "Lectures & Addresses", Routledge, 1908.
[33]Kidd. 40ᵃ.

CHAPTER TWO

ETHICAL JUDAISM COMPARED WITH OTHER BELIEFS

THE essential difference between the ethical teachings of Judaism and those of other religious systems is brought out clearly from the words *ethics* and *morals*. The first word is derived from the Greek *ethos;* the second, from the Latin *mores*. Both mean *customs* or *habits* which, in ancient Greece and Rome, were regulated by the Law and Order of the State. In contradistinction to this civil origin of good behaviour, Judaism points to the will of God, as it is perceived in the human consciousness, as the source of all morality. Those ancient ethical systems, which dispensed with religion, failed to take cognizance of the voice of duty as the paramount guide of all men— a voice which speaks to each man at all times, if only he be willing to listen and obey.

This divine origin of ethical behaviour at once raises our teachings to a sublimity to which other codes, independent of the divine element, aspire in vain. Our system of moral conduct seeks to move us to noble action by an impulse from *within;* an impulse which we may describe as conscience, not by a compulsion from *without*, which we call Law. The well-known utterance of Rabbi Antigonos of Socho makes this quite clear: "*Be not like servants who minister to their master upon the condition of receiving a reward; but be like servants who minister to their master without the condition of receiving a reward; and let the fear of Heaven be upon you.*"[1]

Our ethical teachings have been able to produce the

[1] Abot i. 3.

17

ideal man because they interwove religion and morality and insisted that man owes duties to his Creator, as well as to his fellow-men. A symbol of this union between Belief and Action is the fact that the Ten Commandments, almost equally divided between these twin duties of man, are depicted in our synagogues as engraved on *one* tablet and in equal perpendicular columns. Judaism does not countenance any distinction between these two fields of man's responsibility, laying greater stress on man's duties towards his fellows, lest they be given second place. To emphasize this, Rabbi Hanina b. Dosa, one of the saintliest of men, declared: "*He in whom the spirit of his fellow creatures takes delight, in him the Spirit of the All-Present takes delight.*"[2] The order of this statement is significant. The duties man owes to his fellows take precedence; but only when these are harmoniously combined with his duties towards God, will man reach perfection and qualify for "*a portion in the World to Come*".[3]

It is because the mainspring to noble action is, for the Jew, not from *without* but from *within*, that man is depicted, in Judaism, as a free moral agent, not as "*a miserable sinner*" tainted with a sin perpetrated by Adam. He has the power to eschew wrong and to do that which is right. This path towards perfection—though strewn with many attempts not always successful—are, in the long run, never futile in their quest to conquer the evil inclination within him. The very pursuit of perfection ennobles; for when one's wagon is hitched to a star there is less likelihood for the wheels to be in a rut. The fact that one of the philosophers of our day, Bertrand Russell, named his book "*The Conquest of Happiness*" indicates that happiness (as, indeed, all other human virtues) must

---

[2] Abot iii. 13.

[3] See Lev. xix for an ethical presentation of faith, followed by the statement "*I am the Lord*".

be *fought* for before the victory of its possession becomes ours. Man will complete the work of Creation when he becomes a moral personality, a perfect being whose life and thought testify that he has been coined in the likeness of his Maker. Just as the *summum bonum* of man consists in moral perfection, so will *"the Kingdom of Heaven"* be established on earth when Right is everywhere regarded as Might.[4]

The fact that Judaism endows man with the power to discern between that which is right and that which is wrong—regarding him as a being blessed with the will to choose one and avoid the other—must be borne in mind when we consider the ethical doctrines of antiquity. The conscious effort to improve our natures, expressed in philosophic vocabulary as *meliorism*, best expresses the nature of Jewish Ethics.

In this, our teachings come nearest to the views expressed by Immanuel Kant, who, perhaps more than any other thinker, has left his stamp upon modern ethical thought. His main stress was that all sense of *conscious* purpose must be altogether eliminated from the equation of moral conduct. This insistence is expressed by our sages in one word—*lishmah*—which means that good deeds must be done not for some temporal or material reward, but should be determined only by the fact that their practice is an earnest of our obedience to the will of God, as well as of our love for our fellow-beings. The moral and the divine *"ought"* is the categorical imperative. Judaism fills this categorical imperative with positive conduct by holding before man a divine network of six hundred and thirteen commandments, which may best be described as precision tools for the carving of noble characters. The fulfilment of these precepts is made possible by climbing the many rungs on the ladder of per-

[4] Mic. iv. 1-5.

fection, from the apex of which the Messianic Kingdom will loom into sight. Jewish Ethics are the realization of Jacob's dream: "*And he dreamed, and behold a ladder set up on the earth, and the top of it reached to heaven: and behold the angels of the Lord ascending and descending on it.*"[5]

The eternal glory of Judaism is that it dignifies man not as a tool in the hands of powerful elements, compelled to practise flagellation of the body and asceticism of the spirit in order to placate blind furies and exacting deities, but as a moral personality that can subdue his passions and make them subservient to his will. Man instinctively acts upon motives. These motives will be elevated and will lead to sublime doing if the teachings of self-restraint and self-sacrifice emphasized in the Jewish design of living are brought into full play. This is where Jewish Ethics part company with that school of thought which denies man the liberty to range himself in opposition to the evil forces seeking his debasement.

Man, in Judaism, is not tainted with "*Original Sin*"; "*Original Virtue*" is his lot.[6] Free will thrusts equally aside the theory of *Determinism* preached in some modern schools of thought. For without this freedom, moral life is robbed of its morality.[7] It is God, the source of all morality, that makes Jewish ethics part of religion. For the Jew to be immoral is tantamount to a renunciation of his faith. In his aim to make life a moral consecration, the Jew is aided by precept, ceremony and symbol. These are designed as religious means of self-discipline that appeal also to his imagination and enlist his noblest faculties in the practice of virtue.[8]

[5] Gen. xxviii. 12.
[6] See the interesting essay on "The Doctrine of Original Virtue", by S. Levy, in "Original Virtue" (1907).
[7] See the Jewish Encyclopaedia, s.v. Jewish Ethics.
[8] See the writer's "Jewish Customs" (1950), where Jewish observances are examined from the spiritual and ethical angle.

The more we study the abstract treatises of the ethical teachings of others, the more clearly does the *religious* basis and foundation of Jewish Ethics emerge. Far from reducing social life to a series of accidental happenings and to policies of expediency, Judaism raises the whole *gamut* of human conduct to God and to those moral values whereby alone we can best serve Him. In describing man as a free moral agent Judaism parts company with Nietzsche and Schopenhauer, as well as with early Christianity, who regarded wealth as immoral, even considering poverty as a virtue.

The logic of Judaism refuses to share the belief that the desire for possessions is in itself immoral, especially if the desire be under control, and the possessions used for worthy purposes. Wealth entails duties which give it divine sanction. The protection of the weak by the strong ennobles the character of the protector. Charity is regarded not as a *concession* on the part of the rich, but as the practice of what is only fit and proper. The Hebrew term for charity—*Tsedakah*—literally means the *right* of the poor to share in the good things which God has bestowed on the more fortunate. "*Thou shalt surely give him . . . because that for this thing the Lord thy God will bless thee . . .*"[9]

I. ETHICS OF CONFUCIUS

What Jewish Ethics stand for will be better understood from a glance at the teachings of others. It must be emphasized, however, that the aim of this survey is not to disparage the significant contributions towards civilization made by the philosophers of China and Persia, Greece and Rome. This would be unfair and even defeat the purpose of this book, which is to inspire Jews with

[9] Deut. xv. 10.

3

religious pride and refute our detractors ever busy at
tearing Judaism to shreds. It is necessary to see what
constitutes non-Jewish ethical teachings in order to
appreciate our own system the more.

The main distinction consists in the fact that the others
free ethical conduct from all thoughts of religion, whereas
in Judaism they are indivisible.[10] Their teachings, being
individualistic, or "*otherworldly*", do not offer any
valuable practical solution to the perplexities with which
modern political, industrial and economic life bristles.
The ethics of our faith, primarily religious and social, can,
if translated into everyday life, speed the coming of the
Messianic Kingdom when Justice will be enthroned in
the world. This era has been glowingly described by the
"sweet singer of Israel" as the time "*when mercy and truth
will meet together, and righteousness and peace kiss each
other*".[11]

This distinction emerges most strikingly from a glance
at the teachings of Confucius. Confucius built up in China
a system of common-sense ethics based upon communal
life but without any religious ideals. This may have
satisfied the attitude of that country but was not powerful
or inspiring enough to pass beyond the confines of the
Far East. Confucius taught man not to lend an ear to the
promptings of base desire and not to withhold good from
them to whom it is due. Man must not lift up his heart
with pride; nourish no guile; speak no frivolous word;
intrigue no evil against anyone nor quarrel with his neighbour. He must not desist from listening to reproof, not
strive to be rich, nor close his door to charity. All his life,
man must sow peace among his fellows; for hatred ruins

[10]To cite one illustration. In Lev. xix, wherein a summary is
given of some of the ethical teachings of Judaism, the words
"*I am the Lord*" occur 16 times.
[11]Ps. lxxxv. 11.

happiness, banishing sleep and robbing food of its savour. Pride is hateful, insincerity an abomination, and an evil tongue wickedness. Envy should come into play only when the virtues of another are admired. If one meets a wise man, his superiority should be acknowledged; his wisdom should serve as a spur to emulation.

Inferiors should be treated with courtesy. If poverty be our lot, then should we school our belief to regard this penury as a blessed discipline, as an instrument of our ennoblement. If we are rich, we should not be tempted to boastfulness, lest one day we, too, may become poverty-stricken. Poor and rich come naked into this world; the grave awaits them both. Let one therefore, Confucius urged, be grateful for the breath of life that pulsates within him, counting his many blessings. None will deny that these lessons will retain their worth as long as humanity endures. They speak with the accent of eternity and breathe those imponderable values and verities which transcend time, mirroring as they do the yearnings of the greatest minds of all ages. Nevertheless, they lack the impress of Jewish Ethics, which made "*Imitatio Dei*" the target and lodestar of human thought and action.

II. ETHICS OF BUDDHA

In admiring the exacting ideals taught by Buddhism, we are forced to a conclusion similar to that arrived at when considering those of Confucius. Buddha was a prince garbed as a mendicant friar who preached a gospel of love and charity for all creatures, including animals. The chief planks in his semi-religious ascetic platform are: total resignation and self-effacement in the presence of care, suffering and death—ills which rule the entire domain of life. The ideal life contemplated by Buddha is that of one who has *absolutely* separated himself from the world. This separation is to be not only from the vices of life and its debasing luxuries but also from all amusement and exercise, from business and the holding of property, and from unnecessary conversation. In short, almost the whole of existence is evil to Buddha; throbbing life, with its passions and pleasures, its desires and deeds, all come under his scathing ban. His aim was a state of nostalgic "*otherworldliness*" expressed in the one word *Nirvana*. The only relief he had to offer to the despair and delusion often attending life, was the sympathy and compassion we should exercise towards others.[12]

However much men may venerate Buddha himself, his doctrine appears to be that the sole motive for self-improvement is the selfish motive of obtaining a better future for oneself. The only really satisfying motive appears to be that of getting rid of individual life by the total extinction of desire—a thought that must remain alien to the noblest minds. It is certainly alien to Jewish thought. With its stress on the beauty of tranquillity and the virtue of kindness, Judaism is in full agreement. On its insistence, however, that personal life is an evil—with that Judaism must part company. This view vitiates Buddhism, as far as the Jew is concerned. "*And He saw that it was good*"[13]—this is the *Kol Ya'akov*, "the voice of Israel". Life, and all it holds, is potential of joy and goodness. This is the conviction of Jewish ethics, springing from a faith which bids its adherents to "*serve the Lord with joy and to come before Him with gladness*".[14]

[12]See Dr. C. Gore: "Philosophy of the Good Life". Everyman's Library (1935).
[13]Gen. i. 18.
[14]Ps. c. 2.

III. ETHICS OF ZARATHUSTRA

Of ancient ethical systems, the teachings of Zarathustra perhaps most closely approximate those of Judaism. According to them, the life of man, in spite of the evils which beset it and the abuses which prevail, is of eternal and immeasurable worth. Dr. Gore in his book "*The Philosophy of the Good Life*", summarizes the teachings of Zarathustra thus: "The responsibility of saving one's soul, or of realizing one's being, is the supreme responsibility of men and women as free and rational beings. The adventure and the opportunity is for man as man, not for any class or any race; for there is a good purpose running through creation. The supreme Lord Wisdom, the Creator, the Final Judge, omniscient and omnipotent, is the only God to be worshipped and is one day to come into His own in His whole creation, awarding just judgment of eternal bliss, or eternal woe, on all men according to their deeds.

"The vocation of man is to put his whole self, his body and soul, his thought, mind, and deed at the service of the Holy Wisdom, by prayer and by work, and by living the peaceful, beneficent life. He must love truth and peace and fight hard against those who follow lying and deception, hating them with a holy hatred even while seeking their conversion. There is no way of fellowship with God by charms or sacrifices, but only by the way of *likeness* to God. And what He is, one knows. Transcendent and supreme He is; yet by His attribute and holy spirit, also *immanent* in the world and in men of good will. We know His character of truth and justice, purity and goodness and pity and we can live according to His spirit which works in us in devout obedience."

One cannot help being struck by the resemblance between these teachings and those of Judaism, independent as they were, no doubt, of each other; but here again there is one striking divergence. For whereas Judaism began as a strictly *national* faith, dreaming of being adopted by the whole world *"in the latter days"*[15] as the one true belief, Zoroastrianism began with *universalistic* hopes and ended in becoming the belief only of Parseeism, a sect which, both quantitatively and qualitatively, little influenced civilization.

IV. GREEK TEACHINGS

It is not within the scope of this book to pass all the known ancient systems of right conduct in review; but something must be said about that vigorous ethical system, developed under a sky that fills the soul with joy and beauty. "The influence of Greece on the civilization of the world it is impossible to ignore and difficult to exaggerate. In no department of civilization, except perhaps in that of art, has its influence been greater than in ethics, or the science of the conduct of life."[16] The Greeks taught that life should be valued for the happiness it offers to the individual or society; that good should be loved for its own beauty and that which is just should be admired for its inherent nobility. Greek ethical teachings are both aristocratic and utilitarian, taking no heed of the willing slave, the suffering poor, or the unexpected stranger.

Moreover, each city in Greece had its own traditional ethical standards, each considerably at variance, each seriously weakened by demoralizing mythologies. Like

[15]Isa. ii. 3.
[16]loc. cit. Gore: "Philosophy of the Good Life".

the other systems glanced at already, that of the Greeks lacked the energizing force and motive of the highest purpose of life. They, too, omitted from their province the Author of all being who commanded men to be holy because He Himself is holy. Thus Greek ethics lacked moral content, being devoid of the Will of God and resulting in an essentially unspiritual exposition of human behaviour. As Rashdall in his "Ethics" observes: "The view that moral judgments are essentially *rational* is the view of Plato and the Platonists of all ages, as well as of the greatest Schoolmen and also of old English rationalists such as Cudworth, Cumberland and Clarke, of Kant and Hegel, and of almost all modern Idealists."

V. JEWISH ETHICS IN CONTRAST

From this comparative sketch of other ancient faiths, Judaism emerges ennobled. Opposed to Buddhist self-extinction on the one hand, and Hellenist self-expansion on the other, Judaism strives for self-elevation under the uplifting power of a Holy God. The term which the Torah uses for moral conduct is significant: "*For if ye shall diligently keep all this commandment which I command you,* to do it, *to love the Lord your God,* to walk in all His ways, *and* to cleave unto Him"[17] ‎(ללכת בכל־דרכיו ולדבקה בו)‎; a verse which the Rabbis[18] explain thus: "*As God is merciful and gracious, so be thou merciful and gracious; as God is righteous, so be thou righteous; as He is holy, so do thou strive in all ways to be holy.*"

Judaism is almost alone in its insistence on *holiness* in all things, even in the most mundane matters of life. The Rabbinic advice was: "*Be holy even in the prosaic act,*

[17] Deut. xi. 22.
[18] *Sifre* Deut. xlix.

performing all thy deeds in the name of Heaven." For this
reason does Jewish teaching condemn unchastity in look,
thought or act; regarding profanity of speech an unpardonable offence against Him who made all speech
possible. The Jew was taught that "*the Lord, thy God,
walketh in the midst of thy camp; . . . therefore shall thy
camp be holy, that He see no unseemly thing in thee, and
turn away from thee*".[19] One will find that whereas
throughout the dark Middle Ages, coarseness and
lewdness prevailed among high and low in non-Jewish
circles, a spirit of modesty and charity prevailed in the
Jewish home, raising it into a model of sanctity—an
inspiration to modesty in demeanour and to the practice
of the love and charity which their faith taught. "*And
let them make Me a sanctuary, that I may dwell among
them.*"[20] By keeping their home life pure, they kept away
destruction from their habitations.[21] "Their homes become
not their graves"—the earnest plea of the High Priest on
the Day of Atonement.

Though Judaism makes the idea of a Holy God the
mainspring of noble conduct, it has avoided the pitfalls
of the ancient systems. For it has not made life austere
and joyless, begrudging man of life and laughter. The
Shechinah only dwells in the spirit that knoweth the joy
of successful achievement; it is only gladness that brings
man nearer to God. "*And thou shalt rejoice before the Lord
thy God . . .*",[22] and again: "*And thou shalt rejoice in thy
festival . . .*"[23] Rabbi Berokha, who prided himself on
his austerity, was told by Elijah that, of the crowds he
beheld in the market-place one day, those destined for
eternal life in the World to Come would be two jesters.

[19]Deut. xxiii. 15.
[20]Ex. xxv. 8.
[21]Ibid. xii. 23.
[22]Deut. xvi. 11.
[23]Ibid. 14.

Why? Because they employed every means to cheer the depressed and to increase the world's tale of joy.[24]

By this joyous discipline, Judaism sought to impress upon man that his body should become a ready servant of his will, performing with ease and pleasure all the work that, as a mechanism, it is capable of doing. Jewish Ethics, to borrow the words of T. H. Huxley, in his description of a liberal education, strive to create a perfect man "whose intellect is a clear, cold, logic engine, with all its parts of equal strength and in smooth working order; ready, like a steam engine, to be turned to any kind of work—to spin the gossamers as well as to forge the anchors of the mind".

Judaism seeks to store the mind with a knowledge of the great and fundamental truths of Nature and of the laws of her operations. It seeks to create the being who, no stunted ascetic, is full of life and fire; whose passions are trained to come to heel by a vigorous will, the servant of a tender conscience.[25] The perfect Jew is one who has learnt to love all beauty and to hate all vileness; who respects the feelings and the possessions of others as if they were his own; who loves his neighbour not only like himself but because he *is* part of himself[26]—the real meaning of Leviticus xix. 18.

This never-ceasing emphasis on moral perfection is the core of Judaism. The practical sense of our faith looks askance at metaphysical discussions of God and the Universe. Its counsel of perfection is *"to know Him in all thy ways"*,[27] to obey His commandments and become

---

[24]Taanit 22[a]

[25]Cf. Abot iv. 1.

[26]Lev. xix. 18. Cf. Jer. Tal. Nedarim ix, where this command is illustrated by the fact that the whole body quivers with pain even when only the finger is cut.

[27]Prov. iii. 6. Bar Kappara found in these three Hebrew words— בכל־דרכיך דעהו —the quintessential teachings of the Torah; see *infra*.

God-like in the process. Life is given to man by God, and it is his task to shape it after the divine pattern revealed on Sinai. To choose life and to shape it—this is the demand of Judaism. All that we have—body and soul, wealth and want, pain and pleasure, life and death—must become stepping-stones on the road to holiness and perfection; so many rungs on the ladder placed on earth on which to climb heavenwards. The meaning of the words *"which God created to do"* (Gen. ii. 3) is: He created the world; but it is our task to make it and ourselves perfect.

The all-embracing nature of Jewish Ethics takes every aspect of life into its wide net—science and art, industry and commerce, literature and law. They teach that the Messianic Age will dawn only when all the forces of material, intellectual and social life have been harnessed into the service of humanity, when all the prophetic ideals and the visions of the seers of humanity, spread large across Holy Writ, have been realized. Zion's heights of human perfection will have been attained when holiness is combined with duty, and when all service is performed from disinterested motives. This is Jewish teaching *in excelsis*, in its most exalted form.

The great problem for the Jew wherever he lives, but especially in the State of Israel, is to restore life to its pristine glory, by being a gate of opportunity and a school of character formation. A greater truth has not been vouchsafed to mankind than the vision Jacob beheld in his dream when, a fugitive from a brother's wrath, sleeping under the starry sky of an Eastern night, with stones as his pillow and the ground as his bed, he saw a ladder standing on the earth, its topmost rung reaching heavenwards and from which the Voice of God was heard.[28] Jewish Ethics are ladders on which man

[28]Gen. xxviii. 12.

can rise from rung to rung, outsoaring the shadows of his own imperfections, enabled to bask in his momentous potentialities towards progress and the achievement of immortality. In short, its complete ascent helps man to become a real *"son of God"*.

CHAPTER THREE

ETHICAL TEACHINGS IN THE BIBLE

"Speak unto all the congregation of the children of Israel and say unto them: 'Ye shall be holy: for I the Lord your God am Holy'" (Lev. xix. 2).

FEW are the Biblical commands thus introduced. This is significant. For it implies that the duty of being holy devolves upon *each* Jew and not upon a cloistered sect of hermits only. The Jew must be holy not only in the synagogue and in the home but also in the office and in the workshop. Judaism is something more than a badge and a birth-mark; it is a life, a civilization. The virtues of truth, justice and mercy that are associated with our conception of God must be woven into the daily pattern of life. The mere accident of birth does not qualify one to be of the elect; it only designates him for *enrolment* among the elect. God signs the covenant, but we have to seal it—to seal it with a life of service.

I. CLEANLINESS NEXT TO GODLINESS

"What makes a Jew?"—is a question that is often asked. The answer—*two* things: membership of the Jewish brotherhood, and the loyal fulfilment of those obligations which that membership imposes. Most of these ethical duties are enumerated in the nineteenth chapter of Leviticus, which commands the entire nation to be holy, just as the Decalogue addressed itself to each individual. Here is a brief summary of what this chapter and other

pronouncements of a similar nature require of us. To abstain from all things which defile, physically or spiritually; to avoid forbidden foods; to shun heathenish modes of disfigurement over the dead; to bar intermarriage with those of other faiths. The Torah expects us to be learned and proud members of *"a kingdom of priests and a holy nation"*[1] in which holiness is not a mystical or an abstract idea but a directive and dynamic principle in daily life.

The perfect Jew must be kind in thought and deed, must observe all his holy days, sanctify his life by daily prayer, etherialize his home by piety and ceremony. He must honour his parents and respect the aged and the learned; he must be considerate to the needs of the poor and not withhold payment from the labourer when his task has been done. The ethically-minded Jew must have an unsullied record for clean living and moral thinking and be the possessor of an untarnished reputation for straightforwardness and integrity in business and in social relationship.[2]

Our aim as Jews should be to make manifest to the unthinking mind the reality of the divine, to establish the truth that Nature is more than matter and mere blind force, that man is more than the breath of his body and that life is more than mere existence. Obedience to his ethical precepts will make the Jewish way of life fruitful so that it becomes an inspiration, the source of a sustained effort after right doing. Our aim as Jews should be to proclaim the supremacy of the moral law, denouncing fearlessly the folly and the shame of those who violate it, and winning assent for the doctrine of self-renunciation as the basis for the conduct of life and the way to its mystery.

[1] Ex. xix. 6.
[2] Num. xxxii. 22.

An ideal *difficult* to attain? Yes, but not impossible. The Talmud assures us that man grows in holiness the more he aspires to be moral and pure. "*He who tries to be pure, is helped from on high.*"[3] What is the purpose of our religious duties if not to aid us in this climb towards perfection? Take the intricate system of ablutions governing the purity of family life and the sacred nature of its intimate associations (*tohorat hamishpahah*) as a case in point. Could proof be more conclusive that, for the Jew, life is one long sacrament? The Jew has practised what he has preached, never being tempted to make a demarcation between the pure moral life and the clean physical life. It will come as a surprise to the Jew to be told that: "*The deliberate cult of dirtiness, as a thing pleasing to God, is one of the most amazing things in social history, and makes us realize what a queer religion Christianity was fifteen hundred years ago.*"[4] Biblical Ethics teach us not to hate our body or to shun life's lawful pleasures; so to do, is to be deemed a sinner.

It was one of the meekest of Christian saints, the renowned St. Francis of Assisi, who confessed that his end had come prematurely on account of the austere mode of his earthly life. One hermit is reputed to have boasted that he never washed his face. We read of a convent in which the nuns used to shudder at the mention of the word "*bath*". St. Jerome, the editor of the Vulgate,[5] who lived as a hermit in Syria, tells us that his skin was so coated with dirt that people thought he was a Negro. Those who have read the monotonous homilies of the once celebrated Isaac of Antioch know how much he extols asceticism and glories in the squalor in which

---

[3] Yoma 39ᵃ.
[4] Dean Inge in the "Evening Standard" in one of his popular Essays published some years ago.
[5] The Latin translation of the Bible.

his life was spent. Lecky, an historian of great repute, writes: "The cleanness of the body was regarded as a pollution of the soul and the saints who were admired most were those who had become one mass of clotted filth." So much for the legend of "*the dirty Jew*". The truth is that it was the Jew who kept the world pure in its darkest periods, who taught the duty of holiness and who agreed with the Roman sage that "*unless a vessel is clean, whatever is poured into it will turn sour*".

The source of Jewish strength has been our Bible, which has taught man that he has been endowed with a body, mind and spirit which must be mobilized in the service of God. The Torah emphasizes the fundamental virtues of family life—the seed-plot for all that is best in human experience. In the conception of the *immanence* of God in all activity and in the blending of the secular and the religious—which is the characteristic of our faith—the Jew has found the authority for which he craved as well as the standards to apply to his social well-being. Patterning his life on divine holiness infused him with confidence that he has work to do and a contribution to make towards the welfare of "*the families of the earth*". It taught him to live in harmony with his surroundings, but to rebel against them when belief and morality were at stake. Biblical Ethics aim at a body healthy and educated to exercise its skill and at a mind trained to think clearly and accurately—a mind fed with a knowledge of God as He works in the world and in the lives of men.

The end of all our teachings is to create a *perfect* man, who should be a lover of beauty and a hater of all violence; a man who will be the proud possessor of a developed and disciplined will; who will view all things in a heavenly light; who will, to use Spinoza's famous phrase, always live "*sub specie æternatatis*". It was Judaism, much before Roman times, that taught mankind that "*mens sana in corpore sano"*, that "a healthy soul accompanies a healthy body", with this difference, however: a noble soul can even be accommodated in a crippled body. Such is the aim of the Torah with its vision of all men being citizens of a *"Civitas Dei"*, *"a kingdom of heaven"*, whose marble towers and lofty pinnacles could be seen amidst the smoke and grime of our industrial lives. To live *the good life*— that is the target of all our codes. So to live that even on the edge of the grave we can look *back* without remorse upon our life and the society we helped to fashion. But to look *forward*, at the same time, without fear, to that larger society for which we are bound.

II. THE BIBLICAL PATTERN

After this summary of Biblical ethics, let us concentrate on certain aspects of these teachings.[6] It need not be explained that the ethics of the Bible are not the result of an historical examination based upon *data* collected by observation of the actual conduct and habits of man and nations. Neither do they enter the realm of philosophy with its systematization of ethical theory and practice. They deal with the principles and virtues that should shape human conduct, presenting a scheme of action applicable to the various relationships of life. Supreme among the sources of fundamental ethical laws are the Ten Commandments—a sublime summary of human duties binding upon all mankind; a summary unsurpassed for simplicity, comprehensiveness and solemnity. "In the simplest language, the Decalogue lays down the fundamentals of man's duties towards God and his duties towards his

---

[6] In the latter half of this book, which will deal with *"Applied"*, or *"Practical"* Ethics, many references to our Codes will be cited.

fellow-man. These few brief commands cover the whole sphere of human conduct, not only of outer actions but also of the secret thoughts of our hearts. In simple, unforgettable form this unique code lays down the fundamental rules of worship and of justice for all times and for all men."[7]

Ranging as they do from the culture of nomadic shepherds to the urban civilizations of the Prophetic period, the ethical demands of the Bible cannot be regarded as a unit; yet one central theme unites them. This is: the unity and the holiness of God in whose image man was stamped and whose priest-people Israel was appointed. Vital as this concept is, Judaism is more concerned with man's conduct than with his metaphysical speculations. *"Learn to do well: seek justice, relieve the oppressed, judge the fatherless, plead for the widow."*[8] This is the keynote of our Torah. Man is free to choose whether he will, or will not, live according to this pattern.

The Rabbis have little patience with him who forgets that he bears the divine likeness and acts foolishly. *"He who devotes himself to the mere study of religion (Torah) without engaging in works of charity and love, is like one who has no God."*[9] It is not theory but practice that counts in Judaism.[10] "Which is the small section in which are to be found all the quintessentials of Judaism?"—asked Bar Kappara. His answer, as we have noted already, was the verse in Proverbs *"Know Him in all thy ways"*.[11] For this reason, the Talmud admits the great and early figures of the Bible like Enoch, Noah, Abraham, and the other heroes of tradition as men who fulfilled all

[7] The Pentateuch: J. H. Hertz (Soncino Press).
[8] Isa. i. 17.
[9] Ab. Zarah 17[b].
[10] Abot i. 17.
[11] Ber. 63[b].

the *Mitzvot* and lived the perfect Jewish life long before
the Revelation on Sinai.

In Judaism, the ideas about God are synonymous with
right conduct, both being intertwined and expressing the
ideal of holy *living* and holy *doing*. Ethics and Religion are
one and the same. Man, in whose being divinity is
reflected, must be true to the Law of God, wherein he will
be taught how to model his ways after the divine pattern.
He will find in its precepts that the God whom Israel must
revere is the apotheosis of all ethical qualities. *"For the
Lord your God, He is God of gods and Lord of lords, the
great God, the mighty and the awful, who regardeth not
persons, nor taketh reward. He doth execute justice for the
fatherless and the widow and loveth the stranger in giving
him food and raiment."*[12] The Torah, true to its function,
as an infallible guide to perfection, begins with an act of
kindness—God clothing Adam and Eve—and concludes
with another gracious act—the burial of Moses.[13]

III. THE THREEFOLD ETHICS OF THE TORAH

Biblical ethics conveniently fall into *three* categories.
These are: the Ethics of Love, the Ethics of Justice and
the Ethics of universal humanitarianism. With each of
these groups let us deal briefly.

THE ETHICS OF LOVE

The Ethics of Love are summarized in the injunction:
"Thou shalt love thy neighbour as thyself".[14] The word

[12]Deut. x. 17-18.
[13]Sot. 14ª. In this connection, it must be pointed out that just
to care for the dead, whilst being impervious to the needs of
the living poor, is not to be godlike. God not only buried
Moses; He clothed Adam and Eve, too.
[14]Lev. xix. 18.

"*neighbour*" includes those of other races and creeds, being irrespective of whether they are good or base, kind or cruel. Our duty is to love them. If he is deaf or blind, he is entitled to our consideration.[15] The reputation of another should be inviolable.[16] Tale-bearing, wicked insinuations, hatred of another even in our heart, are all proscribed.[17]

Love declares unethical the revengeful and relentless disposition, and pronounces as abominable dealing in false weights and measures.[18] Love extends to reverence of old age and embraces the dumb creatures pacing earth as having claim on our consideration. Love precludes malice and bitterness, prejudice and intolerance. We are not to rejoice when our enemy is dejected, nor to be dejected when he is elated. Kindness and sympathy should know no bounds. "*If thou meet thine enemy's ox or his ass going astray, thou shalt surely bring it back to him again. If thou see the ass of him that hateth thee lying under its burden, thou shalt forbear to pass by him: but thou shalt surely release it with him.*"[19]

It is particularly when one is in need, when one's well-being is threatened, that the expressions of love on the part of a neighbour count for most. The ethics of love demand that care be taken of the defenceless and the weak. We receive constant reminders to care for the widow and the fatherless, especially when our fortunes go well with us, for then are we most likely to forget the needs of those less fortunate. The burden of their loss must be made to weigh easier for them to shoulder. As for the poor in general, not only are they to be supported but they

[15]Ibid. v. 14.
[16]Ex. xxiii. 1.
[17]Lev. xix. 17.
[18]Ibid. vv. 35-36.
[19]Ex. xxiii. 4-5.

should not be made to feel the stigma of charity.[20] The stranger, too, must be made to feel that he has full share of our consideration: *"And a stranger shalt thou not oppress: for ye know the heart of a stranger, seeing ye were strangers in the land of Egypt."*[21] In thirty-six places does the Torah urge consideration for the stranger. Hence says a Rabbi: *"to divert the right of a stranger is to divert the right of God"*.[22]

Another teacher considers the crime of robbing a stranger to be worse than that of robbing a Jew.[23] *Kiddush Ha'shem*, like *Imitatio Dei*, is only observed when one displays kindness to all. Of Rabbi Johanan b. Zakkai it is told that he would be the first to greet a non-Jew. Other Rabbis are also described as the possessors of similar courtesy. It was a saying of the Rabbis[24] that since the paths of the Torah lead to peace, we should do acts of grace even unto those not of our faith in order to establish peace and goodwill among all men. God says: *"Both the Gentiles and the Israelites are My handiwork. How can I, then, let the former perish on account of the latter?"*[25] For this reason did He stop the Song of the Sea with the protest: *"My handiwork is drowning in the sea—and you dare to sing a song?"* (Ex. xv).

The same pattern of benevolence and justice forms the theme of the prophets whose counsel was pity for those who suffer, the cultivation of a humble and contrite spirit and a peace-loving disposition. The key-note of the prophetic appeal was an age of peace and righteousness.[26]

---

[20]cf. Ps. xli. 2. See Yer. Shek. v. 4; Lev. R. xxxv. where we are told that R. Jonah dealt very wisely and considerately with those who applied for his assistance.
[21]Ex. xxiii. 9.
[22]B. Metz. 59[b].
[23]B. Kama 113[a].
[24]Gittin 59[b].
[25]Sanhed 39[b]; Meg. 10[b].
[26]Isa. ii. 2-4.

Israel's choice of being the *"witnesses of God"* implied no favouritism but a greater responsibility.[27] Idolatry forfeits this divine selection and is productive of oppression and ingratitude. The covenant between God and Israel must be sealed with righteousness and loyalty.[28] The main aim of prophetic teaching is expressed for all time in the proclamation of Micah: *"It hath been told thee, O man, what is good, and what the Lord doth require of thee: Only to do justly, and to love mercy, and to walk humbly with thy God."*[29] The same prophet depicts a day of gloom when people cease to honour those near and dear to them. *"When the son dishonoureth the father, the daughter riseth up against her mother, the daughter-in-law against her mother-in-law and a man's enemies are the men of his own house."*[30] The prophets urge that civic loyalty, even to a foreign ruler, is a patriotic duty;[31] that iniquity is attended by falsehood and the shedding of blood.[32] All teachers in Israel denounce adultery and lying, pride and illegal gain. All abhor gluttony and intemperance, greed and frivolity.[33] Those who are presumptuous, scoffing at things holy, are threatened with destruction.[34]

Though each prophet speaks with a different accent, all are unanimous that Judaism demands love and not sacrifice and that its aim is to unite all hearts in service and fellowship. *"Behold, to obey is better than sacrifice and to hearken than the fat of rams."*[35] Emphasis is repeatedly laid on the view that a law does not become ethical because God has commanded it, but because it *was* ethical was it

[27]Amos iii. 2.
[28]Hos. ii. 21-22.
[29]vi. 8.
[30]vii. 6.
[31]Jer. xxix. 7.
[32]Ibid. ix. 2-5.
[33]Isa. v. 22; Jer. ix. 22-23; Amos vi. 4-7; Hab. ii. 9-11
[34]Isa. xxix. 20-21; Ezek. xiii. 18-19
[35]1 Sam. xv. 22.

raised to the status of a command. Take the command of *"thou mayest not hide thyself"*[36] as a case in point. Even if the Torah had not commanded this it would have been included in our Codes at a later stage. All we are asked to do should be born out of sheer love for men and in obedience to the Will of God.

THE ETHICS OF JUSTICE

No division ultimately exists between the ethics of Love and those of Justice—the *second* of our three groups. They are both correlated, being based on the Brotherhood of Man, itself a corollary of the Fatherhood of God. The distinction between them is slight, though subtle. Whereas the ethics of Love deal expressly with acts of kindness, the ethics of Justice concern themselves with acts of human rights. The ethics of Love express the loftiness in man's nature; the ethics of Justice aim at protecting the rights of others. Justice is a prerequisite to love. When man's failings go checked, his nobility and generosity have a clear road to self-expression.

The purpose of justice is to curb wrong-doing. That is why many of the commands in the Torah are couched in the negative form. What man *should* do is the province of the first group of ethics. Within the domains of Justice it is to warn man what *not* to do that he may be innocent in the eyes of God and man.[37] Since God *"judges the world with righteousness"* and has *"established the foundations of the earth on justice"*,[38] man, in his pursuit of holiness and perfection, must do likewise. Each age is faced with its own problems of evil and injustice, yet those early Torah principles by which society was to be governed are as

[36]Deut. xxii. 3.
[37]Num. xxxii. 22.
[38]Ps. xcvi. 13.

vital and as inviolable to-day as when first proclaimed in those nebulous but formative years of human progress.

"*Justice may pierce the mountain*" and take its inevitable course, but the guilt of the doer of damage is to be assessed by his motives. The Talmudic interpretation of the words "*an eye for an eye*",[39] is that they merely enjoin monetary compensation. Such compensation, commensurate with the accidental destruction of life or limb, must be accepted as authentic, because it is truest to the spirit of the Torah. To ensure that the execution of justice may not be impaired by possible human weakness, the Torah has many a warning for the judge. "*And they shall judge the people with righteous judgment: thou shalt not respect persons: neither shalt thou take a gift: for a gift doth blind the eyes of the wise and pervert the words of righteousness. Justice, justice shalt thou follow, that thou mayest live.*"[40]

It is this ideal of justice which the Prophets made as their central theme, castigating vigorously those who stray from the path of equity. It is clear that the accusation of being "*respecters of persons*" cannot be levelled against them. Turn to their utterances wherever you will, you will hear their fulminations against those who "*grind the face of the poor*" and batten themselves on the need and suffering of others.[41] Prophets hurl their denunciations against the strong who crush the weak; against the insolent who abuse the meek and against those judges who blind their eyes with bribes and rewards. Their fury was felt by the crowned heads of Israel and Judea. "*Thou art the man*" was the accusation flung at King David by the prophet Nathan.[42] Firmly did our Prophets denounce

[39]Ex. xxi. 23-25.
[40]Deut. xvi. 18-20.
[41]Amos. vi. 1-7.
[42]2 Sam. xii. 7.

those leaders and rulers who used their authority to serve their own interests only and not of those whose welfare should have been their prime concern.

THE ETHICS OF HUMANITARIANISM

The third group of ethics expresses the humanitarianism and universalism of Judaism. The Jew who translates these into practice places himself in the category of a citizen of the world, practising righteousness at all times and moulding himself, more and more, after the pattern of his Creator. "Israel's dream", according to Renan, "is a future full of peace for the whole of mankind, a perfect kingdom, whose chief city will be Jerusalem, whither all people will flock to worship the Almighty. Such a religion, though occasionally inclined to be national in tendency is, on the whole, universal."

Long before Renan, Rabbi Akiba and Ben Azzai both stressed the universal nature of Judaism. Is it not significant that in the passage of Micah[43] quoted above, the Hebrew word for "*man*" is *adam*? Not "*Jew*" but "*man*", mark you. God has told every man (*adam*) what He expects each individual to do. The Jewish people is only the depository of the divine truths He has communicated to the whole of mankind.

This catholicity of Jewish Ethics receives confirmation on almost every page of our sacred literature. There the assurance is given that the righteous of *all* nations are qualified for entrance to the Life Hereafter. Could tolerance go further than the observation cited in the Talmud in the name of Rabbi Johanan b. Zakkai? "*What the sin-offering once meant for Israel as atonement for its sins, the practice of loving-kindness and good deeds mean for*

[43]vi. 8.

the rest of the world."[44] Another Rabbi maintains that "*he who denies a belief in idolatry may be regarded as a Jew*".[45]

What greater proofs of the universal nature of our belief than that David is made to descend from Ruth the Moabite, that the architect responsible for the construction of the Temple came, on his father's side, from heathens,[46] that the renowned teachers of Shammai and Hillel, namely Shemaiah and Abtalion, were proselytes; that Rabbi Akiba and Rabbi Meir were also said to have been of heathen ancestry; and that Onkelos was a *ger tsedek*, one who had embraced the Jewish fold? Judaism, to conserve its universalistic approach to life, had to be nationalistic. A renunciation of its identity would have spelt a destruction of the people of Israel—the source of humanitarianism among men. For Jewish Law to have acted otherwise would have been as suicidal and as foolhardy as to cure a headache by the removal of the offending head in which the pain is lodged.

This nobility of conduct finds an echo in the other books of the Bible, especially in the books known as *Siphre EMET*,[47] the Books of Job, Proverbs and Psalms. Man is not a puppet, dancing to a whimsical deity who pulls the strings. He is majestic, little lower than the angels, endowed by God with knowledge and freewill, subject to His laws, liable to correction and punishment when the exercise of this freewill leads him to betray God's plan of the good. In the Psalms, the good *man* is stressed, not only the Jew. "*Happy is the* man *that hath not walked in the counsel of the wicked.*"[48] Job, likewise, is

[44]B. Bathra 10[b].
[45]Meg. 13[a].
[46]1 Kings vii. 14.
[47]In Hebrew, the letters א, מ, ת, are the first letters of the Books איוב, משלי, תהלים. Of course this name is merely a mnemonic, as *all* books of the Torah are books of Truth.
[48]i. 1.

concerned with the principles of *men*, all of whom have been made by God.[49] *"If I did despise the cause of my man-servant, or of my maid-servant, when they contended with me, what shall I do when God riseth up? And when He remembereth, what shall I answer Him? Did not He that made me in the womb make him? And did not One fashion us in the womb?"*[50]

The perfection of human conduct as the aim of Biblical ethics receives its culmination in Psalms xv. and xvi. The reverse side of the picture is shown in Proverbs.[51] *"A base person, a man of iniquity, is he that walketh with a froward mouth: that winketh with his eyes, that scrapeth with his feet, that pointeth out with his fingers. Frowardness is in his heart, he deviseth evil continually, he soweth discord. Therefore shall his calamity come suddenly."* The Book goes on to tell us that: *"There are six things which the Lord hateth, yea, seven which are an abomination unto Him: Haughty eyes, a lying tongue, and hands that shed innocent blood: a heart that deviseth wicked thoughts, feet that are swift in running to evil: a false witness that breatheth out lies, and he that soweth discord among brethren."*[52] The Book of Proverbs also describes the ideal woman in the last chapter,[53] a chapter included in our prayer-book for the husband to recite in his home at the approach of the *Shabbat*.

IV. THE UNIQUE FORM OF JEWISH ETHICS

Enough has already been adduced to prove that in Judaism religion and ethics are inseparable, both bound

[49]Chaps. xxiv. xxxi.
[50]Ibid. xxxi. 13-15.
[51]vi. 12-15.
[52]Ibid. vv. 16-19.
[53]xxxi. 10-31.

up with the Eternal. They are not, as in the Greek and in the other systems of philosophy of the ancient world, separated from a faith in God. It was later Hellenic literature that subscribed to Biblical ethical teachings in order to win over the pagan world to monotheism. In the endeavour to destroy paganism, certain primitive ethical principles were laid down as guiding maxims for those who were not Jews, the main three being the prohibitions of idolatry, immorality and murder.[54] These later developed into the many other laws of ethics binding upon every human being.[55] Priesthood of Israel's One God was thrown open to all that walk in His ways and who have made holiness their aim in life.

This priesthood, attainable by all who so willed it, is to be illustrated and realized by Israel as "*the Kingdom of priests and the holy nation*".[56] As "*a holy nation*", Israel's public and private life was one continuous consecration. Justice, truthfulness, solicitude for the weak, obedience and reverence for those in authority, regard for the rights of others, a forgiving and a candid spirit, aflame with love for man and consideration for beast, charity and humility —these are to be some of the characteristics flowering forth from the Jewish life dedicated to God.

It has often been urged by those who seek to detract from the eternal value of our Bible, that the motive for noble conduct in the Pentateuch is a desire for material possessions. In other words, that Jewish ethics are based upon the barter system of religion, the mercenary stipulation of "*Do ut das*" practised by the Romans and the Greeks. This view is false. Firstly, because only *two* commandments in the Bible—the Fifth Commandment[57]

[54]Known as the Seven Noahide laws, in Hebrew the
שבע מצוות שנצטוו בני נח
[55]Sanhed 56ᵃ.
[56]Ex. xix. 6.
[57]Ex. xx. 12.

and the commandment referring to the sending away of the mother bird before taking the fledgling[58] contain any mention of reward. Secondly, because the Code of the Pentateuch addresses itself primarily to the *nation*, rather than to the *individual*. In its early formative years, when Israel was emerging from the spiritual serfdom enforced by Egypt, the nation had to live under a strict discipline.

The purpose of the Torah was to make Israel a fit receptacle for the divine truths taught at Sinai. It was the conviction of the Lawgiver that only the ideal of life blazoned forth in the Torah would make Israel its worthy exponents. For this reason, were certain measures introduced to ensure greater discipline and more ungrudging observance. The motive of our precepts on conduct was never a desire for prosperity or the fear of disaster. It was a desire for ethical self-realization and a yearning to be regarded as a priest-people. It has oft been conclusively proved that the limpid stream of Pentateuchal morality flows from the historical relation of Israel to God, without any motives of ulterior rewards and penalties.

V. A JOYOUS FAITH

The ethical teachings of the Bible are of a joyous kind, not ascetic in outlook, or clouded by the thought of "*original sin*". Judaism created the phrase, *Simchah shel Mitzvah*, performing joyfully the duties and responsibilities of being a Jew. In our Bible, the world is beautiful, life is precious. Both have their centre in God who "*moves in a mysterious way His manifold wonders to perform*"; who secures the co-operation of those He has made in the work of keeping the world beautiful and good.

[58]Deut. xxii. 6-7.

It is the privilege of man to range himself on the side of the divine. As long as he is on the side of God, he will neither totter nor stumble. Strength will be his and armour and confidence his shield. He will fall should he lapse from rectitude, allowing his evil inclination to obtain the mastery over him, superseding good by evil. *"But the way of the wicked shall perish"*[59] was a warning issued in the infancy of civilization—a warning which can be disregarded only at man's own peril. The wages of sin will always be punishment.

We can now understand the statement of Rabbi Shimon b. Lakish. God said to Israel at Revelation: *"If you keep my Torah, well and good: if not, you will cause the world to become null and void again."*[60] Without ethical conduct expressing the Will of God, man's greatest incentive to noble living would be gone. It is useless to appeal to natural instincts in order to be good and pure. Nature is a fickle mistress, a tyrant doing her work independently of all that happens around. One Rabbi thus strikingly puts it: *"Stolen seed grows as well as seed which has been bought."*[61] Nature concerns itself little with ethics, but God takes a benevolent interest in all that happens here below. *"How manifold are Thy works, O Lord! In wisdom hast Thou made them all."*[62] It is no exaggeration to say that our Torah-way of life has been responsible for our preservation to this day—a survival which "has encroached upon Time and exhausted Eternity". *"Great is the Torah"*, said Rabbi Eleazer b. Hyrkanos, *"for were it not for the Torah, heaven and earth would not have been created."*[63]

Before turning to the other main source of ethical

59 Ps. i. 6.
60 Ab. Zarah 3a.
61 Ibid. 54b.
62 Ps. civ. 24.
63 Ned. 32a.

conduct the Talmud,[64] it must be re-emphasized that
the goal of Biblical teaching is to perfect the whole world
into a *Malchut Shamayim*, "an heavenly kingdom". The
Jew must not forget his mission—to keep alive the ideals
of justice, compassion and humility in human society
and to hold aloft the banner of universal brotherhood and
universal peace. "*This people whom I have formed shall
declare My praise.*"[65] This thought of our mission should
be our challenge as well as our opportunity. Our challenge
—because our survival is due only to the fact that we must
be in the forefront of all those who labour in all good
causes. Our opportunity—because in an age which has
made science usurp the throne of faith, we must teach
the world again that "*not by might, nor by power, but My
spirit*"[66] will salvation come to mankind. Not in the wind
or in the earthquake of mechanized and brutal warfare
will the Lord be found, but "*in the still small voice*" of
Jewish Ethics which dreams of a world in which truth
and righteousness shall kiss each other. Mankind has
learnt that science can sharpen the fangs of ferocity as
much as it can alleviate human pain. Atomic energy can
be used for life or death.

A knowledge of Jewish teachings in our daily action
will enable each Jew to make a distinct and valuable
contribution towards the weal and happiness of mankind.
Thousands of years ago, the world was enriched by the
proclamation of the Jewish prophet, Malachi: "*Have we
not all one father? Hath not one God created us? Why
do we deal treacherously every man against his brother,
profaning the covenant of our Father?*"[67] Biblical ethics

---

[64]Only such quotations that lay down principles of conduct
    will be quoted here; more specific teachings will be cited in
    later chapters.
[65]Isa. xliii. 21.
[66]Zech. iv. 6.
[67]ii. 10.

were at their apex when this protest was made by the last of the forty-eight prophets who brought the message *"Thus saith the Lord"* to a people eager to hear the Biblical injunction, be it of a positive or a negative nature. They knew that the purpose of such an injunction was to add stability and happiness to their lives.

CHAPTER FOUR

ETHICS IN THE TALMUD

I. THE DIGNITY OF LABOUR

ONE of the aims of the Talmud is to interpret the ethical ideals of the Bible through precept and example and to stress the importance of applying them to life. To take example first. The Decalogue stresses the dignity of labour by commanding us to work for six days before resting on the seventh. For the Rabbis not only preached the dignity of labour but wedded action to affirmation. They refused to receive payment for their ministrations, preferring to join the labouring ranks. Here are a few examples (in a later chapter, others will be cited):

Rabbi Joseph turned a mill; Rabbi Hanina was a shoemaker; Rabbi Abba, a tailor; Rabbi Simeon, an embroiderer; Rabbi Nehemiah, a potter; Rabbi Abba Hoshayah (known for his power of Midrashic exposition), a dyer; Rabbi Abin, a carpenter; Rabbi Joshua b. Hanaya made clasps; Rabbi Joshua b. Illui, a cooper. So one could add example upon example also from medieval records where men like *Rashi*—the commentator *par excellence*—was a vine-dresser and the illustrious figures of the Golden Age in Spain, Yehudah Halevi and Maimonides were physicians. From recent times, also, examples can be given. Famous Rabbis of Central Europe, like the *Hafetz Hayyim*, eked out a bare livelihood from the humble shops managed by their wives or from the sale of their books at a minimum of profit. Though we would now question the moral right of asking the wife to be the family bread-winner, yet the point here stressed is that a knowledge of the Torah was not allowed to become a source of livelihood.

All this proves that the Talmud attempts to make the ideal *real*. Professor J. Z. Lauterbach[1] writes: "The aim of the Rabbis was to make mankind progress along lines of ethical perfection, leading towards the goal of a united humanity. In order to make people strive for moral improvement, they made the ethical concepts of lawgiver and prophet, sage and teacher, the *basis* of the Law. The prophets and seers guide our conduct from afar, like lighthouses on the promontories of life. The lawgivers and judges, formulating their practical rules and decisions, place in our hands the humble candles whereby we see how to take the very necessary daily steps of life. It is from these humble steps that the great journey towards the goal of a united humanity is made up."

One of the lasting contributions of the Talmud to ethics is the moral type of leader it created. Each *Mitzvah* received a deeper meaning in the sphere of daily life, so that the Jew develops a healthy outlook whilst avoiding the *otherworldliness* of the ancient systems of the mystic East or the chastened sentimentalism of the practical West. The *Halachah* breathed content and added motive to the commands of the Torah by enlarging the scope of duty and by lifting the *letter* of the law into the realm of spirituality. The Rabbis emphasized that it is the *motive* which decides the value or character of any good deed. "*An evil deed*" they taught,[2] "*that is done from a good motive is better than a good deed inspired by an evil motive*". Since man has the power to control his acts,[3] he must see

---

[1] "The Ethics of the Halachah", Central Conference of American Rabbis, Vol. XXIII, 1913.

[2] Nazir 23[b]. See also Sanhed. 106[b] (קודשא בריך הוא לבא בעיא).

[3] Abot iii. 15.

that the responsibilities he performs with his hands are duties prompted by the heart. God judges man by the intentions which spring from his heart. This stress on *motive* in the moral life is expressed epigrammatically in an observation of a Rabbi[4]: "*The righteous have their desires in their power; the wicked are in the power of their desires.*"

II. THE ETHICS OF KINDNESS

As an example of the ethics of our *Halachah*, take the laws governing Charity (*Hilchot Tsedakah*). The word *Tsedakah* teaches us that Judaism does not consider it a favour for the poor to have their condition improved but an inalienable right. The Rabbis were so advanced in their views of Social Justice that they were convinced that indiscriminate almsgiving aggravates the misery of the recipient besides preventing other measures from being used that would be more beneficial to all concerned. It is the duty, as well as the prerogative, of him who has some of the blessings of this world not to rest content so long as others suffer for want of those very things he can spare. The Torah[5] anticipated the maxim of the text-books of the Communists and Socialists—"*To each according to his needs; for each according to his powers.*"

Epigrammatic as this advice may sound, we prefer the warmth of the Biblical command: "*If there be among you a needy man, one of thy brethren, within any of thy gates, in thy land, which the Lord thy God giveth thee, then shalt thou not harden thy heart, nor shut thy hand from thy needy brother; but thou shalt surely open thy hand unto him, and surely lend him sufficient for his need in that which he wanteth. Beware that there be not a base thought in thy*

[4] Ber. 61[b].
[5] Lev. xxv. 35; Deut. xv. 8.

heart saying: 'The seventh year, the year of release is at hand': and thine eye be evil against thy needy brother, and thou give him naught: and he cry unto the Lord against thee, and it be sin in thee. Thou shalt surely give him, and thy heart shall not be grieved when thou givest unto him; because that for this thing the Lord thy God will bless thee in all thy work and in all that thou puttest thy hand unto. For the poor shall never cease out of the land; therefore I command thee saying: 'Thou shalt surely open thy hand unto thy poor and needy brother in thy land'."[6]

From this extract was the giving of alms amplified by the Rabbis, and later reduced to a fine art by Maimonides in the chapters on *Tsedakah* in his *Mishneh Torah.* It is apparent that Talmudic ethics proceed upon the principle that whatsoever is alive has a *right* to be alive and to be *kept* alive. Maimonides (*Mattenot Aniyim X*) places that form of charity in the first rank which puts the needy person into business for himself, making him self-supporting. Even the latest innovations of modern countries, with their National Health schemes, Old Age pensions, insurance against sickness, measures against unemployment, precautions against contagious disease or industrial accidents, limitations of the hours of employment and the prohibition of child labour and all the other concomitants of democratic statecraft, are sketchily outlined in the social legislation in the Talmud.

One writer[7] sums up his study on this subject thus: "What impresses us most in this study is the governing force which the religion of Israel supplied and the remarkable humanizing influence it exerted on the dispersed Jewish community during the centuries when

---

[6] Deut. xv. 7-11.
[7] "Social Legislation in the Talmud", Torah Va'Avodah Library. In this booklet, Dr. Epstein combines scholarship with lucidity.

Roman civilization was being shattered. These communities were able to acquire in most countries a large measure of self-government and independent municipal rights. They were, in fact, little empires within an empire, theocratic empires in which the One and Only God ruled supreme. To interpret His will, there was the Torah—the Written Law and the ever-expanding and adapting oral tradition, by which the Law was amplified and adjusted, so as to bring the details of social life into the subjection to the Divine will and, at the same time, into harmony with the changing environment.

"Living amidst an unfriendly population, subject to violent currents of hate and persecution, the Jewish communities had a severe struggle to maintain the ideals of justice and mercy, righteousness and equity, which they drew from the Bible and Talmud. It was not always possible for them to regulate the social relations of rich and poor, employer and employed, debtor and creditor, rulers and ruled, buyer and seller, sinner and saint on the lines they desired. But the Jewish leaders, undaunted by all obstacles and difficulties, struggled bravely on, and thus kept the people from being submerged. In what they accomplished, they not only anticipated much that is best in the social ethics of modern civilization: but what is more, have provided the Jewish State of the future with valuable material for the setting up on earth of a Kingdom of God."[8]

Every ethical utterance of the Talmud is alive with human kindness and is motivated by the ideals of holiness and love—the most powerful incentives to good living. The command: "*And thou shalt love the Lord thy God*" (Deut. vi. 5) is explained by the Rabbis thus: "Act in such a manner that God will be beloved by all His creatures."[9]

---

[8] Ibid. p. 19. This was written before the setting up of *Medinat Israel* on Iyar 5th 5708.

Yoma 86ª; Sifre Deut. xxxii.

The ideal Jewish life must be a successive *Kiddush Ha'shem*, a constant endeavour to avoid perpetrating any action calculated to profane the holiness with which Judaism has been vested. A Rabbi[10] does not hesitate to brand *Hillul Ha'shem*, the desecration of the name of God, as "*the gravest sin*", a sin which can only be expiated by death.[11]

Since the fountain-head of *halachic* ethics is true humanity, no distinction was suffered between man and man, though race and creed may divide them. To commit fraud against non-Jews was considered more obnoxious than its perpetration against a fellow-Israelite. It was more likely to lead to a defamation both of Jews and Judaism.[12] Many are the illustrations in our classical literature of the considerate treatment meted out by the Jew to the stranger in his midst.[13]

The Talmud[14] insists that the Golden Rule pronounced by Hillel: "*What is hateful unto thee, do not to thy fellow*", is a cardinal principle of Jewish Law which is applicable to all men. It is instructive to understand why the Rabbinic Golden Rule is couched mostly in the *negative*, and not in the *positive* form advocated elsewhere. Judaism is primarily a discipline aiming at the curbing of unbridled instincts. Such discipline concerns itself more with what people must *not* do rather than with what they *should* do. Rabbi Akiba, who elaborated the teachings of Hillel, was more explicit: "*Whatever thou hatest to have done unto thee, do not do unto thy neighbour*". Hence do not hurt him; do not speak ill of him; do not reveal his secrets to others;

---

[10]Sanhed. 107ª.
[11]Yoma 86ª.
[12]Tosefta B. Kama. x. 8. See also Hull. 94ª; Sheb. 39ª; Makkot 24ª.
[13]This humanitarian attitude towards believers of another faith is absent from the Christian Scriptures and the Koran.
[14]Shabb. 31ª.

let his honour and his property be as dear to thee as thine own.[15]

In this vein spoke also Ben Azzai: "The Torah, by beginning with '*This is the book of the generations of Adam*' (Gen. v. 1), makes it clear that the command '*Thou shalt love thy neighbour as thyself*' (Lev. xix. 18), refers to *all* people who must be included as '*thy neighbour*'."[16] "All righteous people, not only Jews", says another sage, "shall enter the eternal Kingdom." The Psalmist (cxviii. 20) did not specify the Jew, when he said: "*This is the gate of the Lord; the righteous shall enter into it.*" All citizens, irrespective of belief, are entitled to a share in the amenities of a township on which the maintenance of concord depends. All the poor of the town must be supported; *all* their dead given a decent burial; *all* their mourners comforted; and *all* their sick visited.[17] No Jew can be called *righteous* who is not good unto all.[18] So important is the respect we must pay to *all* our fellow-pilgrims on earth that most of the Biblical prohibitions may be transgressed on its account[19] (משום כבוד הבריות).

III. LOGICAL APPROACH TO LIFE

Those who ridicule Talmudic Judaism for its hair-splitting legalism must be oblivious of our judicial code, shot through with ethical pronouncements of universal brotherhood. They must be deaf who cannot hear the denunciations of fraud and of every device which takes

[15]This quotation is from Abot iv. 15 and Abot de R. Nathan xxvi —a work which, in the edition of Schechter, is a mine of ethical teachings that should be more known and explored.
[16]Gen. R. xxiv (end).
[17]Gittin 64[a].
[18]Kidd. 40[a].
[19]Kidd. 40[a]; Ber. 19[b]; Abot iv. 3; Bezah. 32[b].

undue advantage of the ignorance of another, whether he be Jew or Gentile. Fraudulent deals; betting; gambling; cornering markets; raising the price of foodstuffs; loans on usurious terms; breaches of contract in commerce, as well as in social life; acts of carelessness, which expose men and things to damage and danger—all come under the condemnation of our Rabbis.[20] To insult another, to put him to public shame, is to be guilty of taking his life.[21] This statement, of purpose is couched in Rabbinic hyperbole, in order to point out the seriousness of the crime.

The spreading of evil reports, even if they have some vestige of truth, is branded as calumny. Our moral codes expose the shifts and subterfuges with which dishonesty and hypocrisy are paraded as piety and sincerity, revealing them in their true guise and character. To listen to slanderous gossip and to cause suspicion by intentional or thoughtless remarks about others, is regarded as violations of our cardinal teachings.[22] In the passage of time, Judaism may somewhat have changed its outward appearance, but the fundamental ethical values have not been withered by age nor staled by custom. The divine truths they communicate to men have not been surpassed.

Lauterbach cites copiously from the *Halachah* to prove that the Talmudic sages may be considered the true successors of the Prophets, to whose utterances they gave practical embodiment by detailed legislation. To contend that our *Halachah* is merely legislative in character, narrow-minded, pedantic and devoid of the true spirit of religion, is to declare oneself a fanatic. Such opinions of our legal code, depicted usually as being mainly

---

[20]B.B. 90b; Sanhed. 25b; Hull. 94a—to quote only a few of many passages dealing with these sins against society.
[21]B. Metz. 58b.
[22]Pes. 118a.

concerned with *outward* conduct, confined solely to those
who believe in and practise Judaism, are based on
misconception and bias. "This accusation of narrow-
mindedness", says Lauterbach, "does not apply to
Rabbinic Judaism but to those who cannot appreciate the
beauties of our *halachah*. Furthermore, their criticism is
based not on direct knowledge, but on works from
opponents of Rabbinic Judaism."[23]

We have seen that the ethics of the Bible and of the
Talmud both speak with one and the same voice, being
the same in essence and in principle. The Rabbis continued where the prophets left off.[24] They were of the
belief that their task was to emphasize what the Torah
teaches and to urge the implementation of its duties in
daily life, since the last pronouncements on moral conduct
had been made there. Their slogan might well have been:
"*Deeds, not Creeds*". These maligned Rabbis of old were
more shrewd observers of the human scene than are their
detractors of to-day. They realized that the loftiest ideal
loses its purpose if unaccompanied by action. "His
preaching much, but more his *practice* wrought, A living
example of the truths he taught."[25]

Anybody can coin beautiful phrases; but in everyday,
practical life the question is: "What influence does such
eloquence exert on life and conduct?" The Rabbis had a
logical approach, and they differentiated between grain
and chaff, between flower and fruit. "*Not the teaching is
the thing, but the action thereof* ",[26] they taught. Learning,
for which the Jew had a passion that set his heart and

[23]loc. cit.
[24]B. Bab. 12[a]: נטלה נבואה מן-הנביאים ונתנה לחכמים "When
prophecy was taken away from the Prophets, it was given to
the Sages."
[25]The quotation is from Chaucer's "Canterbury Tales"; see
the Prologue.
[26]Abot. i. 17.

mind aglow, was important only because it led to action.[27]
Everywhere, the stress is that the *deed* must be the
inseparable companion of the spoken word. Once a
promise has been given, it must not be broken
lightly.

This *practical* touch of the Rabbis can best be seen in
their emphasis that no man can reach perfection *all at
once*:—"*Natura nihil facit per saltum*". Nature itself
proceeds along its way, step by step, as the pageant of
the varying seasons shows. "Let a man occupy himself
with the study of Torah and the Commandments and the
teachings of the Rabbis; for these will direct his steps to
God." Being realistic, rather than otherworldly, they
were always ready to make concessions—provided that
the true purpose of the Torah was still maintained.[28]
They realized that "*to try to grasp everything is to succeed
in grasping nothing*".[29] It was, therefore, senseless "*to
publish such decrees which communities could not be expected
to carry out*".[30]

Above all, they protested against individuals and nations
that preached love but practised hate, that were true to
the description which Isaac gave of Jacob: "*The* voice *is
the voice of Jacob; but the* hands? *They, surely, seem those
of Esau?*" (Gen. xxvii. 22). Rabbinic teaching aims at
universal peace and at the establishment of the Messianic
era on earth. Only when this era has dawned, but not
before, will many of the commandments have outlived
their utility.[31] Even sacrifices, save that of the *Korban
Todah*, the "*thanks-offering*", will no longer be required.
All festivals and fast-days, except Purim and the Day of

---

[27]Kidd. 40[b]; B.K. 17[a]: תלמוד גדול, שהתלמוד מביא לידי מעשה.
[28]Examples of these will be given in later chapters.
[29]Ket. 10[a]: תפסת מרובה, לא תפסת.
[30]B. Bath. 60[b] אין גוזרין גזרה על־הצבור, שאין רוב הצבור יכולין לעמוד בה
[31]Nidd. 61[b]: מצוות יבטלו לעתיד לבא

Atonement, will be abrogated. May not this be taken as proof that the purpose of our ritual observances is to usher in the "*Kingdom of Heaven*" on earth?

IV. HUMANITY IN JUDAISM

As we wend our way through the labyrinthine mazes of the Talmud, the conviction is borne upon us that the Rabbis, whose statements are there recorded, were no harsh and vigorous legalists. They sought to judge each man "*on the side of merit*" (לכף זכות)[32] and taught that none should pass judgment on his friend until he was placed in a similar position.[33] Pervading the entire body of *Halachah* is a sublime motivation, and the virtues extolled by the Sages are forbearance, patience, compassion, charity, fellow-feeling, kindliness, consideration and kindness. It is quite understandable that when they speak of God, which they do almost on every occasion, they refer to Him not as a stern Lawgiver, nonchalant and callous, but as *Rahmana*, the all-merciful, loving Father. This is significant. It proves that, complex and technical as the legal sections of the Talmud may be, these are at the same time permeated by a deep sense of humanity and justice.

It would be no exaggeration to claim for the *Halachah* (the term describing the fruition of many centuries of meditation, yearning and discussions of the perfect life) that it exerted as great an influence on the Jew as did the Bible. None will disagree with Prof. Louis Ginzberg[34] that "the most contradictory judgments have been passed on

[32]Abot i. 6.
[33]Ibid. ii. 5.
[34]"The Palestinian Talmud", p. LXIX; quoted in Rabbi Louis Newman's "Talmudic Anthology", New York, 1945.

the Talmud—its theology, ethics, system of law and its literary form. There can, however, be only *one* opinion on its great influence upon Jewish life and thought for about two thousand years. Biblical Judaism was limited to one small country and to a time of cultural homogeneity of the Jewish people: but the Talmud made it possible for Judaism to adapt itself to every time and place, to every state and society, and to every state of civilization."

As we continue our study of Talmudic ethics, it becomes clear that the Rabbis regarded the performance of the *Mitzvot* not as ends in themselves but as stepping-stones to godliness. It was because "the Holy One was pleased to make Israel worthy that He gave them a copious Torah and many commandments; as it is said (Is. xlii. 21): "*It pleased the Lord, for His righteousness' sake, to magnify the Torah and to make it honourable*".[35] This purpose of our *Halachah*, with its network of regulations, emerges even more strikingly from a passage in the *Tanhuma: "Does it then make any material difference to God whether one ritually slaughters a beast before eating it, or if he eats it without Shehitah? Or do you really think it is of such vital concern to Him if one eats unclean things? No. The regulations governing our food laws were given, so that men through their observance, became purer and holier beings."*

It is natural that not only the laws themselves but all the wealth of details that grew around them were vested with divine authority. For these helped to teach the Jew to control his desire and appetite, apart from furthering in him a regard for hygiene and a striving after holiness. "It cannot be emphasized too often that in dealing with the laws of the Torah, the Rabbis delved deep in order to discover their underlying ethical purpose. Even ritual

[35]Makkot 23[b].

laws, perhaps the least expected moral sources, were made to yield moral laws!"[36]

The two loaves on the table on the eve of Sabbath must be covered when the *Kiddush* is recited. Firstly, because the double portion of *Manna* which came down on the sixth day (of which the two *Hallot* are reminiscently symbolical) was covered with a fine layer of dew.[37] Secondly, perhaps, to teach the virtue of consideration; for although the loaves were placed on the table as soon as the table-cloth was spread, they now find themselves "*by-passed*" by the wine which appeared on the table afterwards. Accordingly, we cover them that they should not, as it were, witness our slight of them. If inanimate things are so considerately treated, how much more so should man?

Or take the laws governing the *Tephillin*. If, by chance, the phylactery of the head (*shel rosh*) be taken out of the bag first, it must quickly be covered up, and that of the hand (*shel yad*) be donned with a blessing. The reason is the same. Do not hurt the susceptibilities of anything. The training thus received will help to carve characters and refine natures. Similarly, the lessons of sympathy are stressed time and again. No blessing of *She'heyanu* is pronounced by the *Sho'het* at his first *She'hitah* or by the *Mohel* at his first circumcision. Why? Because both these acts involve some pain to the animal and the child respectively. That is also the reason why this blessing is not recited when donning, for the first time, shoes that are new, or when making the blessing on the counting of the Omer on the second eve of the Passover festival. In the first instance, leather could only be obtained from the

[36]loc. cit. Those who will turn to this essay will see that the present writer is indebted to Prof. Lauterbach for much of the material in this chapter.

[37]See Exodus xvi. 14ff.

hide of an animal; in the second, the ceremony of the *Sephirah* awakened far too many poignant memories of a Temple in ruins and of the transient glory that was once ours.

Here is another illustration. In Leviticus xiv. 36, we are told: "*And the priest shall command that they empty the house, before the priest go in to see the plague, that all that is in the house be not made unclean; and afterwards, the priest shall go in to see the house.*" From this seemingly arid verse the Rabbis deduced that even the most trifling article belonging to another must be spared. Why should the man about to be pronounced unclean be deprived of his possessions? So strong was the conviction that inherent in every Biblical command is a moral purpose that even failure to discern it did not affect their attitude toward that law. They contended that the disciplinary value of implicit obedience is in itself a means to the acquisition of virtue. It is not relevant whether the Rabbis forced their ethical teachings into the Biblical commands. What we are concerned with is that the Rabbis approached the study of the Torah ethically.

V. SOME TYPICAL INSTANCES OF ETHICS IN THE HALACHAH

Passages in the *Halachah* which can serve as illustrations of this statement are many. The following will add emphasis to the main thesis of this chapter. Take the two verses of Leviticus (xiv. 40, 42): "*Then the priest shall command that they take out the stones in which the plague is, and cast them into an unclean place without the city . . . And they shall take other stones, and put them in the place of those stones; and he shall take other mortar, and shall plaster the house.*" From these verses, the Rabbis inferred

(Negaim xii. 6; Sifra 73ᶜ top) an ethical maxim: *"Woe unto the wicked, and woe also unto his neighbour"* (אוי לרשע, אוי לשכנו). Thus from the midst of an *Halachah*, seemingly bereft of any ethical teachings, the sages of the Talmud plucked flowers of moral behaviour.

Again, the *Sifra* (88ᵈ) has this comment on Lev. xix. 14: *"Thou shalt not curse the deaf, nor put a stumbling-block before the blind, but thou shalt fear thy God: I am the Lord"*: Lest you plead: "I meant well, giving him only friendly advice (עצה טובה)", the divine warning is that since you advance your motives as a defence, God knows what is in your hearts. This is the reason why the phrase *"I am the Lord your God"* acts as a refrain almost to every command in this chapter of Holiness.

To the *Sifra* (93²), we turn again for a most striking ethical observation. Commenting on Lev. xx. 26: *"And ye shall be holy unto Me: for I the Lord am holy, and have set you apart from the peoples, that ye should be Mine"*, the sages add: "Whence do we derive that one should not say: I do not like to wear *Shatnez* (a web mixed of wool and linen and explained in Kil. ix. 8 as an acrostic— דבר שהוא שוע טווי ונוז). I do not like to eat the flesh of the pig . . ." Rather: "I do like to do these things; but what can I do since my Heavenly Father has decreed in His Torah: *"And I have set you apart from the peoples, that ye should be Mine?"* (ואבדל אתכם מן־העמים להיות לי). Discipline manifests greater obedience and self-sacrifice.

Instructive is the Rabbinic interpretation of the concluding words לא תוכל להתעלם—*"thou mayest not hide thyself"* of Deut. xxii. 3. In the Torah, the words *lo tukhal* refer both to *physical*, as well as to *moral* inability. A good example of the former is in Exodus xviii. 18: *"Thou wilt surely wear away, both thou, and this people that is with thee; for the thing is too heavy for thee. Thou art not able to perform it thyself alone."* The Hebrew reads:

כי כבד ממך הדבר, לא תוכל עשהו לבדך. It is obvious from the context that not being *able*, in this instance, means sheer *physical* inability.

On the other hand, the inability mentioned in Deut. xxii. 3, of not turning "*a blind eye*" to the stray ass or lost article of "*thy brother*", can only refer to *moral* inability. For *physically* it is possible to do so; moral compunctions, however, make this impossible. The word *tukhal*, though strictly unnecessary in this context, was inserted to emphasize the moral compunction and the religious imperative. "*Thou art not (morally) able to hide thyself*." *Physically* you can. To all *outward* appearances you can. But being an ethical command (דבר המסור ללב), you *may* not and *must* not hide yourself.

Wherever we look at Jewish law, we see that ethics and religion are indissolubly linked. Take the command in Deut. xiv. 21: "*You* shall not eat anything that died of itself (*nevelah*); for *thou* art a people holy unto the Lord." The characteristic Midrashic comment (*Sifre* Deut., § 104 (95ᵃ) is: קדש עצמך במותר לך: דברים המותרים ואחרים נהגו בהם איסור, אי אתה רשאי לנהוג היתר בפניהם In which other Codes will we find such tender consideration for the feelings of others? And all this in the midst of an *Halachah* or *Nevelah!*

Another example of the Hebrew verb *Yakhol* (to be able) being used of *moral* inability is in Deut. xxiv. 4: "*Her former husband who sent her away, may not take her again to be his wife, after that she is defiled*"— לא יוכל בעלה הראשון אשר שלחה לשוב לקחתה, להיות לו לאשה אחרי אשר הטמאה. Here, too, it is not the *physical* inability that is alluded to in the words *lo yukhal*, but the moral imperative that is stressed. Her former husband cannot remarry her after she had married again and was released by her second husband's divorce or death. Such an act would be deemed an "abomination (תועבה) before

the Lord". The lesson stressed is that a *moral* imperative shall make a base action as impossible of fulfilment
just as a total lack of physical strength incapacitates
action—an idea which raises Jewish teachings to sublime
pinnacles. This view is also corroborated by Gen. xliii.
32. *"Because the Egyptians might not eat bread with the
Hebrews* (לא יוכלון)*; for that is an abomination unto the
Egyptians."*

The ethics of the *halachah* denounce a sin committed
in secret as they do one which is perpetrated in public.
According to Rabbi Isaac (Kidd. 31ᵃ): *"He who commits
a sin in secrecy, is as if he had thrust aside the feet (the
Presence) of the Shechinah. For it is said: 'Thus saith the
Lord, The heaven is My Throne, and the earth is My
footstool; where is the house that ye may build unto Me?
And where is the place that may be My resting-place?'"*
(Isa. lxvi. 6). Helpful, as usual, is the comment of *Rashi
ad locum:* "For him who sins in private God is not
omnipresent, otherwise he would not have transgressed.
Accordingly, it is as if he thrusts aside the Presence of
God from his immediate circle, leaving part of the world
devoid of His existence."

The well-known statement of Rav (Bezah 9ᵃ) that:
"Wherever the Rabbis prohibited an action for the sake
of appearances, such an action is also forbidden in the
intimate secrecy of one's innermost chamber" (כ״מ
שאסרו חכמים מפני מראות העין, אפילו בחדרי חדרים אסור)
may have been inspired from a Biblical passage. From
a study of the *eleven* sins, cursed in Deut. xxvii. 15-25,
it would appear that although the words *"in secret"*
(בסתר) are mentioned in reference to the *first (Cursed be
the man that maketh a graven or molten image, an abomination unto the Lord, the work of the hands of the craftsmen,
and setteth it up in secret*), and in one other instance
(v. 24) they are to be implied likewise in the case of the

remaining *ten* sins. Since God fills the whole world with His glory, there can be no distinction between wrongs done publicly or privately.

These are but a few of the characteristic utterances of a lofty ethical nature found embedded in our *halachah*. To recount them all would be to fill a library. In their teachings, the Rabbis included those of other faiths into our consideration and humanity. All are equally children of God. *"It is forbidden to steal the mind of any creature, even if he be a worshipper of idols"* (Hull. 94ᵃ) is one remark typical of many others. When the Talmudic sages ruled that *"the saving of a life thrusts aside the observance of Sabbath"* (Yoma 35ᵇ), they illustrated this decision with the story of the frozen Hillel. The significance of this story is that the Rabbis themselves were the first to implement any decision they made, terming those who held back from saving life on account of some religious scruple, as one who was a pious idiot[38] (חסיד שוטה)

VI. LIFE AND LAW

In later chapters, we shall tell of this Rabbinic ethical approach in laws governing employer and employee, buyer and seller, benefactor and beneficiary. That passion for social righteousness, which set the soul of our prophets aflame, also ignited the hearts of those who were the architects of our *halachah*. It has been well remarked that

---

[38]Cf. also Sifre Deut. 72 (89⁶) for the statement of R. Joshua b. Korchah on Deut. xii. 17 and Josh. xv. 63, where the same distinction is made, this time in Tannaitic source, between physical and moral inability. I am grateful to the Rev. S. Levy, M.A., for drawing my attention to numerous examples of such distinctions. Cf. Targ. Onkelos to Deut. xii. 17; xiv. 24; xvi. 5; xvii. 15; xxi. 16; xxii. 29; xxiv. 4, where Onkelos says: כי באמת היכלת בידו, אבל התורה לא נתנה לו רשות

"*this combination of law and religion resulted in giving to the Law something of religion. One cannot believe in God and be dishonest to man.*"[39] The high regard for human life figures conspicuously in our teachings. It is because man bears the impress of God that the highest value was attached to human life. The saving of a life in danger thrusts aside all laws and precepts.[40]

Only *three* grave sins were singled out as exceptions which may never be violated even in cases where life was at stake. These were: idolatry, immorality and murder.[41] It was held that when these three crimes were perpetrated, the life given by God for His service was forfeited. Significant is the reason why human life was considered more important than the commandments. In every human life, there is a possibility of service to the cause of humanity. Consequently, the saving of *one* life may be the saving of a *whole* world. When man was created, he was created alone. Why? "*To teach us that he who destroys one life destroys a whole world.*"[42] Not only was the law abrogated when there was *positive* danger to life, but also in cases of threatened peril was a suspension of observance permissible.[43]

This consideration on the part of *halachah* needs emphasis these days when clamours are often heard that to be rigidly faithful to the Torah means the suspension of the intellect, to be tied to ritualism by the dead hand of tradition. The aim of Judaism (as perfected by Rabbinic teaching derived from the Revelation at Sinai, הלכה

---

[39]Tosefta Shevuot iii. 5. וכחש בעמיתו—אין אדם כוחש בעמיתו עד שכופר בעיקר

[40]"*Pikkuah Nephesh*", Yoma 82ª.

[41]Sanhed. 74ª: Pes. 25ª: כל עבירות שבתורה, אם אומרין לו עבור ולא תהרג, יעבר ולא יהרג, חוץ מע״ז, ג״ע, ושפיכות דמים

[42]Sanhed. 37ª.

[43]Yoma viii. 8: אפילו ספק נפשות דוחה שבת. This is derived from the command לא תעמד על־דם רעך (Lev. xix. 16).

למשה מסיני) is to secure the co-operation of all to contribute towards the welfare of mankind and so to bring earth nearer to heaven. The preservation of each individual soul means the addition of another moral factor to the cause of humanity. All men may be described as pieces of a gigantic jig-saw puzzle, which although at times awkward and angular are, nevertheless, indispensable towards the creation of the composite picture. To thrust aside temporarily a *Mitzvah* in order to preserve a life was regarded in consonance with the *spirit* of the command of the Torah.

No legal device, this, but a broad-based interpretation of an immutable law. The Rabbis had no hesitation in declaring that, holy and binding as the strict observance of the Sabbath be (regarding him who flagrantly desecrated it as having excluded himself from all consideration as a Jew), the holiness of this day must recede into the background when the Angel of Death is nigh. *"The Sabbath was given to you, not you unto the Sabbath"* is a quotation from a Jewish source[44]. The saving, one Sabbath day, of poor Hillel by Shemayah and Abtalion, whose lectures he could not attend on account of poverty, is enhanced by the reason given by these two Titans of learning of their act: *"Better to save one who will observe many Sabbaths, than to save only one Sabbath and thereby destroy a soul."* To put the letter of the law above its *spirit*, is to destroy the purpose for which the Sabbath was given—a day of physical *re-creation* and spiritual rejuvenation (*Shavat Va'yinaphash*).

This wide interpretation of Sabbath observance was applied to other essential Biblical commands. The *leitmotiv* of our ethical system is the command of God: *"Ye shall therefore keep My statutes and Mine ordinances,*

[44]Mekhilta on Ki Thissa, from which, probably, the statement in the N.T. was derived.

which if a man do, he shall live *by them; I am the Lord.*"[45]
Man must *eat* to *live*, not *live* to eat. He has the duty to
look after his physical and mental welfare as he has the
responsibility to be solicitous for the well-being of others.
Interesting in this connection is the shrewd remark of a
Hasidic Rabbi, to whom one complained that *"So-and-so"*
desecrated the Sabbath and ate all kinds of forbidden
foods. "You have been given two eyes. One with which
to see your own *faults*, the other with which to behold the
virtues of another." Glancing at the physical robustness
of the complainant, the Rabbi added this: "My friend,
I would advise you to look after your own *soul* and the
body of another, rather than make yourself censorious of
another man's *soul* whilst feeding carefully your own
body." The duties man owes to his fellow-being could
not have been more masterfully stated.

The trend of our *halachah* will earn admiration if we
bear in mind the Jewish conception of man[46] and the
contribution he is asked to make towards the welfare of
humanity. Because the Jew does not belong to himself
alone but is a unit in a universal brotherhood, he has no
right to dispose of his own life when circumstances
overwhelm him.[47] His death at his own hands, though it
may spell the conclusion of his own misery, may be the
cause of untold misery to those he leaves behind. Jewish
ethics are insistent that the pleasure and relief which we
seek for ourselves must never be obtained at the expense
of others. The Jew is taught to take his joys in a subdued
manner, chastened by the thought that the loudness of
his behaviour may wound the susceptibilities of those
cradled in a more refined school.

[45]Lev. xviii. 5: Sanhed. 74ª.
[46]See Appendix I at the end of this book.
[47]Lauterbach, loc. cit. See B.K. 91ᵇ, where Rabbi Eliezer is
    reported as having said that God will hold him responsible
    who takes his own life (מִיד נפשותיכם אדרוש את־דמכם).

As a precaution to the taking of one's own life, no Jew is allowed to undermine his health by fanatical asceticism and constant fasting. The emaciated body and the rough hair-shirt are not the *insignia* of the Jewish saint. Life was made to be enjoyed, in moderation of course. Our lips are trained to frame the benediction "*Blessed be the Lord, day by day*" (Ps. lxviii. 20). It is told[48] of the Schools of Shammai and Hillel that they would save the nicest things they came across during the week to enjoy them on the Sabbath day. God wishes us to combine religion with pleasure, to divide the festive day into two halves, one to be spent in the service of God, the other half for our own enjoyment (חצי לי׳ וחצי לכם).

It may well be that another reason for the observance of the Dietary Laws, apart from the main stress on holiness found in Leviticus xi. 43-47, is the principle that it is forbidden to eat or do anything which is likely to impair one's state of health.[49] So important is this prophylactic principle that a Rabbi is of the opinion that even such foods that come under the ban of forbidden things (מאכלות אסורות) are temporarily permitted if, by their means, life may be prolonged.[50] In fact, such acts that are conducive to physical health are considered prime religious duties. Those practices that may lead to a weakening of the faculties are deemed sinful and obnoxious, and contrary to Jewish thought. Interesting is the suggestion made by some scholars that antediluvian man lived so long because he ate the healthy vegetarian

---

[48] Bezah 16a.

[49] B.K. 91b: אין אדם רשאי לחבל עצמו "No man may do injury to himself".

[50] Hullin 10a (חמירא סכנתא מאיסורא). See also Taan 11a: היושב בתענית נקרא חוטא "He that makes fasting habitual, is deemed a sinner." If he is a teacher of children, for instance, he will not be able to devote of his best to the task at hand if he spends his days in chastising his body.

food produced by the rich soil prior to its deterioration
by the waters of the Flood.

It is a natural step from not being allowed to injure
peace of mind by deprivation due to religious considerations, to the other demand of the *halachah*. This is, not to
destroy anything even if it belongs to us—not to mention
if such destruction involves the property of another.
This principle is known as *bal tashhit* (בל תשחית) and is
based on the provision made in Deuteronomy xx. 19-20.
This passage is important and must be quoted. "*When
thou shalt besiege a city a long time, in making war against
it to take it, thou shalt not destroy* (לא תשחית) *the
trees thereof by wielding an axe against them; for thou
mayest eat of them, but thou shalt not cut them down; for
is the tree of the field man, that it should be besieged of thee?
Only the trees of which thou knowest that they are not trees
for food, them thou mayest destroy and cut down, that thou
mayest build bulwarks against the city that maketh war
with thee, until it fall.*" It may well be that apart from the
symbol of the torn heart,[51] the custom of *Keriah*[52] for the
dead may have first been a concession as well as a protest
against the pagan practice of tearing the hair as well as
the garments in the presence of the dead (Deut. xiv. 1-2).

From this prohibition against destroying anything
potential of serving a good purpose, it follows that none
has a right to squander his fortune. Even for charitable
causes is such uncontrolled action forbidden if the result
of this excessive philanthropy be that the distributor of
his wealth now becomes a burden to society. Charity, too,
has a limit beyond which it is not wise to go. "Let him
who distributes his possessions to charity not distribute
more than one *fifth* thereof, lest he himself become
dependent on others for support" says a Rabbi. The

[51]Joel ii. 13.
[52]The tearing of part of a garment for a dead relative.

reluctance with which the Jew regarded dependence on the bounty of another can be gauged from the prayer he utters at the conclusion of each meal: *"We beseech thee, O Lord our God, let us not be in need either of gifts of mortals or of their loans, but only of Thy helping hand, which is full, open, holy and ample: so that we may not be ashamed nor confounded for ever and ever."*[53]

More than any other principle regulating Jewish moral conduct is that which teaches that each human being is a member of the larger family of mankind. Accordingly, all that he does must be surcharged with consideration for the interests of others. His joy must not cause misery to others, nor his grief be a source of woe to those around him. The aim of our *halachah* is not *negative* only. Urgent as it be not to cause anxiety to the honour and well-being of others, it is imperative to care for the prestige of another and for the preservation of his peace of mind. This principle is in consonance with the many reminders in the Talmudic records of the dignity of man.

Where the honour and welfare of others are at stake, Biblical and Rabbinic commands take second place.[54] The Rabbis, who advanced no statement unless they corroborated it with Biblical support,[55] cite an interesting illustration from Exodus xxi. 37. *"If a man steal an ox, or a sheep, and kill it, or sell it, he shall pay five oxen for*

---

[53]Singer's Prayer Book, p. 281. In connection with the principle of *bal tashhit*, of not destroying anything that can be of any use, it has been contended by some Rabbinic authorities that if a bonfire, like the *Hadlakah* on Lag B'omer at the grave of R. Simeon b. Johai at Meron, in Galilee, gave pleasure to the spectators who had assembled from far and near to take part in the *Hillula* festivities, the articles thrown into the flames cannot be considered to constitute an act of wanton destruction; see Zevin: "*Ha'Moadim B'halachah*", pp. 299-304.

[54]Shabb. 81[b].

[55]The reason being to show that Talmudic ethics are sparks from the divine flame of the Torah.

an ox and four sheep for a sheep." Why this difference in
the penalty? Is not the crime the same in either case? No,
says a Rabbi.[56] This verse teaches us that so considerate
is the Torah for the dignity of man (though circumstances
have tempted him to steal and be branded as a thief) that
it has, of purpose, altered each penalty to fit not only the
crime but also to compensate for the trouble and the lack
of dignity such a theft involved. The fine in the case of a
sheep was smaller, *four* instead of *five;* because when the
thief purloined the sheep he was probably compelled to
carry it on his shoulders to avoid its escaping capture.
Such an act involves trouble and humiliation on the part
of man coined in divine likeness and now serving as a
carrier for a dumb and frightened animal.

In the case of an ox, such a procedure was impossible,
the ox being too heavy for man to carry. Because no loss
of propriety was incurred in the act of leading the ox away
from the possession of another, the penalty was increased
to *five* oxen. There is also the further reason that the ox
may have been needed for his labour in the field; for this
reason the loss to the owner is all the more. Fanciful?
Yes, but is it not evidence of the ethical approach of our
Rabbis in their elucidation of the Bible from whichever
angle this approach was made?

These statements from Biblical and post-Biblical
sources of Jewish moral conduct, convince us that the aim
of our religion is to add joy to life and dignity to man.
The Bible shows consideration towards the thief who,
even when he was sold for his theft as a slave on not being
able to pay the restitution required, was not to be treated
as an ordinary slave or to have to suffer the opprobrium of
serfdom for more than six years. The slave, who had gone

[56]B. Kama 79[b]. The Talmud makes it clear that this law of the
"*four or five*" applies only in the case when the animal has
been sold or slaughtered by the thief before it was restored.

into voluntary servitude, must not be further humiliated by his master and made to undergo degrading work. On the contrary, so many restrictions hedged the ownership of slaves, especially if he were Jewish, that the phrase was coined in Talmudic circles: "*He who purchases a slave purchases, in reality, a master unto himself.*"[57] "The master can only lay claim to the servants' toil, but his honour and dignity belongs to the servant. He is a fellow-man in all respects."[58] Even when speaking of the Canaanit slave, a Rabbi explains that "the slaves were entrusted to us to employ their service, but not as objects of our derision."[59]

The period when Jews possessed slaves stands out in our *Halachah* as one which was more humane and enlightened than the state of society of our most democratic countries to-day. It is to the glory of Jews that not only did they treat the slave humanely, but as a people they were the first to roll off the reproach of owning another human being as their slave, sold to them in body and soul. There are to this day over five million slaves in various parts of the world—a world which has not yet taken to heart the words of Job: "*If I did despise the cause of my man-servant, or of my maid-servant, when they contended with me—what then shall I do when God riseth up? And when He remembereth, what shall I answer Him. Did not He that made me in the womb make him? And did not One fashion us in the womb?*" (xxxi. 13-15).[60]

[57]Kidd. 20ᵃ: כל הקונה עבד עברי כאילו קונה אדון לעצמו
[58]Lauterbach, loc. cit.
[59]Niddah 47ᵃ. Ham, the son of Noah, is the first to be designated as "*a slave*" in the Torah, because the shameful treatment meted out by him to his father branded him as unfit to be responsible for his own actions. He required a *lord* and *master* to regulate his life.
[60]This chapter deserves study, as one of the first utterances of a noble spirit, excruciated on the rack of pain and tormented by the mystery of suffering, yet full of love for the down-trodden.

VII. BUSINESS MORALITY

In the *Halachah*, consideration for him employed in our service borders almost on the point of tenderness. Not only must we pay him the stipulated wage before the sun goes down each day upon labour's task completed, but his health, personal comfort and sense of decency must receive priority of attention and care. The person employed is asked not to *botch* his work but to show all regard for the rights of his employer. He was exempt from the recital of all but the most necessary prayers when actually employed on his work, and even those could be recited in an abbreviated form.[61] Furthermore, the hired labourer was exempt from paying damages for an article spoiled by him accidentally in the process of working at it. When one compares this considerate regard with the practice current in some circles of deducting from the wages of those employed even when the damage was accidentally incurred, we can see how far in advance Judaism still is of the vaunted sophistication and advertised enlightenment of society in our own days. In this aspect of life, as indeed in all others, the Talmud can justly claim: *"The Rabbis have forestalled thee in this."*[62]

As a deterrent to dishonesty in commercial relationships, the Rabbis coined many a striking thought. One of the most impressive is that each soul, after it has winged its flight from earth to heaven, will be confronted with the question: *"Hast thou been faithful in business?"*[63] *"Hast thou conducted thy economic transactions at the expense of faith (באמונה)?"* The Hebrew is capable of

---

[61]Berachot 46a.
[62]Shabb. 19a: כבר קדמוך רבנן
[63]Shabb. 31a: נשאת ונתת באמונה

both translations and contains a censure against *"pious"* hypocrites who make a *"business"* of their faith.

The temptations in the path of rectitude being so many in business, it was necessary to prescribe in detail. When one is already negotiating for the purchase of an article, it is morally wrong for another to step in and bid a higher price so as to retain it for himself.[64] Neither is one allowed to compete with a shopkeeper in the same street, unless it be that he wishes to sell the essential commodities of life at a much cheaper rate.[65] The reason for this is not difficult to see. The opening of a new store may serve as a wholesome deterrent to the *"cornering"* of the trade by one merchant. Strict as the *Halachah* is against the unfairness of *"cutting prices"*, yet it was considered not only legal but meritorious to help the consumer to obtain the essentials of life as cheaply as possible. The Rabbis considered it illegal to derive profit from the sale of food.[66] We read of inspectors vested with authority to regulate the market prices of all food and drink.[67] To sell adulterated foods, to give false descriptions of the articles sold, to sell *trefah* meat even to a non-Jew (let alone to a co-religionist on the pretence that it is *Kosher*)—all come under the ban of unethical conduct. In the latter case, the Gentile may have, of purpose, gone to a Jewish shop in order to obtain *Kosher* meat either for himself, or for another Jew.[68]

The question is debated whether a shopkeeper, in order to induce children to come again for their custom, may give them little gifts each time they come to purchase goods for their mothers. Is such conduct ethical, though

---

[64]Kidd. 59[b]: עני המהפך בחררה

[65]When the intention is to benefit the customer, competition is allowed, within moral limits of course.

[66]B. Bath 90[a]: אסור להשתכר בחיי אכל נפש

[67]Ibid. 89[a]: see also Lauterbach, loc. cit.

[68]Hullin 94[a].

the children benefit as a result? To give the appearance
of wishing to buy, whilst not having the slightest intention
so to do, steals the mind. To bid for an article in order to
wrest it from another—especially when he has no money
to obtain it for himself—is a breach of strict moral
conduct. Similarly, it would be wrong if an owner of
adjacent property were to ignore the right of his adjoining
neighbour (bar Metzra) to acquire the field he wishes to
sell and to dispose of it to a third person. Should he do so,
he may be compelled later to re-sell it to his former
neighbour for the purchase price only. For did he not
ignore his claim to purchase the field before any other
could so do?[69]

VIII. THE AIM OF THE HALACHAH

One other matter calls for notice. There are many
things which may not be condemned by the law, yet are
culpable in the eyes of ethical teaching. These are actions
which violate the moral standard, though not actually
infringing upon the civil law.[70] As an example, we may
quote the law of the Shemitah, the seventh year of Release
(Deut. xv. 1-6). Though the debt is automatically released
with the advent of the seventh year, no debtor may take
undue advantage of this law. Whenever possible, he
should pay his debt before the arrival of the Shemitah
year.[71] When the Rabbis suspected prevarication, they
organized the device of the Prozbul, a declaration made in
court before the execution of a loan to the effect that the

[69]This right is termed by the Talmud (B. Metz. 108[b]):
דינא דבר מצרא
[70]This category is known as דברים המסורין ללב "things that are
left to the dictates of the heart".
[71]Shebiit x. 9. "The Rabbis are pleased with him who does so:
המחזיר חוב בשביעית, רוח המקום נוחה הימנו

law of limitation, by the entrance of the Sabbatical year, shall not apply to the loan to be transacted.[72] This was no subterfuge but an honest attempt to make a law of the Torah conform to the spirit which first created it.

It was also taught that since the *Shemitah* was contingent on the Jubilee year, the first was not applicable when the latter was no longer in force. Similarly, the various laws concerning the *Erubin* were so many honest attempts at keeping in the minds of the people the purpose of the Law. The permission to cook a little extra on the festival-day if it be a week-day in order to have food left over for the morrow, which is a Sabbath, when no cooking was allowed, is called *Eruv Tavshillin*.[73] The provision to unite families living in one court into one household by placing a meal in a common-room accessible to all was known as *Eruv Hatzerot*. These were devices true to the principle of *"that he may live by them"* (Lev. xviii. 5). Without these modified interpretations of the Biblical laws, a conscientious fulfilment would be well-nigh impossible in the changing conditions of life on account of the hardships they entailed.

The main purpose of the intricate network of the *Halachah* was to keep the nation alive through all its vicissitudes. The word *Halachah*[74] suggests "Progress" and is meant to serve as a guide in daily life. The world has not yet *progressed* to those sublime standards of holy living and action patterned in our codes. The Jew, who faithfully adheres to the standards blazoned forth before his trail in his Codes, Biblical and post-Biblical, will be armed with a moral strength that will overpower those

[72] Gittin 36[a].
[73] Bezah 15[b]. See writer's article s.v. in "Jewish Chronicle", April 27th, 1951.
[74] Derived from the root הלך "to go".

that rise up against Him. He will echo the words of
R. Yehudah Halevi: *"Men revile me; but they know not
that the shame endured for Thy sake, O God, is naught but
honour."* To study our ethical codes is to possess ourselves with a further source for strength and pride in our
Judaism.

CHAPTER FIVE

ETHICS IN MEDIEVAL TIMES

The ethical teachings contained in the classical works of
our medieval Jewish philosophers elaborate those of the
Bible and the Talmud. Their essential characteristics are
the same. All their utterances breathe love and compassion
for all men alike. All insist on the *sine qua non* of unsullied
and unselfish motives in the doing of an action. All stress
the perfection of man and the stability of this world
(*yishuvo shel olam*) rather than the acquisition, as a result
of good deeds, of "*a portion in the World to Come*". One
need only dip into the books of moral conduct produced
after the close of the Talmudic age,[1] especially during the
Golden Age in Spain,[2] as well into those compiled as near
as possible to our own times, for proof of these claims.

I. PHILO (30 B.C.E.-40 C.E.)

Though Philo was neither a Talmudic teacher nor a
medieval scholar, our sketch of Jewish ethics in post-
Talmudic times may conveniently begin with him.
Allegorical commentaries on the Torah and moral
treatises on Moses and the patriarchs—whom he holds
forth as types of universal religion—form the bulk of
Philo's literary legacy to mankind. He followed the Greek
philosophers not only in the medium, Greek, but also in

[1] Circa 500 C.E.
[2] In the early centuries of the second thousand of our Common
Era.

the incentive they gave to ethical conduct and the desire of man for happiness. This happiness consists not in the possession of material goods and civic honours (pleasant and desirable as these may be), but is to be found in a life lived in accordance with that which is best in man.[3]

To attain this beatitude of body and spirit, Philo emphasizes the need of *"imitating God"*, an effort which will banish the baser feelings of human nature such as self-love and self-conceit. His principal works popularly present Judaism as a philosophical religion, primarily intended for those Hellenistic Jews fascinated by the views of Aristotle and Plato. Living in the most formative years of civilization, when a new religion appeared on the horizon, his ideas, especially that of the *Logos*, or the *Word*, played an outstanding *rôle* in the development of Christianity. It was natural that the early Church Fathers used the *Logos*—which Philo describes as the instrument of God's activity and His immanent manifestation in the Universe—as an authoritative source for their doctrines of a Saviour and a Trinity. As we are appraising not his philosophy or theology but the contribution he made towards the study of ethics, a discussion of Philo's contribution to Christian ideology is beyond the scope of this book.

Grappling with the problem of Freewill and Providence, he maintained that man is endowed with a conscience which serves as his accuser, judge and adviser.[4] Man is empowered with freewill, though everything is foreseen,[5] so that he might be held responsible for his actions. Without this power of deciding his own actions,

---

[3] See the article "Philosophy, Jewish", in Vallentine's Jewish Encyclopædia, 1938, and the publications of the East & West Library on some medieval Jewish philosophers.

[4] The reader will find material on the subject of this chapter in the article "Ethics" in "The *Jewish Encyclopædia*".

[5] Abot iii. 19.

Jewish ethics would be shorn of its worth. Reward and Punishment would be meaningless. Philo follows the reasoning of Plato that man has a mind twofold in scope. Being *rational*, it is directed towards the universal; being more often than not *irrational*, it seeks the particular and the transient.

The ideal man will extirpate desire and plant virtue in its place. At no time does Philo advocate asceticism as the *norm* of life. Those who wish to sever themselves from the hustle and bustle of this life in order to inhabit the realms of contemplation, can do so after they have discharged their responsibilities towards mankind.[6] This goodness, which must extend to solicitude for animals, constitutes for Philo, as it did for Plato in the "*Ideal Republic*", the highest of cardinal virtues. He praises those ethical virtues, first met with in the Bible and later elaborated by our *Halachah*, such as self-control and self-sacrifice, as the main enemies of illegal desire and debasing pleasure.

He conceives piety, not in bodily flagellation or mental mortification but as the state of mind which flowers into sincere prayer. Its fruits are hope, joy, peace and forgiveness. Philo underlines the urgency of Repentance, convinced that it is human to err. The evil spirit has been placed in man as a means to perfection by overcoming its temptations to stray from righteousness. He agrees with Rabbinic teaching that the best test of repentance is the avoidance of the same sinful act in the future. "*It is not the speculation (Midrash) of a Biblical command that is essential, but the practice thereof.*"[7]

Philo serves as a good introduction to the medieval

---

[6] See his "*Vita Contemplativa*", believed to have been composed by him as a result of his experiences as a member of the Essenes.

[7] Abot i. 17: לא המדרש עיקר אלא המעשה

moralists into whose lives and works we are about to provide a fleeting glimpse. They, like him, though in a much lesser degree, were influenced by the teachings of Greek philosophy to which they added the Arab philosophy of their day. All seem linked by one laudable aim: to bring into line the ethical teachings of the Torah and the Talmud with the advanced views of their age.

II. SAADIAH BEN JOSEPH (882-942 C.E.)

Saadiah heads the list of a long succession of scholars whose avowed object was twofold: to reconcile Arabic and Greek learning with Jewish teaching and thus make Judaism more precious to its instructed adherents. All these great men, from the ninth till the twelfth century, enriched the mind of mankind. Saadiah, however, was the first to demonstrate that one need not suspend the intellect in order to be a conforming Jew. He himself, as is evidenced from his militant attitude towards the Karaites, was a staunch upholder of Rabbinic Judaism.

The scope of this book precludes even a summary account of the great legacy to Jewish learning he bestowed during a short and eventful life. Only one book, his masterpiece, is germane to our subject, namely, *"Emunot Vedeot"*, the *"Book of Beliefs and Dogmas"*.[8] In this great work, a serious attempt was made, for the first time, to provide adequate solutions of the many problems raised

---

[8] It was written in Arabic, under the title *Al-Amanat w'al-It'iKadat*, and was translated into Hebrew with the name האמונות והדעות. See Dr. A. Altmann's work on *Saadia* in the East & West Library (1947). It was Alexander Marx in his "Essays in Jewish Biography" (J.P.S. 1946) who first called attention to the fact that the Genizah fragments discovered in Cairo give 882 (not 892) as the year of his birth.

for thinking Jews by the study of Greek philosophy in its Arabic dress.

Saadiah appears as a pioneer who systematizes and interprets his ancestral faith in the light of the learning of his day, dealing with the ethical problems of Freewill, Providence, and Reward and Punishment and others of a similar nature. His unshakable belief in the righteousness of God solves the problem of evil. The fundamentals of his metaphysics are the existence and the unity of God. The ascetic who goes to extremes is condemned, even when such an attitude is born of the desire to be pious and learned. True happiness comes from a firm belief in the Torah and its Revelation.

It must be reluctantly admitted that his contribution to Jewish Ethics is slight and elementary, but what he did add is vital. To this day, the book has remained one of the most cherished in our cultural library because of the genius possessed by the author in those fields of learning which only began to develop in the ninth century. One cannot agree with Lewis Browne when he writes:[9] *"To laymen, however, both Jewish and Gentile, the book can have little meaning now, fumbling as it does with metaphysical problems which have long since lost their urgency."* This book will always be valuable as a reliable source to those who study the origin and development of Judaism and its ethical codes.

III. SOLOMON IBN GABIROL (1021-1058 C.E.)

Gabirol crowded into his thirty-seven years the reputation of being at once poet, philosopher, moralist and grammarian, but his direct contribution to Jewish ethics is slight. He wrote a slender book on the importance

[9] "The Wisdom of Israel", 1949, p. 269.

of moral qualities in which he deals with the principles
and conditions of virtue, the goal of life and the result of
moral conduct.[10] In two divine gifts, man is on the side
of the angels, in his gift of speech and in his power to
reason. He is most true to the ethical teachings of his
faith when he expresses the belief that evil is not *innate* in
human nature but that man has the power to make it
subservient to his better self. The soul comes pure from
its heavenly source. It is the task of religion to bring
about a happy fusion between the soul and the higher
world which men should people. Written in Arabic, its
aim is to show that human impulses can either be trained
for virtue, or if unchecked, lead to vice.[11]

The other work on which his fame rests is the *"Source
of Life"* (מקור חיים),[12] a work mainly devoted to the
central problems of medieval metaphysics. To ibn
Gabirol, not only the ordinary material objects but also
the spiritual substances are composed of matter and
form.[13] The real and perfect unity is in God. Matter and
form constitute a unit and the closest unit is to be found
in intelligence. In this reasoning, he shows the influence
of the Neoplatonic school, which he harmoniously
combined with Jewish feeling.

This synthesis he also achieved in his celebrated hymn
"The Royal Crown" (*Keter Malchut*), some of which is
incorporated in the *Sephardi* ritual of *Yom Kippur* as
well as in his *"Choice of Pearls"* (מבחר פנינים). His fame,
however, like that of Saadiah, does not rest on his

---

[10]*Tikkun Middot Hanephesh*. His "Selected Poems" have been
   published by the Schiff Classical Library (J.P.S. of America),
   and contain translations by Israel Zangwill.
[11]See "The Wisdom of Israel", pp. 284-301, for a selection from
   Gabirol's writings.
[12]In Arabic, *Yanbu al-Hayat*.
[13]See the concise article "Philosophy", by S. Rawidowicz in
   Vallentine's Jewish Encyclopædia, p. 515ff., London, 1938.

contribution to Jewish ethics. It lies elsewhere, largely because his work does not exclusively refer to Judaism. It is so obviously saturated with Greek-Arabic philosophy that it cannot be counted as an essentially Jewish work. Nevertheless, Gabirol cannot be omitted from a history of the march of Jewish ethical learning.

IV. BAHYAH IBN PAKUDA (11TH CENTURY C.E.)

Bahyah was the most popular Jewish religious philosopher in the Middle Ages as well as the first to write a systematic account of Jewish ethics. In his *"Duties of the Heart"* (*Hovot Ha'levavot*), intended primarily as a corrective against ritualism on which much emphasis was laid in his day (to the exclusion seemingly of much that was true to the spirit of Judaism) he sets himself the great task of explaining the nature of his faith and the ethical impulses such a belief engendered. The book is divided into ten sections (*Shearim—Gates*), corresponding to what the author considers the *Ikkarim* (*Fundamentals*) of Judaism.

It clearly bears the impress not only of deep piety but also of the thought current in his day.[14] The basis of true conduct and service to God is not the *total* surrender to Talmudic studies, to ritual and mechanical observances but inward faith, sincerity and uprightness. Though Bahyah, following the Islamic ascetics, is inclined to regard abstinence as a virtue, he looks askance at its extreme form, commending joyful optimism instead.

Written in Arabic, it soon became the most popular ethical treatise in the Middle Ages. To this day, study-

---

[14] See "Wisdom of Israel", pp. 302-320 for characteristic extracts. The ten "Gates" are שער היחוד, הבחינה, עבודת האלהים, הבטחון, יחוד המעשה, הכניעה, התשובה, חשבון הנפש, הפרישות, ושער אהבת י׳

circles are held with the book as their text, passages from it being regularly recited by pious Jews as part of their devotional exercises during the first two solemn days of the Jewish Year and on Yom Kippur itself. Its popularity is well deserved. It is religious in character and deals in a practical way with the duties and responsibilities of our faith. The aim of moral discipline is to love God *"with all our heart, soul and might"*. This ambition can be fulfilled by study and self-discipline. Gratitude to God is the main theme, an attitude of mind, he contends, which will engender in man a passion for religious and ethical acts.

He agrees with the views of Gabirol, though his own approach is ethical rather than metaphysical. Humility is the highest quality of the soul because it causes its possessor to be generous towards all and to overlook the shortcomings of others, being always ready to forgive when sinned against. Bahyah's deep psychological understanding of human nature, his emphasis on self-contemplation, his moderate asceticism, together with the original style in which he wrote have won for him an immortal niche in the hall of classical literature. Extracts are not the best *media* through which to give a worthy impression of the book, yet the following passage is so characteristic that it claims quotation.

"A man should commune with himself in reference to the desires of his heart and his worldly tastes. A careful consideration of the ends they serve will lead him to look with contempt on fleeting possessions. His thoughts and desires will then be fixed on the highest good and on what is of eternal value to mind and soul. He will learn to strive only for what is actually necessary of the things of this world. He will desire to be kept both from poverty and riches so that he may have enough for a simple, healthy life. He will yearn after wisdom and spiritual possessions, of which none can rob him.

"Another subject for self-communing is the question whether we have made proper provision for the journey we must one day make to another world. Only a foolish traveller will wait until he is actually on the road, before making provisions for his necessities. The wise man will prepare his '*food for the way*' well in advance. We must prepare for death whilst we live by storing up '*good deeds*'.

"Another subject that should not be neglected in our contemplation, is the inclination of the soul to seek the fellowship of men. The advantage of occasional solitude and temporary separation from men is the avoidance of association with their evils and follies and of not being always influenced by their example. To speak much is calculated to lead to the talking of slander and the telling of untruths, even on occasion to the taking of false oaths. One of the Hasidim said to his disciples: 'The Torah permits our swearing by the name of the Creator to what is true; but I counsel you not to take an oath by the holy name of God, whether to the truth or to a lie. Say simply "*Yes*" or "*No*".' Too much social intercourse leads to boasting and the display of knowledge. The pure of heart will love solitude; but here again the temptation to complete solitude must be guarded against. Living in the society of philosophers, of the pious, and of great men, in general, is of tremendous advantage to our moral well-being.

"One should consider well, in communing with the soul, whether he has made the best use of any wealth that he may possess. Has he always done good with it? One should meditate constantly on the many ways in which one man can help another, only doing unto others that which he loves others to do for him. Man should rejoice in the happiness of others and grieve in their sorrow. At all times he should be full of compassion for them, warding off from them to the utmost of his power any-

thing that may injure them. Has it not been said: 'And
thou shalt love thy neighbour as thyself'?"[15]

V. YEHUDAH HALEVI (1085-1142)

Like Gabirol, Yehudah Halevi was not only a poet but a
philosopher. Unlike him, he made his metaphysics
subservient to his intense Jewishness. In 1140, he wrote
his masterpiece the *Kuzari*[16] in the form of a dialogue
between the King of the Crimean Kingdom of the
Khazars and the Rabbi who converted him from paganism
to Judaism. In this book, for which he obviously used
Saadiah as a model, he presents the reader with a vivid
and excellent summary of Jewish traditional beliefs and
their ethical implications.

In the course of writing this classic, two truths dawned
upon him. One: that as a basis of Jewish belief the continuity of Jewish tradition outweighs philosophical
arguments. Two: that the preservation of Judaism is
contingent on the possession of our national homeland.
His *"Ode to Zion"*, which is included in the liturgy of
Tisha B'av, has ranked him as our first national Poet-
Laureate. His personal claim to attention here lies in the
distinct contribution he made to our ethical teachings.

It is not necessary to quote excerpts from the
Kuzari, for the book has been translated into almost
every European language.[17] Let only a few observations

[15] Lev. xix. 18.
[16] In Arabic, in which it was written, it is called *Kitab Al-
Khazari*.
[17] The "East & West" Library has recently given us an abridged
"Kuzari", by Prof. Heinemann; but the best English translation is still that of Prof. H. Hirschfeld. See also representative
selections in Lewis Browne's "Wisdom of Israel", pp. 321-325.
The best of extracts, however, cannot take the place of a study
of the book itself in its Hebrew version.

suffice.[18] The anti-philosophical attitude and deep religious sense of Yehudah Halevi strengthened his scepticism concerning the faculties of reason to grasp unaided the idea of God. In Judaism, he emphasizes, History and Tradition are the *only* sure sources of truth as well as of the knowledge of God. It was from this angle that Halevi arrived at the conclusion of the important *rôles* which nationalism and the Hebrew language must both play in any explanation of the survival of our faith—a survival to be described not so much as the *history* of a *miracle* but as the *miracle* of *history*.

To him, Judaism was the *only* true religion, based as it is on the Torah and Revelation and not on the rationalism of Aristotelian philosophy or on the uncertainties of Neoplatonic thought. For one reason or another, mainly perhaps because of his ardent nationalism (a feature so strong in Jewish life to-day with the establishment of the *Medinat* Israel), Judah Halevi is the most widely-read medieval writer on Jewish ethics. His views are discussed among scholars perhaps more than those of any other writer, with the exception of that other great star in the Jewish horizon—Maimonides.

VI. MOSES MAIMONIDES (1135-1204)

Maimonides was a faithful follower of Aristotle whom he calls *"the philosopher of all philosophers"*.[19] Not only does he subscribe to the metaphysics of this Greek thinker, but he is also influenced by his doctrine of ethics. There is this important difference, however. In Maimonides, ethics and religion are indissolubly linked, morality being

---

[18]See Vallentine's "Jewish Encyclopædia", p. 518 (s.v. Philosophy), 1938.

[19]הֶחָכָם שֶׁבַּחֲכָמִים; See especially the *"Guide for the Perplexed"*.

best attained through a faithful observance of the *Mitzvot*.
This point he makes clear in his introduction to *Abot* as well
as in various passages of his *Sepher Hamitzvot*, his *Mishneh
Torah*, and especially in his *"Guide of the Perplexed"*.[20] He
will always be thankfully remembered as the great harmon-
izer of Greek and Jewish thought, the golden link between
the culture of the West and the wisdom of the East.

His ethical teachings have been described as those of
Aristotle clad in a Jewish garb and supported by quotations from Bible and Talmud. In his ethical system, he
harmonizes God's omniscience and foreknowledge with
man's freewill, stressing that the highest aim of man lies
in concentrating his intellect on God. Significant is the
fact that his vast compendium begins with the section of
Knowledge (*Deot*). Those trained in philosophy can best
obtain the highest knowledge of the glory of Judaism
and come into mystic union with God. The first necessity
towards moral and intellectual perfection is to subdue
physical urges and render the body subservient to reason.
Neither the wise who lack virtue, nor the virtuous who
lack wisdom can claim to be absolutely perfect. The Jew
must lead a regular life, eschewing evil and choosing good.
The power of choice and freewill is his. He must seek
medical advice in sickness, observe bodily hygiene at all
times and be pure and clean in his thoughts and deeds.

Being a renowned physician, he wrote in Arabic a work
on the *"Health of the Soul"* (*Tab Al'Nafus*), in which he
emphasized that to have perfect peace of mind and
contentment, the health of the soul must be looked after
as much as the well-being of the body. What food and
fresh air are for the body, moderation in joy and grief and

---

[20]See *"Eight Chapters"* IV; *"Guide of the Perplexed"*, III. 33;
Hilchot Deot, and *Hilchot Tshuvah*. A book by Yellin and
Abrahams gives, in a small compass, a worthy estimate of this
great figure.

a well-balanced outlook are to the soul. Pity for all created things is the sign of a healthy soul; so is the respect of the life and property of others. These views, to cite only a few, have exercised the greatest influence on all subsequent writers. No other teachings have been more unstintingly praised, so critically examined, so bitterly attacked both during his life-time and long after his death.

The essential differences between Maimonides and the Aristotelian school of ethics can be briefly described. The latter treat the moral aspect of life as of incidental concern. To the Jewish thinker, metaphysical speculation is basically a side issue and his concentration is on the ethical side. To Maimonides, Judaism was the main inspiration of all his work. Ardent supporter as he at first was of Aristotle's "*First Cause*", the moment he discovered that this theory had no real relationship with this world he took leave of Aristotle and created a new metaphysics which claimed support from the mystical principles of Plato.

Maimonides could not wholeheartedly agree with the Greek philosopher who conceived speculation as the sole aim of being, and who taught that things divine could be understood only by means of the rational faculties of man.[21] Maimonides did not deny the general truth of this theory. He contended, however, that since man has been endowed with evil instincts, passions, appetites and distractions, both of a mental and physical nature, he must secure the aid of something more than logic to conquer them. For this reason he adumbrates and develops the Aristotelian "*Mean*."

To surmount these obstacles, there must come into operation the workings of practical reason which will serve to regulate human action and provide for the

[21]See the essay of Dr. I. Epstein in the "Memorial Volume to Maimonides", pp. 59ff., 1935 (Soncino).

physical needs, enabling us to proceed undeterred towards our goal. These actions are in themselves neither good nor bad. Their moral worth is determined solely by the extent to which they help or hinder man in his realization of the highest perfection.[22] Maimonides emphasizes that the attainment of *intellectual* perfection is in measure with the acquisition of *moral* perfection. Real knowledge, in his view, is not merely the possession of a logical brain but of the knowledge of God. *"Thus saith the Lord: Let not the wise man glory in his wisdom, neither let the mighty man glory in his might. Let not the rich man glory in his riches, but let him that glorieth glory in this: that he understandeth and knoweth me"* (Jeremiah ix. 22-23).

Maimonides displays a definite ethical trend in all his writings, brooking no gulf between belief and action. According to him, all *Mitzvot* have their *source* in God. Their *object* is the ennoblement of man and his perfection. They purposefully form part of the divine plan to teach good morals, increase knowledge and improve actions. He seems to have blazoned a path for St. Thomas Aquinas[23] in subordinating, in his prophetical expositions, natural knowledge to Revelation, though clearly recognizing the light of reason as a source of knowledge besides the light of grace.[24] The object of this world, created *"ex nihilo"* and by the *fiat* of God, was moral perfection. He attacks those schools of thought which see more evil than good in this world. *"The evils which men do to each other"*, he points out, *"are vastly greater than any natural*

[22] Ibid.

[23] Whose *"Summa Theologica"* quotes several times the *"Guide"*, and who calls Maimonides, R. Moses *"Aegiptione"*, "the Egyptian" (sic), a reference to the domicile of Maimonides in Cairo for many years.

[24] For a cross-section of the teachings of Maimonides, *vide* Browne's "Wisdom of Israel", pp. 347-375, but especially A. Cohen's "Teachings of Maimonides" (Routledge, 1927).

evils which befall them. Whatsoever is formed of matter must suffer the ills inherent in matter, and even here man himself must bear most of the burden of blame."

These evils, he emphasizes, are negative, being merely the absence of good (*shelilah*). They are categorized into three kinds: Those which befall man because he is of flesh and blood; those which men themselves bring on one another by use of force and inhumanity, evils, by the way, which vastly exceed the other kinds. Thirdly, those evils which are caused by greed and lack of insight into the real values of life. Being the doctor of the *soul*, as well as of the *body*, Maimonides prescribes the enthroning of the spiritual as against the material and the intellectual as against the instinctive.

He is, however, a practical idealist. For though he ranks the welfare of the soul above that of the body, he agrees that the well-being of the body must take pride of place, if the other is to be possible. "The well-being of the soul can be promoted by correct opinions communicated to the people according to their capacity, either in plain form or by allegory. The well-being of the body can be attained by the proper organization of the relations in which we live, one to another; namely, by banishing violence from our midst and by directing our actions only for the welfare of mankind." Maimonides demands that we judge all things not from our own personal point of view but from that of mankind. Our lives depend just as much upon the lives of others as theirs depend on ours.

"The greatness of Maimonides", writes Browne,[25] "lay in his prodigious capacity not alone for amassing knowledge, but also for sifting and essaying it. His first major work, a comprehensive commentary on the *Mishnah*, begun when he was twenty-three, already revealed the

[25]Ibid. p. 348.

striking independence of his mind. He heaped scorn on all who *'being ignorant of science, and far away from knowledge'* took every saying of the ancient Rabbis *literally*." Many of these sayings, he insisted, were purely figurative. He was a rationalist and his *"Guide of the Perplexed"* reveals him a rationalizer of religious beliefs who exerted a tremendous influence on medieval scholasticism. To Jews, he will always be a guide to ethical conduct, a beacon shining the way to speculative heights. His message is that all the evils we encounter are not in nature or in life but often in ourselves and in our own actions. God, nature and life are good. Man must therefore become perfect with the help of Judaism.[26]

VII. ELEAZER B. JUDAH B. KALONYMUS (1160-1238)

The principal work of this Cabbalist, Talmudist and liturgical poet was the *Rokeah*, a treatise on Ethics and Jewish law influenced largely by the mystical tendencies of his great teacher, Rabbi Judah *He'hasid* of Regensburg.[27] The name of the book was deliberately chosen. The word Rokeah occurs in the Bible[28] where it is translated *"perfumer"*, and this prompted him to try and impart to the daily life of the Jew the fragrance of

---

[26] A digest of *"The Teachings of Maimonides"* has been compiled by A. Cohen, London, 1927. More recently, Hutchinsons has published a noteworthy study on the *"Guide"* by Prof. Leon Roth (1949).

[27] Died in 1200. Though acquainted with the rationalistic philosophy cultivated by his colleagues in Spain and North Africa, he preferred to steep himself in mysticism, convinced that thus alone could he attain true wisdom and perfect solace. His *"Book of the Pious"* is a rambling treatise full of moral reflections, theosophical flights, and pleasant superstitions. See "Wisdom of Israel", pp. 387-389.

[28] Exodus xxx. 35.

religion. His object has well been described thus:[29] "*Just as the holy anointing-oil scented the lowliest vessels of the sanctuary, so the goodly direction of the* Rokeah *sought to sweeten and glorify the humblest life.*" To him, as to the French philosopher Amiel, religion without mysticism was like a rose without perfume. Though he advocated the most meticulous observance of Jewish ritual, he always emphasized the finer aspects of our moral standards.

Rabbi Eleazer not only *preached* ethics; he *lived* it. His wife and children had met a cruel death at the hands of the Crusaders in 1196, at Erfurt; yet he writes in his Introduction: "*Forgive them that speak ill of thee and avenge not thyself upon him that injures thee.*" When one thinks of the tragedy of his life, a tragedy often enacted in the lives of many others of our ancestors, one recalls the question of Leopold Zunz: "If a sad event depicted for two hours in the theatre is called a tragedy, what should we say of a tragedy that has lasted for two thousand years and has not ended yet?"

Our ethical codes do not depict a Deity, transcendental and remote from "*the vale of tears,*" in splendid isolation from those He has formed. In the pages of the *Rokeah*, God appears as the "*Holy One*" whose holiness is an everlasting challenge and an inexhaustible inspiration to human society. God is part of our very selves. To sin against Him is a *Hillul Ha'shem*. Since He is within us, our life should be one of holiness and self-denial.[30] Touching and beautiful is his comment on Prayer: "Fix thy mind upon Him when thou prayest and say to thyself: 'How honoured I am to be allowed to offer a Crown to the King of Glory, since I am but clay'. Therefore think reverently on God while the breath of

---

[29] In an interesting essay on the book in the Jubilee Volume of Jews' College, 1905, by the Rev. Morris Joseph.
[30] Ibid. p. 179.

life is still within thee; for His eyes run to and fro throughout the earth."

The Rokeah[31] describes the ideal Jew as one who bears patiently "*the yoke of the heavenly Kingdom*", who is ever humble and self-denying, who scorns the vain pleasures of this life and who lives by his faith. The perfect Jew has gentle speech for all, rejoices in the good fortune of another, loving him and always ready to lend a generous hand without thought of public recognition for his kindness of heart. "*Walking with God*", another term for Holiness ripens into noble deeds. The thoughts of the ideal man will resemble "*a mass of heated metal glowing with the fires of this love*".

Fired by his own example, he counsels resignation when faced with divine chastisements. May not these well be stepping-stones and gateways to noble opportunities serving as purifying agents and pledges of divine love?[32] Each utterance of this remarkable book has the true accent of Jewish ethics. Let this quotation serve as illustration: "If a man has sinned, let him repent with all his might, praying earnestly to receive pardon and to sin no more. If trials come upon him, let him greet them with joy. Even when he has repented he is not, on that account, to expect impunity. He may still have to expiate his transgressions in suffering. The glad submission with which he receives his punishments is to be regarded as part of his penance and atonement."

The Rokeah further counsels us to shun worldly delights as so much vanity and vexation of the spirit and exhorts us not to indulge in the luxury of woe or to welter in a sea of sorrow for its own sake. True service to God

---

[31]It was usual for an author to be known after his book. See a fascinating essay on this theme by Schechter in his "Studies in Judaism" (First Series).

[32]Rabbinic phrase is יסורין של אהבה; cf. Ber. 6a.

means to flood the soul with light, not to enshroud it in gloom. The Rabbinic phrase is "*Simhah shel Mitzvah*". The words of Emerson[33] may well sum up the practical wisdom of this great classic: "*It would be hard to put more mental and moral philosophy than the Persians have thrown into a sentence: 'Fooled thou must be, though wisest of the wise; then be thou fool of virtue, not of vice'.*" Both Rabbi Eleazer and his *Rokeach* will always occupy an honoured place in the history of Jewish ethics, serving as sublime patterns of conduct and impressing upon us that man is a dual composition of mind and matter capable of the rarest virtues.

VIII. THE CONTRIBUTION TO ETHICS OF THE CABBALAH

The mystical philosophy which so deeply influenced the Middle Ages and which is known as the *Cabbalah*, probably began in the seventh century of our era. It reached its culmination in the *Zohar* whose composition belongs to the thirteenth century.[34] Among the amalgam of ideas, beliefs and doctrines drawn from all sources, Jewish and non-Jewish, there jostle the views of neo-Pythagorism; Neoplatonism, Gnosticism and Philonism with those of Biblical and Rabbinical exegeses and ethical maxims. "The whole material appears under a Jewish colouring of an intense religious sanctity and a devoutness which has made the study of the *Cabbalah* the pursuit

---

[33]Quoted in his essay on "Illusions".

[34]Tradition had claimed Rabbi Shimon b. Johai as the author, because the work begins with his utterance. Recent scholarship, however, has established that Moses de Leon of Spain was the editor of this mystical commentary on the Pentateuch in the thirteenth century c.e. See the "*Zohar*", edited in 5 volumes by H. Sperling and M. Simon, and published by the Soncino Press in a scholarly English translation.

of the most saintly and most pious sections among the Jews.

The first impetus to the intensive study and development of the *Cabbalah* in the Middle Ages came from a desire to break away from the supposed rigid and arid formalism of Talmudic Judaism which had given the mistaken impression to many that Judaism is more of an external and legalistic system and little of a religion of the spirit. The *Cabbalah* was a revolt against this religious petrifaction in favour of a more vital dynamic religion of an inward and first-hand type."[35] It is this revolt that is, in itself, its major contribution to our ethical codes.

In its doctrine of the "*Eser Sephirot*" (Ten Emanations), an attempt to portray a cosmic realm in which there exists an unbroken intercourse on the wings of prayer between God and His world, the moral perfection of man is made to influence the ideal world. Study is exalted to the rank of an aid by which man can escape the machinations of Satan. Righteousness is described as the dew which vivifies a parched humanity. Study and Service to mankind, *Torah and Avodah*, are the forces responsible for the full and the happy life.

Evil, which can be conquered, man having freewill, is necessary to the divine scheme of existence. Without it, there can be no good. Various attempts are made at solving the age-old problem of good and evil. Insistence is laid on the fact that the words of the Torah must be interpreted not always in a literal but often also in a mystical sense. Every word of the Bible was made to yield by various devices[36] some esoteric meaning. This

---

[35]J. Abelson, in Vallentine's Jewish Encyclopædia, s.v. *Cabbalah*.

[36]The devices chiefly used are *Gematria, Notarikon and Temurah* —permutations and combinations of letters, numerical values and other fanciful advices favoured especially by the *B'aal Ha'turim* in his commentary on the Pentateuch.

method of numerical dialectics may have helped to confuse the minds of many scholars; but does it justify the bitter attack made by one writer who brands it "as a *confused* body of notions furtively growing in Israel for over a thousand years, claiming to contain the wisdom secretly *"received"* (*Cabbalah*) by successive saints to whom it had been divinely revealed?"[37]

The *Zohar*, which contains such passages as "Every man should so live that at the close of every day he can say: 'I have not wasted my day';" and again, "that there is no spot on earth devoid of the presence of God"— among others equally beautiful, does not deserve, either the condemnation of Grätz that *"it is lunacy raised to the degree of a science"* or that of Browne that: "Actually it was made up for the most part of abstruse irrationalities picked up third-hand from various peoples who had come in contact with the Hindus."[38]

Contradicting himself on the next page,[39] Browne is more fair to the *Zohar* when he says: "With all his insistence on the primacy of ecstatic union with God, the compiler of the *Zohar* could not forget the importance of service (*Avodah*) to mankind. Apparently, even to this impassioned theosophist, faith had meaning only in so far as it was supported by works."

When one considers the centuries during which mysticism was at its peak—the period of the Crusades, covering the eleventh, twelfth and thirteenth centuries— one is surprised not so much at the superstitions that have

[37] L. Browne in "Wisdom of Israel", p. 379. Browne seems to have been too much under the influence of Grätz, whose bias against the *Cabbalah* was undeserving. This prejudice of Grätz, together with some unfortunate misstatements of historic events, has robbed his monumental work of much of its value as a reliable source of information.
[38] Ibid.
[39] Ibid., p. 380.

crept into *cabbalistic* writings but at the fact that despite the inordinate absorption in ritualism and mysticism which characterized these tragic centuries, the Jews never ceased to ponder the problem of ethical conduct.[40] An equally inspiring source for right living is to be found in the many ethical wills left by some of the greatest scholars and saints of medieval times, like Nahmanides (1194-1270), Judah b. Asher (1270-1349), the Gaon of Wilna (1720-1797), and many others.[41] These "*Wills*" contain intimate and paternal guidance throwing light, in addition, on the character of the writer and on the conditions of his times.

Among the notable works of this kind are the *Sepher Ha'Hanagah* (Book of Conduct),[42] by Asher b. Yehiel, and the *Sepher Hamusar* (Book of Morality)[43] by Joseph ibn Caspi, containing his famous programme of Jewish education. One must not, of course, omit the endless mine of ethical conduct to be found on almost every page of Joseph Karo's "*Shulchan Aruch*" (1488-1575) and in the earlier compendium "*Mishneh Torah*" of Maimonides.

IX. THE INFLUENCE OF HASIDISM

The importance of this movement, originating in the eighteenth century among the Jews of Eastern Europe, lies in its central tenet that *everything*—mind and matter, good and evil, the birds and the bees and the rocks and the rills—are all so many manifestations of God. From

---

[40]The reader will find a digest of its moral lessons in the "Talmudic Anthology" by Newman and Spitz, and especially in Martin Buber's "Or Haganuz" (Schocken, 1947).

[41]A most interesting collection has been edited by Israel Abrahams in his "Ethical Wills" (J.P.S. of America).

[42]Better known as "*Orhot Hayim*" (Paths of Life).

[43]Or *Yoreh Deah* (Teacher of Knowledge).

this it followed that God could be worshipped at all times and everywhere, not necessarily according to a fixed formula but with whatever words came into one's mind.[44] All the world, like the Bush seen by Moses in his vision, is aflame with God; but only he who *sees* takes off his shoes and draws nigh to the site, realizing that he is treading on holy ground.

The chief emphasis of the *Besht*[45] was that zeal, prayerful devotion and humility were more acceptable to God than intellectualism. The most ignorant man could draw as near to God as the most learned. Since access to God was so easy, one ought to be full of joy. The adherents of *Hasidism* stressed that there was a mystical ecstasy in the communion of God and man which must be fed on the joyful affirmation of life, on the practice of compassion, charity and love and on democracy and brotherhood between rich and poor as well as on the moral values of Judaism. "*Hasidism is Judaism*", says one authority,[46] "with particular points of interest, emphasis and practice. It is a free and intensely emotional expression of Judaism adapted to the common people. Hasidism is more than a *cult;* it is a *culture*. While it has its unique message, it is as complex and as varied as the life and outlook of the millions who have been its adherents."

[44] See "Wisdom of Israel", p. 459. The reader who wishes a more reliable estimate of the contributions of Hasidism and mysticism to Jewish Ethics must consult the authoritative works of Martin Buber (Hasidism) and Scholem, ("Major Trends in Jewish Mysticism.")

[45] A word abbreviated from *Baal Shem-Tov*, the name given to the founder of Hasidism, Rabbi Israel b. Eliezer (1700-1760). See Martin Buber (*Or Haganuz*), pp. 1-104.

[46] See "*The Hasidic Anthology*" by Newman and Spitz (New York, 1934), for an Introduction to the history and teachings of the movement and a comprehensive collection, under alphabetical order, of some of its wise maxims and gnomic utterances. See also "Wisdom of Israel", pp. 459-500.

The brevity of this note on Hasidism must not serve as an index of its invaluable contribution to Jewish ethics; but where others have written so comprehensively, it would be folly to add anything new. The subject has fascinated some of the greatest scholars of modern times, like Schechter and Buber, Horodetzky, Cahana and Scholem because Hasidism has enriched the life of our people for the past two hundred years at every point. The movement has made notable contributions towards the philosophy of the Jewish life, preserving striking expressions of outstanding personalities on the major subjects of belief, philosophy and experience. It has also added to our literature a rich legacy of fabled beauty and exquisite quality.

Realizing its power, when purged of the dross of fanaticism and the cult of mercenary *Tsaddikim*,[47] to endow the Jewish masses with vitality and religious ecstasy, an attempt has been made in our own days by Martin Buber to preach a neo-Hasidism which purports to be a return to the fundamentals of the movement.[48] But as one writer observes,[49] "The principles and conclusions of neo-Hasidism are as different from those of the old movement as Buber with a twentieth-century outlook differs from the *Besht* and his day." Some revival of the early Hasidic spirit is a *desideratum* in these prosaic and sordid days. For it would ennoble the new Jewish Life in *Medinat Israel* and also exert a tremendous impact far beyond the boundaries of the Third Jewish Commonwealth.

---

[47]The name adopted by descendants of the founders of the movement who established dynasties vying in regal splendour those of the courts.

[48]"*Hasidism*" in East & West Library, 1947.

[49]Vallentine's Jewish Encyclopædia, p. 139 s.v. "*Chassidim*", a brief article by Dr. S. Grayzel, a noted American Jewish historian.

X. MOSES HAYYIM LUZZATTO (1707-1747)

We must content ourselves with a reference to one other great figure who made a noteworthy contribution to Jewish ethics. Moses Hayyim Luzzatto was perhaps the last saintly scholar to write in the medieval spirit. His piety and mysticism are all the more remarkable when it is realized that he lived in a century in which his contemporaries were Voltaire, Rousseau, Heine, Swedenborg, Zinzendorff and the Wesleys.[50] The fact that he imagined himself the recipient of heavenly revelation from great Biblical personages under whose influence he wrote his cabbalistic writings does not in the least detract from the value of his classic, the "*Mesillat Yesharim*". To this day, it is studied widely and with great advantage for the attainment of the ethical life. (It will be recalled that Joseph Karo also had a medium which he called *Mishnah*, and which prompted him to write.) This work is deservedly popular and has been translated into most modern European languages on account of its lasting contribution to the godly life. The extracts cited below will give some indication of the rare spirit that has communicated to subsequent generations the truths flashed forth to him from heaven.

The bias displayed by Grätz towards anybody who manifested mystical tendencies is seen from the fact that although he acknowledges Luzzatto as the Master of Hebrew and the poet of genius who allowed himself to be misguided by the Cabbala, not the slightest reference is made by him to the *Mesillat Yesharim*, one of the gems

---

[50]See "Wisdom of Israel", pp. 440-451, for some selected passages from his classic "*Mesillat Yesharim*" (*Path of the Righteous*), first published in 1740 in Hebrew, and translated into English by M. Kaplan (J.P.S., Philadelphia, 1936).

of our ethical literature. Yet it is to this classic that Luzzatto owes his fame. In it, he triumphantly vindicates the spirituality of Judaism as did Bahyah ibn Pakuda before him.[51] The book elaborates a remarkable statement made by Rabbi Pinchas b. Yair, one of the saints in the Talmud, a statement which has been called "*The Saint's Progress*".

Here it is: "The knowledge of Torah leads to awareness; awareness to zeal; zeal to cleanliness; cleanliness to abstinence; abstinence to purity; purity to saintliness; saintliness to humility; humility to fear of sin; fear of sin to holiness; holiness to possession of the holy spirit; the possession of the holy spirit to the power to resurrect the dead."[52] Luzzatto attractively expounds each of these grades, stopping short at the last rung of this ladder of holiness, lest he be suspected of those cabbalistic pursuits which he had been made to swear that he would abandon. Into this little masterpiece are compressed the brilliant style of the author, his deep spirituality and his humble saintliness. To read it is a literary delight; to ponder its truths a spiritual experience.

His introduction to the book is significant for its enormous value to the study of Jewish ethics: "I have not written this book to teach the reader anything new. Rather is it my aim to direct his attention to certain well-known and generally-accepted truths. The fact that they are well known and generally accepted is the cause of their being overlooked. This book, if it is to be of any benefit, has to be read more than once. A single reading may give the impression that it does not enlarge one's

[51] In his "Duties of the Heart".

[52] Ab. Zarah 20[b]: Sotah ix. 15. He was the son-in-law of R. Simeon b. Johai, to whose shrine at Meron, in Northern Galilee, annual pilgrimage is made at Lag B'omer, his reputed *Yahrzeit*.

stock of ideas; to derive any benefit from the book, it should be read and reread, time and again. Then only will it lead us to reckon with those truths which we naturally forget, as well as teaching us to take seriously the performance of those duties which we usually try to avoid."[53] Could more disarming sincerity be found in any other author?

"One who is saintly", proceeds Luzzatto, "is inevitably suspected of being a dullard. This fact has its evil consequences both for the learned and the unlearned. It will be exceedingly hard to find saintliness among us, since neither the learned nor the ignorant are likely to cultivate it. The learned will lack saintliness because they do not give it sufficient thought; the ignorant will not possess it because their powers of understanding are limited.

"The majority of men will conceive saintliness to consist in reciting numerous Psalms and long confessionals; in fasting and ablutions and in ice and snow. Such practices fail to satisfy the intellect and offer nothing to the understanding. We find it difficult properly to conceive true saintliness, since we cannot grasp that to which we give no thought. Although saintliness is latent in the character of every normal person, yet without cultivation it is sure to remain dormant."

It is in this vein that the book is written. It is a case of *"deep calling unto deep"*. Tradition has it that when the Gaon of Wilna had finished reading the book for the first time, he exclaimed: *"Were Moses Hayyim Luzzatto alive to-day, I would go on foot to Safed to learn Torah and morals from him."* Rabbi Israel Lipkin of Salant, the founder of the *Musar* Movement[54] in the middle of the

[53]See an article on the *Mesillat Yesharim* in "The Jewish Review", Nov. 4th, 1949 (London), by Rabbi Dr. L. Rabinowitz.

[54]He established special lectures on the ethical implications of the *Halachah* at the leading *Yeshivot* of Russia and Poland.

nineteenth century made this book the subject of concentrated study in the renowned *Yeshivot* of Europe.
Professor S. Schechter is no less appreciative of its worth:[55]
"The Jewish public took but little notice of Luzzatto's
'One hundred and thirty-eight Doors of Wisdom', but it
did appreciate at once his noble '*Paths of the Righteous*',
preaching morality and holiness."

The book will make no appeal to those who believe in
a system of ethics divorced from divine sanctions. To
those, however, who see ethics as part of religion and who
realize that the impulse behind it is the desire to fulfil the
way of God, the book will remain a perennial source of
religious inspiration. It is because of the soundness of
this view that we have deemed it right to seal this chapter,
dealing with the ethical stars in our medieval firmament,
with one of the brightest of them all—Moses Hayyim
Luzzatto. Let him who wishes to convert an occasional and
fleeting glimpse of goodness in thought and deed into an
abiding and permanent vision turn to the pages of the
"*Mesillat Yesharim*". He will find in it much of spiritual
worth, having communion at the same time with a rare
spirit the like of which the world has seldom seen.

[55]See "Studies in Judaism" (2nd Series, p. 281).

CHAPTER SIX

ETHICS IN MODERN TIMES

FROM the writings of a selected few, each representative of a school of thought in his own day, we shall be enabled to appreciate the distinct contributions they made towards the development of Jewish ethics. The scope of this book cannot include a comprehensive summary of Jewish thought throughout twenty centuries; otherwise many great names, here of necessity omitted, would have been included.[1] Chosen for mention are those that have some unique and constructive point of view to offer. Before we begin with the contribution of Mendelssohn, with whom the modern era in Jewish history may be said to begin, there are three names which call for passing notice.

I. LEVI B. GERSHON[2] (1288-1344)

Levi b. Gershon was the first to write a classical religious-philosophical work in Hebrew to supplement and correct the presentation of Judaism made by Maimonides in his *"Guide"*. His *"Milhemet Ha'shem"* (Battle of the Lord) is a classic which reveals him intellectually akin to Maimonides. Like him, he was a great Talmudist and an expert mathematician, philosopher

---

[1] An ambitious but sketchy attempt has been made by A. Lichtigfeld in *"Twenty Centuries of Jewish Thought"* (London, 1938), consisting of brief extracts from the works of writers on metaphysics and ethics of Judaism over two thousand years.

[2] He was commonly known as Gersonides, or *RaLBaG*, after the first letters of his name.

and astronomer. He differed from him, however, in his uncompromising rationalism, apparent not only from the book just mentioned but also from his commentaries on most of the books of the Bible. Like Maimonides again, he, too, was often attacked for his outspokenness in religious belief; but his work is a further proof that truth will ultimately prevail. From an ethical viewpoint, his work is significant in that he maintained that the thoughts and actions which Judaism seeks to guide and control are those based on the mind as well as the heart. Our love of God must never allow emotionalism and sentimentality so to dominate our lives as to disregard a rational approach to faith. Judaism is essentially a religion in which belief is inseparable from reason.

II. HASDAI CRESCAS (1340-1412)

Hasdai Crescas must be mentioned both for the intrinsic worth of his teachings and because he differed radically and vigorously from those Jewish philosophers, including Maimonides and Gersonides, who allowed Aristotle to dominate their own conception of God and the World. He was the last original thinker of medieval Jewry who exercised an influence on the philosophy of Baruch Spinoza (1632-1677). Crescas agreed with R. Yehudah Halevi that when one is considering the imponderable verities in the realm of ethical conduct, the emotional motive should receive prior claim over the intellectual. This explains his constant defence of belief against the attacks of pure rationalism. Religion to him, as to Matthew Arnold centuries later, was *"morality touched by emotion"*.

He was emphatic in his insistence that to achieve moral perfection and consummate union with God which such a state implied, neither theory nor practice *alone* is sufficient. The indivisible fusion of both must be an earnest of the ideal Jewish life. Though all human action was providentially foreseen this did, however, detract from the power of man to choose the good and eschew evil.[3] Echoing an isolated Talmudic opinion, he taught that the dispersion of Israel among the nations was designed to serve as a moral improvement not only of the Jewish nation but, indirectly, of the salvation of all mankind. We, who have witnessed the miraculous foundation of the new Jewish State in Israel, prefer to pin our faith in the emergence of a better world, to live in the "*Light*" which will come again, with the help of God, from Judea. Dispersion is fraught with too much attrition, assimilation and extinction.

III. JOSEPH ALBO (1380-1440)

From Crescas, we pass on to his distinguished disciple, Joseph Albo, who enriched Jewish thought by a work distinguished for clarity and comprehensiveness, by power of exposition and philosophy. His *Ikkarim* (Fundamentals), the popularity of which is still undiminished among scholars, based Judaism not on the *Thirteen* Principles of Faith of Maimonides but on the *three* fundamental beliefs whose denial would signify heresy. These are: The Existence of God, and all that it implies; Divine Revelation, and its corollary, and the belief in Retribution.

This is not the place to discuss his metaphysics. We would only add that what prompted Maimonides, Albo and others to search for dogmas in Judaism was the challenge of Christianity with its minimum of custom and

[3] Thus agreeing with R. Akiba's statement in Abot iii. 19.

observance. Other factors contributing to this reinterpretation of Judaism were the new development of the natural sciences and the radical changes which occurred in the world at the end of the Middle Ages.[4] More about Albo and his philosophical and ethical interpretations of Judaism is readily available in the English translation of his *Ikkarim* by the Jewish Publication Society of America.

IV. MOSES MENDELSSOHN (1729-1786)

The modern era in Jewish thought may conveniently be said to have begun with Mendelssohn, a man of genius who deserved to be called by Jews *"the third Moses"*[5] and by non-Jews, *"a second Plato"*. In the task of reinterpreting Judaism in the light of *Haskalah* and Emancipation it was German Jewry, at the impetus of Mendelssohn, that was conspicuously productive in those pre-Hitler days. The part that Spain played in the Middle Ages was now assumed by the flourishing communities of Germany. By nature, Mendelssohn was the philosopher and the recluse rather than the theologian and the apologist. He was forced into theological controversy by Lavater, a German pastor who tried to convert him to Christianity; to receive, of course, the answer he deserved.

[4] The brevity of this notice of Albo must not be taken as a measure of his invaluable contribution towards a systematic presentation of Judaism. His *"Ikkarim"* ranks among the solid classics of our philosophical works. With Albo we must close our retrospective survey of the ethical teachings of the Middle Ages and pass on to modern times. The omission of other great names, apart from consideration of space, is chiefly due to the fact that their owners did not tread any new path in Jewish ethics but merely repeated what others before them had said.

[5] The first two being Moses the Lawgiver and Moses Maimonides.

In reply, Mendelssohn was driven to make public his views on religion in general and on Judaism in particular. The result was his *"Jerusalem"* (1763), an epoch-making work in which he demonstrated the compatibility of Judaism with the religion of reason. In our faith (and he was staunch in his orthodoxy), he saw no conflict whatsoever between Reason and Belief. There is no need for an enlightened citizen to stifle his reason in order to be religious. Mendelssohn urged Jewry not to give up its *"particularism"* but loyally to practise ceremonial Judaism. Theory must be fed by practice, as the wick is fed by the oil in the lamp. Ethics mean right *doing*, as well as right *thinking*. According to him, the word *Orthopraxia*,[6] instead of *orthodoxy*,[7] would more correctly describe traditional Judaism.

Judaism, a religion primarily intended for Jews but encouraging feelings of respect towards members of other faiths, emphasized that what was demanded of its adherents was not speculation but moral practice. Our ancestors at Revelation stressed *"We will do"* (*na'aseh*) before *"we will understand"* (*ve'nishma*). Then comes the famous passage: "There is not, amongst all the precepts and tenets of the Mosaic Law, a single one which says: 'This shalt thou believe', or 'This shalt thou not believe'. All that the Torah says is: 'This shalt thou do', or 'This thou shalt not do'."[8] Faith, by its very nature, cannot be commanded from *without*. It is essentially a state of mind produced by *inner* conviction.

In this appeal for *deed*, not *creed*, Mendelssohn gives added emphasis to what his illustrious predecessors in the

---

[6] The Greek for "*right doing*".
[7] The Greek for "*right opinion*".
[8] The 613 commandments of Judaism comprise 365 negatives and 248 positives, said to correspond to the days of the year and the limbs of the body respectively.

field of religious ethics had stated. Obvious as this truth must sound to Jewish ears to-day, its revolutionizing nature at the time when "*Jerusalem*" was published can be gauged from the congratulatory message the renowned Immanuel Kant sent to the author, as soon as he had finished reading "*Jerusalem*". Kant[9] wrote that he wished that the lessons of "*Jerusalem*" would be taken to heart by the religions of the world, a comment which speaks volumes.[10]

It must be borne in mind that this book was written at a time when the Ghetto walls were falling and the thirst for assimilation, especially on the part of the more enlightened in Jewry, was overwhelming. The Jewish world was then divided between accepting and rejecting the famous maxim of J. L. Gordon: "*Be a Jew at home, but a man in the street*".[11] Armed as Mendelssohn was with scholarship and authority to stem the onrushing waves of assimilation, these were too strong even for him. Reform Judaism came to Germany not *because* of Mendelssohn but *in spite of* his valiant efforts to vindicate traditional and loyal Judaism.

V.   R. SAMSON RAPHAEL HIRSCH (1808-1888)

The first orthodox Rabbi in Germany to launch a vigorous and scholarly attack against Reform Judaism,

---

[9] Mendelssohn had snatched a prize on a philosophic treatise offered by the Berlin University from Kant who had come a close second.

[10] An English translation of "*Jerusalem*" by M. Samuels appeared in London as early as 1838.

[11] הוי איש בצאתך, ויהודי באהליך. Judah Leib Gordon (1831-1892), was the leading poet of the Haskalah period, displaying a masterly Hebrew style and a definite poetic talent. Had he not allowed himself to become involved in the quarrels between the Hasidim and their opponents (1879), his claim to be the creator of neo-Hebraic poetry would have received universal recognition.

with its emphasis on *"Prophetic"* Judaism and its denial of the validity of Rabbinic Judaism with its accent on custom and observance, was R. Samson Raphael Hirsch. In 1851, he left his position as Chief Rabbi of several communities in Germany to become the Rabbi over a small section in Frankfurt that had seceded from the *Gemeinde*, the larger community, as a protest against the longing for reform that was manifest among the "powers" at the time. From this small beginning, he built up a large congregation, one which was unyieldingly orthodox. Around it he established a network of schools both for secular and Jewish studies. He founded charitable organizations, besides creating a newspaper to publicize his views. In all his writings he displayed a colourful and vigorous personality, manifesting a trenchant and cultured orthodoxy that singled him out as the powerful exponent of views which still exercise tremendous influence in the life of orthodox Jews.

His fame, certainly as far as ethical Judaism is concerned, will rest on his classic *"The Nineteen Letters of Ben Uziel"*,[12] written in German under a *nom de plume*. In this book, he essays to justify the claims of Judaism as an infallible guide to the Jew in the modern world; sympathetically explaining the *inner* purpose of what at first would appear a superficial and incomprehensible command. In this exploratory and speculative mood, he had distinguished followers in the writings of Nathan Birnbaum (1864-1937), Isaac Breuer (1883-1946), and others.

The *"Nineteen Letters"* created a stir and the book was hailed by the orthodox as a brilliant and intellectual presentation of their conception of Judaism. Written in a classical German, fearless and uncompromising in its

---

[12]See the excellent Introduction and Translation in English, by B. Drachman, New York, 1899. The Hebrew version has just appeared in Jerusalem (1950).

defence of *halachic* faith, sympathetic towards Rabbinic institutions and ordinances, it was hailed as the *"Magna Carta"* of orthodox Judaism. It was not long before it gave birth to a new movement, *Neo-orthodoxy*, with its programme of unswerving orthodoxy set in a slightly modernized and aesthetic form. From his writings, one gets the impression that had he assumed the *rôle* of a nineteenth-century Bahyah ibn Pakuda, his presentation of Jewish ethical duties would not bear the title of *"Duties of the Heart"* (*Hovot Ha'Levavot*), but that of *"Duties of the Limbs"* (*Hovot Ha'Evarim*). The emphasis of R. Hirsch was on pious *deeds* rather than on *dreams* of a universal and prophetic Judaism devoid of daily duties.

Not content with the knowledge that his book was regarded with respect by his followers, as was the *"Guide for the Perplexed"* in its day, Hirsch continued to wield the pen in a real *Milhemet Ha'shem*[13] against Holdheim (1806-1860), Wise (1819-1900) and others who, according to him, were cutting at the roots of traditional faith. Abraham Geiger (1810-1874), an intimate friend of his youth and a fellow-student, was now regarded, on account of his heretical views, a bitter opponent whom he must oppose vigorously and unsparingly. Never was there a greater *"dispute for a heavenly cause"*[14] and never one fought with more expert weapons. Hirsch was not content with polemics alone. Together with these, he combined a practical approach to the Jewish life, being the first to establish orthodox schools where the knowledge of a trade, together with a knowledge of Judaism, was taught.[15]

---

[13]"The battle of the Lord."

[14]מחלקת לשם שמים. See Abot v. 20.

[15]Abot ii. 2. The ideal of *Torah Va'Avodah*, or *Torah Ve-Derech Eretz* has always permeated Jewish ethics. It is the dynamic and the mainspring of the *Hapoel Hamizrachi*, the roof organization for the *Bnei Akiba, Torah Va'Avodah* and *Bachad*, to which movements this book is humbly dedicated.

VI. R. ISRAEL LIPKIN [SALANTER] (1810-1883)

What R. Samson Raphaël Hirsch did in Germany in his battle against Reform, R. Israel Lipkin of Salant did in Russia, where the enemy of the traditional Jewish way of life was the *Haskalah* movement which took a heavy toll of the *Yeshivah* students who were of the first to be attracted by it. To demonstrate that orthodox Judaism need yield to none in its philosophic and ethical approach to life, he introduced into the curricula of the *Yeshivot* in Wilna and Kovno, over which he in turn presided, the study of ethical writings such as Bahya's *"Duties of the Heart"* and Luzzatto's *"Path of the Righteous"*. This *Musar*-movement,[16] as it came to be known, was practico-ethical in essence with individualistic tendencies straining after self-knowledge and self-respect. It emphasized that the idea of the *Mitzvot* was to *preserve* life. In any emergency where life was in jeopardy, there should be no qualms in the mind of even the most pious that the divine commandment must for that moment receive secondary consideration.[17] Coming as it did from one who was regarded as the Gaon of his day, such ethical teaching was effective in its refutation of the charge of the *Haskalah* leaders that Jews were governed, as well as stifled, in their intellectual growth by the dead hand of tradition in an age of freedom.

Before we proceed to examine somewhat more in detail the rise and growth of this remarkable ethical movement, an interesting fact deserves mention. It has already been said that whereas in Germany the enemy of

---

[16]*Musar* means *"ethical instruction"*.

[17]We have seen in Ch. iv that the principle of פקוח נפש is prominent in our moral and legal codes.

orthodoxy was Reform, in Russia it was *Haskalah*.[18] Why was this? The reason may well be that the Jews in Russia and Poland enjoyed spiritual autonomy and so were not compelled to model their faith on that of the one dominant around them. In a determined effort to spread enlightenment among the fanatical and help them to take advantage of the winds of freedom that were beginning to blow in eighteenth-century Europe, it was found necessary by the intellectuals of the day to alter the *inner* values of Judaism and to convince the masses that many practices had outlived their usefulness. In Germany, however, no such religious autonomy existed. There, Jews were, more or less, compelled to subscribe outwardly to the *mores* of the day. Accordingly, it was deemed necessary by the exponents of Reform in that country to embark upon a new formulation of the traditional outlook so as to bring the religious life of the Jew into marching line with that of his fellow-citizen of another faith.

Encouraged by the success which attended his initial efforts, R. Israel Lipkin established a special *Musar* retreat[19] which was never to shut its doors, day or night. Thither the followers of his movement might repair, at all times, to commune with God and to spend profitable hours in contemplation of the right way of life.[20] At his instigation, the printing-presses of Wilna and Kovno poured out thousands of copies of various ethical classics of the Middle Ages for the use of the countless study-circles he had established.

Tradition embellishes his achievement by adding that

[18] A Hebrew word, stressing the primary place of intellect and logic (שכל) in the practice of Judaism.
[19] Or "*Shtiebl*", literally "*a small house*"; a name given in Russia and Germany to small groups of organized worshippers. Cf. the Welsh use of "*Bethel*", "small house of God".
[20] This was called "*Tikkun Ha'nefesh*" and serves as a dynamic force in ethics.

he introduced a special tune (*Niggun*) with which those who study works of an ethical nature could accompany their study. This tune differed from the various *Niggunim* heard in the *Yeshivot* over the pages of the Talmud in that it was of a sad, haunting and plaintive kind—one calculated to stir the heart with immortal longings.[21] Imaginary though this may be, it shows that everything was done to stimulate elation and the outpouring of the soul. The student of *Musar* was exhorted to approach his subject in a spirit of trepidation, "as if a sharp sword was hovering between his thighs and *Gehinnom* open beneath him", the advice offered by the Talmud to the Jewish judge (*Dayan*).[22]

In his utterances, he depicted God as zealous to punish evil-doing and faithful to reward righteousness.[23] The most impressionable hour of the day, just before *Ma'ariv*,[24] was chosen for this study. Those who witnessed these scenes record that the assembled students worked themselves to such ecstasy and were so swayed by emotion as to resemble (*Lehavdil*) a revivalist or evangelical meeting of another creed. Verses of the Bible, calculated as the most likely to introduce the mood of contrition and repentance were chosen and repeated so often and so plaintively that the atmosphere became surcharged with an *otherworldliness*. It was in this mood that the evening prayers began, with the result that prayer became not

[21]See Meg. 32ᵃ, where the study of Bible, or Talmud, without a tune, merits condemnation. The real sense of this statement is given in the explanation offered there that it refers to scholars who are not friendly one to another.

[22]Sanhed. 7ᵃ.

[23]So *Rashi* on Num. xv. 41.

[24]The evening prayer recited when labour was done and before the last meal of the day was taken. According to the Talmud, it was ordained by Jacob, just as the morning (שחרית), and the afternoon (מנחה) prayers originated from Abraham and Isaac, respectively (תפלות אבות תקנום); cf. Ber. 26ᵇ.

something mechanical (*Keva*), a burden which must be borne, but an exhilarating experience gladly undertaken.

It would be unfair to give the impression that the movement revelled in emotionalism and neglected the philosophic outlook. One thing is certain. Besides its accent on inner uplift, it had deep and psychological content. Rabbi Israel Lipkin taught that the most effective way to cure vice is to avoid it. Was not the Nazirite told to avoid approaching a vineyard of whose grapes he had vowed not to partake?[25] Those who are prone to flare up in anger are advised to eschew the slightest sign of displeasure and to cultivate calmness and peace of mind. He advised the teachers of *Musar* to exercise much patience in their cure of souls, since it was among the most difficult tasks in the world to bring back the erring to the paths of rectitude. In his book *Or Israel* ("The Light of Israel"), compiled by his disciple R. Isaac Blazer, are gems of the purest ethical kind.

His contribution to Jewish ethics was his insistence on the *practical* application to life of the moral teachings of the Jew.[26] This vigorous activity on his part took the inevitable toll. A Hebrew monthly,[27] begun in 1861 and devoted to *Halachah* and *Ethics*, had to abandon its publication owing to the precarious state of his health. He gave up his post and spent the rest of his days as a wandering scholar, visiting *Yeshivot* where his curriculum was studied and conferring with teachers and students as to the best methods for the implementation of his programme of ethical studies.

---

[25] סחור, סחור, לכרמך לא תקרב—"Make a *detour*; it is not wise for thee to approach too near".

[26] Thus exercising great influence on the pioneers of the *Yishuv* in Israel. It was such ideology that gave birth to the *Kibbutzim* in modern Israel under the *aegis* of the *Hapoel Hamizrachi* and the *Hasidic* Movement.

[27] Called תבונה—"Psychology".

R. Israel Lipkin was unique in that his personality was a singular combination of an ultra-orthodox Jew and a man of the world. He yielded to none in his loyalty to the State, inhumane as it then was to his co-religionists. As an indication of his wide and courageous principles, he advised his followers not to avoid military conscription. National service he included in the Rabbinic maxim that *"the law of a state, must be accepted as law"* (*dina demalchuta dina*). Little wonder that his colossal Rabbinic learning, deep piety and tremendous influence for good have not only singled him out as one of the brightest stars in the firmament of the nineteenth century, but has made him in addition the subject of countless recorded tales.

Many are the striking incidents in his career. The first concerns his love for children, those "feathers plucked from the wings of love and dropped into the lap of motherhood". One day, on his way to the synagogue to attend the *Kol Nidre* service, he passed by a house from which the cries of a small child could be heard. Looking in at the window, he at once saw what was wrong. All the family had gone to synagogue, no doubt leaving the child asleep in his cot. When the child woke up to discover that it was all alone in the house, its terror knew no bounds. Rabbi Israel decided that he could best serve God, even on this holy night, with the saving of a little soul rather than by the saying of many prayers. So he tended the child till its mother returned. It was some time after that the puzzled community learnt the secret of the mysterious absence of their beloved Rabbi from the most solemn service of the synagogue. A similar tale is related of the saintly R. Moshe of Sassov and of other Hasidic Rabbis.

The other two incidents are equally indicative of his *practical* ethics. The story is told[28] that one year, when

[28]It forms the subject of one of David Frischman's vivid Hebrew sketches called *"Sheloshah Sheachelu"*, "The Three that Ate".

the plague of *cholera* was dangerously rampant in his town, the doctors forbade fasting on *Yom Kippur* on the ground that a weakened state would invite the plague to do its worst. When Rabbi Israel observed the reluctance of his congregation to follow this advice, he ascended the *Bimah*[29] on the Day of Atonement, after the conclusion of the morning service, and there and then proclaimed aloud the *Kiddush* over wine and the blessing over the cake, and thus publicly broke his fast.[30]

VII. MOSES SCHREIBER, THE HATAM SOPHER[31]
(1763-1839)

What Rabbi Samson Raphael Hirsch did for orthodox Judaism in Germany, the *Hatam Sopher*[32] did for the rest of those European centres where his authority was unquestioned. This is true not only of Hungarian Jews but of Russian and Polish Jews as well. To this day, many Jews would not worship in a synagogue where the *Bimah* is near the Ark and not in the centre of the building; or where music is introduced at a wedding or memorial service though these occur, of course, not on a Sabbath or festival but on a weekday. Such strictures may seem to savour of the fanatical. Yet when one realizes the spread of the Reform Movement in his day and the breaches it

---

[29]The raised reading-platform in the Synagogue from which the Torah is read, usually in the centre of the building.

[30]Cake was chosen and not bread, because the latter would involve the washing of the hands and a long Grace after meals.

[31]It was common for Rabbis to be known after the names of their books.

[32]The family name *Schreiber* adapted the Hebrew equivalent *Sopher* (Dan. xii. 4), though no longer, as their ancestors did, pursuing actually the profession of scribe. See S. M. Lehrman "A Champion of Orthodoxy", in "The Jewish Monthly", London, October, 1949.

made in the ranks of orthodoxy, one can sympathize with such religious zeal.

His championing of orthodoxy was effective because he stressed the ethical background of the *Halachah* in the famous *Yeshivah* at Pressburg over which he presided with such renown for thirty-three years. To eager disciples, never less than five hundred, he expounded the precise meaning (*Peshat*) of each Rabbinic utterance, bringing out its ethical content rather than encouraging *Pilpul*[33] (verbal dialectics and phraseological acrobatics). In this way, he demonstrated that the Talmud develops the path of perfection blazoned out by Lawgiver and Prophet rather than indulging in hair-splitting discussions just for the sake of argument.

The last twenty years of his life reveal him, both in his writings and in his public utterances, as a doughty champion of orthodoxy. As a preacher, he combined fearlessness with eloquence, sparing not evil-doers, be their rank ever so high. From his printed works,[34] it would seem that he attacked Reform because of its antagonism to orthodoxy, and on account of his conviction that the breaking of any Jewish law is a breach of our legal constitution. He was afraid, and subsequent events have justified his fears, that any trifling with established usage and practice would lead to abuses of a more serious nature. His writings display him as a great lover of Zion, besides proving him to be a foremost authority in Talmudic lore.

He objected to secular study solely because of his conviction that the time to be devoted to Rabbinic

---

[33]Word meaning "*pepper*", reflecting the *spiciness* of Talmudic hermeneutics and the *sharpness* of Rabbinic variance in dispute.

[34]Only three of which have been published from nearly a hundred left in manuscript. *Halachic* literature would be enriched if the others saw the light of publication in due course.

learning, on account of its importance, was not to be lessened by the study of other subjects. The Torah was to be the main preoccupation of the Jew, his meditation "*by day and night*" (Josh. i. 8). Therein alone would he find everything worth knowing.[35] The *Hatam Sopher* was a lover and staunch upholder of the knowledge of Hebrew, in which language he advocated that our essential prayers should be uttered. According to him, the Mishnaic concession to recite certain prayers in the vernacular,[36] was granted only in cases of emergency. It was not to be made an excuse for an ignorance of our national language, the vital link which held a scattered Jewry together.

Such views may have sounded extremist at the time, but we who have witnessed the resurgence of the State of Israel and the revival of Hebrew in our day know that these miracles were inspired and aided by such protagonists of our faith. Once Hebrew is exchanged for the vernacular, he warned, be the reason however plausible and pressing, many other *traits* of "*particularism*", as Mendelssohn stressed, would be lost to posterity. Had his advice been followed, we might have been spared much ignorance of Judaism and the many communal schisms between the orthodox and "progressive" which persist to this day.

As an example of his *Hibbat Ha'Aretz*, his comment on Genesis xxxii. 5[37] may be quoted. Drawing attention to the Hebrew word for "sojourned" (*Garti*), which means "*I have been a stranger*", the *Hatam Sopher* adds: "The patriarch (Jacob), symbol of Israel throughout the ages, stresses that while staying with Laban in another country, far from his own Canaan, it was only possible for him to *sojourn* there, to feel like a stranger, not able to settle down

[35]Abot v. 25.
[36]See Sotah vii. 1.
[37]"*With Laban I have sojourned*"   (עם לבן גרתי, ואחר עד־עתה)

in undisturbed tranquillity. Peace of mind can only come to the Jew who, no longer hated and baited, hunted and haunted, no longer driven from one land and not allowed to enter another, is allowed to strike roots once again in *Eretz Israel*, the land of our *fathers* which we must help to become again the land of our *children*." Only one possessed of noble ethical purpose could write with such feeling of the Land and the Book. The *Hatam Sopher* well deserves to find a place in our ethical picture-gallery. He certainly belongs to those great Rabbis of the last century who were pioneers of religious nationalism.

VIII. THE HAFETZ HAYIM (1838-1933)

No man belonging to our own times more embodied the ideals of Judaism than Rabbi Israel Meir Ha-Cohen of Radun (Poland), better known as the *Hafetz Hayim*. The first book he published was against the sin of slander and tale-bearing. This already proclaimed him as *the* scholar and saint of his age. He, however, would have been the first to disclaim that his mode of life placed him in the front rank of those noble souls of old, whose lives and teachings are among the most precious possessions of our spiritual legacy.

He was the teacher *par excellence*, the foremost exponent of Talmudic knowledge of his day and his heart was full of love towards all. With this prodigious knowledge, he was the humblest of men, a combination at all times as rare as it is welcome.[38] A lover of mankind he certainly appears in all his writings. It was this love which enabled him to harmonize religious fervour with sweetness of disposition,

[38] He has found an enthusiastic biographer in Yiddish and English in M. M. Yashar's *"Saint and Sage"*, New York, 1939—a book which must be read to be enjoyed.

and which made him devote much time to the writing of popular books on the perfection of human character and the cultivation of the virtues. All those who write about him exhaust the vocabulary of praise, rifling their imagination to describe the saint and sage who, for nearly a century, moulded the religious life of his contemporaries.

One writer[39] describes him as "a God-intoxicated personality, an acknowledged and beloved teacher, who imbued Israel with faith and lovingkindness, both by precept and example. His life reveals him as a High Priest of purity and simplicity, of faith and optimism, of consistency of purpose and action. Of few others can it be said that he was that rare combination of traditional Judaism and universal idealism whose heart beat with pure love of God and service to all his fellow-men."

At his death, he was acclaimed by the greatest as well as by the humblest of the age as the saintliest man one could hope to find on earth. Of the many tributes, that of Rabbi Kook—himself a paragon of scholarship and of saintliness, deserves to be reproduced here. "His sole ambition and delight",[40] wrote Rabbi Kook, the Chief Rabbi of Palestine at the time,[41] "was to serve his Creator; he dedicated all his days to the perfecting both of his own life and that of the people, in whose midst he lovingly laboured as one of themselves. Indeed, his character,

---

[39]B. Revel, in a Preface to Yashar's biography.
[40]True to the best ethical teachings of the Talmudic Rabbis, the Hafetz Hayim consistently refused to accept the office of *Rav* of a *Kehillah* and to be paid for his ministrations as such, preferring instead first to open a little grocery store which was managed by his wife, so that he might continue his beloved studies. Later, he closed this store and eked out a very humble livelihood; selling, at the barest minimum of profit, his own books. Never did he grumble, "rejoicing in his lot" (Abot iv. 1).
[41]See *Ha'hed*, Tishri 5694, Jerusalem. It is interesting to observe that it was the Hafetz Hayim who conquered the reluctance of R. Kook to become a Rabbi in Israel.

example and teachings fully qualified him for the task of being the *Moreh Derech*, 'the Teacher of the Jewish Way of Life'. At the sight of so much evil in the world, his generous heart bled."

Realizing that much of this was brought about by man's inhumanity to man, especially by the gossip and slander that passed from mouth to mouth, he was determined to wage "a battle royal" against the hydra-headed monster of *Leshon Ha'ra* (The Evil Tongue). His first effort in this campaign was an exhaustive study of the laws against *Leshon Ha'ra* in the Bible and Talmud. Every point in his attack was based on sound *Halachic* foundations, equipped with arguments as precise as they were complete. This book he called *Hafetz Hayim*, basing himself on the words of the Psalmist (xxxiv. 15-17): "Depart from evil, and do good: seek peace and pursue it. The eyes of the Lord are towards the righteous, and his ears are towards their cry. The face of the Lord is against them that do evil, to cut off the remembrance of them from the earth."

This standard work on an important aspect of Jewish ethics was followed by another smaller work of a cognate nature which he called "*Shemirat Ha'lashon*" (The Guarding of the Tongue). The third of the trilogy, his "*Ahavat Hesed*" (The Love of Kindness), contains legal and ethical expositions of that generosity in thought and benevolence in deed which we should exercise towards one another. No writer combined to a happier degree the art of weaving the sublimest moral purpose into the most ritualistic observance. It was this characteristic which prompted R. Kook to remark about his books that "their equal can be found only among the works of the greatest scholars and moralists of the past."

These works were followed by practical manuals containing digests of the Jewish Codes, written primarily for those Jews who for economic reasons migrated to

America or England, countries that combined a reputation for freedom in the economic and civic domain with apathy and laxity in religious observance. They were composed in order to help them to be loyal to the traditional faith under the changed circumstances due to their migrations. He composed another handbook for the use of those who, being conscripted, found it a struggle to combine loyalty to God with obedience to the State. The first he called *Nidhe Israel* (Israel in Transit), the other *Mahaneh Israel* (Israel in the Ranks).[42]

From both books it is obvious that his deep sympathy for those forced to emigrate in order to seek a livelihood, and his concern both for their economic and religious welfare, as well as for their moral rectitude in the face of temptations to deviate from *Kashrut* and family purity, while serving in the ranks far away from home, were inspired by love and sincerity. He pleaded with scholarly eloquence that the joy of the fulfilment of a *Mitzvah* (*Simchah shel Mitzvah*) makes any temporary thrill of pleasure dwarf into nothingness. True piety brushes aside the bizarre and the flamboyant after which the soul hankers.

This vast ethical output was crowned by his masterpiece the *Mishnah Berurah*, the remarkable compendium of the *Shulchan Aruch* which Karo had based on *The Four Turim* of Rabbi Jacob b. Asher.[43] The compilation of the *Hafetz Hayim* omitted those precepts presupposing the

---

[42] An abbreviated edition was compiled by M. M. Yashar and was distributed to American Jewish soldiers serving in the second World War (1939-1945).

[43] The word means "*Row*": see Ex. xxviii. 17. R. Asher's complete code is called *Arba'ah Turim*, because it contained *four parts:* viz., *Orah Hayim* (on Jewish Ceremonials); *Yoreh Deah* (on forbidden foods and cognate subjects); *Eben Ha'ezer* (on marriage and divorce laws); and the *Hoshen Mishpat* (on civil laws). They were written in the early years of the fourteenth century.

existence of the Temple, as did the work of Maimonides before him. His concern is only for those precepts the observance of which is independent of Eretz Israel. With his finger on the pulse of the times in which he lived, the *Hafetz Hayim* sought to make this code explicit and ethical in its content. The result was the standard work *Mishnah Berurah* (The Clear *Mishnah*), so named on account of the concise commentary attached, together with the scholarly discussion of sources, which he called *Beur Halachah*, "The Explanation of the Laws".

It is significant that Rabbi Kook, himself a great authority on *Halachic* Judaism, pronounced this work so decisive in its conclusions as to have earned for its compiler the distinction of "*one of the foremost authorities on our Halachah whose decisions are binding for all*". Little wonder that such a personality became a subject of legend even in his life-time. When he died, the stories clustering around his memory were legion.[44] The following is eloquent of his outlook towards life.

The story is of a visit paid to him by a wealthy visitor from America who was aghast at the abject poverty of the Rabbi's surroundings. For all he found in the small home were the mere rudiments necessary for eating, sleeping, sitting and studying. "Rabbi", he asked in amazement, "where do you keep your belongings?" With a shrewd smile, the *Hafetz Hayim* replied: "And, pray, where are *your* possessions? You, I am told, are a rich man." The visitor retorted in amazement: "But I am only on a visit to Poland. One does not carry all one has acquired while travelling from one place to another." To which the Rabbi replied: "How truly you have spoken! We travel lightly, leaving our worldly goods behind us. Well, I, too, am but a stranger in this life, advancing with each day

[44]The reader will find some of these in Yashar's biography "Saint and Sage".

a step nearer to my permanent home in the World to Come. Why should I be cluttered with things which I cannot take with me hence?" The visitor left a wiser man. He had learnt much sober wisdom and the secret of happiness and peace of mind from the lips of the unassuming Rabbi.

It was to another visitor that he replied that he was not keen on going to heaven unless he could be assured that there was a copy of the Talmud there which he could study constantly. For of what use were all the legendary accounts of the Hereafter if he could not pursue there his beloved studies?

A quotation from the Master himself will give the reader an idea of his method of approach when dealing with human virtues and vices. When writing on "Chastity",[45] the *Hafetz Hayim* observes: "Wholesome family life is the basic element of the Jewish national structure. Upon its purity depends all that is noble and sacred in Jewish life. The home, as the chief centre of Jewish interest, has been to the Jews more than a castle. It is a *sanctum* which he has ever thought to hallow and beautify. Here he learnt from his childhood the art of moral perseverance, the blessing of self-control, the balancing of his cravings and emotions. Here he was taught how to guard himself against lewdness in thought and in speech, as well as in deed. The purer the tongue, the more sanctified the heart: the more modest the demeanour, the more sublime the life.

Immodesty in the home is like a worm in poppy plants, says a sage of old. The sin of unchastity is grave. Its punishment is extirpation (*Karet*), the soul being cut off from the source of eternal life to wither like a branch lopped off from the tree. For the pleasure of a moment, a

[45] I am indebted to Rabbi M. M. Yashar for the citation of this extract. See "Israel in the Ranks", pp. 113-116.

pleasure that could be procured in a lawful manner, one risks his life eternal. Of the sinful generation of the flood it is said that the patience of God was exhausted when the people sank into moral degeneracy. God is impatient with those who lead immoral lives.

"Vicious environments may cause man to go astray. Associating with evil company may make him feel that he is not alone when he engages in illicit conduct. Often even he who is inclined to pursue the path of chastity feels that he is not strong enough to face the ridicule of his loose friends. He then resigns himself to indecency. A moment's pause for serious thinking would help him check the tide of his passion."

The *Hafetz Hayim* quotes from the Bible to prove his point, enriching his argument with many a homely illustration and concluding a remarkable essay thus: "Unchastity in the mind is counted among the sins of adultery. Man ought to turn away his eyes from sights which may breed lustful thoughts. He should abstain from listening to obscene talk which may stimulate the *Yetzer Ha'ra* (Evil Impulse). If he allows the impulse to occupy his mind and his imagination to play with the gratification of it, he is guilty of sin. To escape falling into it, he should avoid all such pitfalls. Study or prayer are good antidotes and will often help man to regain his moral balance and to maintain it. A life distinguished by sexual purity ranks high in the heavenly scale of merit. Keeping aloof from all manner of unchastity earns one the virtue of saintliness. An old Talmudic maxim states: "*Sanctify thyself in the lawful pleasures of life.*"[46] These considerations deserve the attention particularly of the young man in the ranks, away from home and his dear ones. He must do his utmost to maintain the chastity of his body and soul, not only for his own good but also for

[46] קדש עצמך במותר לך; Yeb. 20ᵃ.

the sake of those who love him so dearly and who pray for his safe return." The *Hafetz Hayim* impressed his seal on Jewish ethical conduct with sympathy and affection for his fellow-men. Those who write after him can only voice imitations of his love for all beings created in the image of God. What Yehudah Halevi said of Gabirol as a poet, can be said of the *Hafetz Hayim* as a teacher of ethics: "*He locked the door of Poetry behind him, and placed the key in his pocket.*"

The historical part of our survey of the march of Jewish ethics from Bible times to our own day which has till now engaged our attention will be followed by an examination of these ethical teachings when applied to life. This summary of modern ethical literature which we have endeavoured to present is far from complete, but those keen to know more have other sources.[47] Before embarking on the second part of this book—Applied Ethics—passing reference must be made to some modern Jewish writers on ethics; almost all, by the way, hailing from Germany and who have stamped their thought on much of the religious life around us to-day.

IX. HERMANN COHEN (1842-1918)

Foremost is Hermann Cohen, an outstanding thinker who devoted his great speculative energy to Jewish philosophy and ethics in his classical work "*Die Religion der Vernunft aus den Quellen des Judentums*".[48] In this

[47]Such as the instructive books of Rabbi Dr. I. Epstein, the Principal of Jews' College and the editor of the Soncino English Talmud (completed 1949). See his "Jewish Way of Life, "Judaism", and other works.

[48]Leipzig, 1919. Copious extracts from this work and from other modern works by Jewish scholars on the philosophy of ethical religion will be found in A. Lichtigfeld's book "Twenty Centuries of Jewish Thought", London, 1938.

learned work, in which much of his argument and outlook on life is based on the philosophy of Kant, he built his system of Jewish thought identifying Judaism with Reason (*Vernunft*). To him, God is the origin of the World (*Ursprung*) and the Proclaimer of morality for all times. In his stress on the moral life of reason, Hermann Cohen saw *"the significance of Judaism for the religious progress of mankind"*. His importance for Jewish ethics lies in his unique achievement of turning back the minds of men to the moral aspects of God and Israel.[49] In his emphasis on the essence of the moral life as residing in the ideal end, that is, in permanent study and assured attainment, he links himself to the great thinkers above mentioned.

According to him, the Sabbath idea, apart from being a religious command, added to the well-being of Society. It meant the limitation of the hours of labour and the lifting of the status of the labourer—from being *"a hand"* to the dignity of a person entitled to enjoy rest and leisure. This is but one example of his fresh approach to the entire body of Jewish beliefs, an approach developed by two other great men of our day, Franz Rosenzweig and Martin Buber.

X. MARTIN BUBER

Martin Buber is that rare type of cosmopolitan philosopher, combining a nationalistic trend with religiophilosophic elements and amalgamating within himself mystic tendencies and Hasidic influences. His presentation of Judaism possesses a much broader aspect than accepted orthodoxy, being more in the nature of religious socialism and the revival of Hasidism than that of a formal con-

[49]See L. Roth in "The Legacy of Israel" on "Jewish Thought in the Modern World".

servatism. In his writings, Buber expresses the Jewish passion for justice, which far from being dead, is one of the most living influences of our time, the little yeast which leaveneth the whole lump.[50]

Jewish ethics differ from those of the Greeks; whereas the latter is *speculative*, the former is *practical*. Martin Buber demonstrates to the thinking world that whatever ideal of spiritual worth has reached the European people is due to the Jewish view of life and purpose of action. In the light of such achievement, the Jew has deserved better treatment than that meted out to him by the nations of the world.

XI. NAHMAN KROCHMAL (1785-1840)

Of the *Maskilim* who attempted to build up a Jewish philosophy consistent with the modern outlook of their time, Krochmal easily takes pride of place. His classic *"The Guide of the Perplexed of our Times"*[51] proclaimed him as *"the father of Jewish Science"*. His object in this work, which was epoch-making, was to reconcile Judaism with modern ideas, as did Maimonides before him. This he does by emphasizing spirituality as the Jewish contribution to culture. The work is important as a guide to the scientific study of Jewish literature by one who called himself *"the eternal student"* (*der ewige Student*). In Hebrew, the two words for a scholar are *Talmid Hacham*, *"a wise student"*—a significant title. To study this work

---

[50]His *Or Haganuz* (Shocken 1947) is not only a compilation of the best of Hasidic traditions, but also a revelation of the tendencies of the author.

[51]מורה נבוכי הזמן was written in Hebrew and published after his death in 1851 by Leopold Zunz, himself one of the founders of the new "Jewish Science". See the excellent edition of Dr. S. Rawidowicz.

is to be provided with a balanced outlook on modern problems.

XII. AHAD HA'AM [ASHER GINSBERG] (1856-1927)

Ahad Ha'am is singled out for reference here because he was the greatest modern Hebrew writer and thinker in whose essays the note of ethical idealism is predominant.[52] His restatement of a prophetic synthesis between nationalism and ethical universalism ranks as a permanent contribution to modern Jewish thought. He clearly stressed the fact that morality in Judaism is not contemplative abstraction but practical well-doing. Judaism is *"not in heaven"* (Deut. xxx. 12) but consists of duties to be performed in the everyday grind of existence. His influence on a host of distinguished disciples colours, to this day, Hebrew literature both in the *Golah* and, especially, in the surging and throbbing life of the world's newest State—Israel. Much of the Israeli ideology speaks in the voice of Asher Ginsberg. He has, indeed, become "one of the people" (*ahad ha'am*).

XIII. A. D. GORDON (1856-1922)

The mention of Israel calls to mind another great worker in the field of practical ethics. A. D. Gordon was the first Jewish philosophic writer and worker of modern Palestine who opposed Marxism and taught the masses

[52] A translation of his selected essays has been made by Sir Leon Simon, together with a biography of Ginzberg. The latest edition is that of the East & West Library (1948), also by Simon, now in active retirement at the University of Jerusalem.

to base their conduct on Jewish nationalism combined with the principle of labour (*Avodah*). In this emphasis on *Torah Va'Avodah*,[53] Gordon contributed to the development of ethical faith its highest ideal, an ideal which should be the basis of the new Jewish ethics in the new Jewish State. Gordon has a flourishing memorial in Degania, where his study is preserved as he left it, and in which the present author turned the pages of this remarkable man's Bible, from which much of his dynamic inspiration was obviously drawn.

XIV. MORITZ LAZARUS (1804-1903)

Moritz Lazarus largely owes his fame to his classical work, the "Ethics of Judaism",[54] a philosophic compendium popular in its own day and not without its worth to-day. He wrote as a Jew, first and foremost. Other writers, such as Heine, Disraeli, Karl Marx, Bergson, Freud and Einstein—to quote only a few of the galaxy of great men who, though stemming from Jewish origin, belong to the world of culture in general—wrote as Europeans who echoed the passion for justice and lovingkindness that enflamed the utterances of the prophets. The stream of Jewish ethics is perennial, constantly refreshed by *"the living waters"* of the Torah and the Talmud, our glorious Jewish heritage of four thousand years.

The words of Browne may well seal this chapter:

[53]The name given to the group within the *Mizrachi* whose programme is study and *Hachsharah*. Cf. Abot i. 1.
[54]See English translation by H. Szold. This work will always rank as a classic on account of two things: its sympathetic treatment of Jewish teachings, and the distinction of its having been one of the very first modern presentations of this aspect of Judaism.

"The Jews who have already contributed so much to the mind of mankind should be left free to contribute still more. Their unique history has endowed them with a peculiar capacity for appreciating the worth of wisdom; and if allowed to function uncurbed, who can tell what that capacity may yet bring forth?" ("The Wisdom of Israel"). Since these words were written, just before their author's lamented death, the State of Israel has proved to the world that the genius of Israel to teach mankind the art of living together is as creative to-day as it was in those ages of long ago. *"Israel is not widowed"*[55] of its power to lead the world back to the path of righteousness and mankind would be well advised to help it in its struggle for rebirth as a holy nation with a divine mission. The student who approaches the study of Jewish ethics in an unbiased manner will be convinced that Judaism can, once again, kindle the star of hope in the world's night of despair and uncertainty.

[55]Jeremiah li. 5.

BOOK TWO:
APPLIED ETHICS

CHAPTER SEVEN

OUR APPROACH TO GOD

In the first part of this book, an endeavour was made to prove that in Jewish Ethics the existence of God is more than an intellectual affirmation. In this, the second part, our aim will be to show that a belief in the Jewish way of life implies the shouldering of moral obligations. The Rabbis, to emphasize this truth, refer to the declaration of the *Shema*, made by the Jew twice daily in his prayers and a third time on his bed just prior to consigning himself to sleep, as the acceptance of *"the yoke of the Kingdom of Heaven"* (*Ol Malchut Shamayim*). To be a true Israelite means to submit oneself resignedly and gladly to a divine discipline which takes into account every detail of life. For Judaism concerns itself with the relations between man and man and idealizes life as a segment of the divine.

Because of the spiritual implications of human relationships, Jewish ethics regards nothing appertaining to man as too trivial to be disregarded. *"Let all thy deeds be in the name of Heaven"*, pleads a Rabbi. This vital concern with the petty and humdrum things of life is no measure of the banality of our philosophy. On the contrary, it manifests the high regard which Judaism has for life, considering *all* things, great and small, essential to the hallowing and ennoblement of human nature. One can serve God in the ordinary things of life as in the most sublime. The Jewish net is cast wide. Man can approach nearer and nearer the standard of perfection traced out for him in a life of obedience to God and His Torah. The avenues for such ennoblement are open to him everywhere.

I. LAWS AND ETHICAL DOCTRINES: THE DIFFERENCE

As we shall be citing many laws of Judaism in order to discover their moral background, it is right at this stage to venture some distinction between doctrine and law. The first category of precepts teaches the eternal principles of Justice, Love and Moral piety as the standard of duty. Law, on the other hand, is the embodiment of these principles and their application to life. Judaism issues this warning: a life that is shaped by the rules of Ethics, without the sanction of religion, tends gradually to become one of weariness, pettiness and frustration.

To free man from this sense of disillusionment, our laws, governing every action of our lives, seek to impart an aspect of "something more" to our thoughts and deeds, teaching us that life is a part of eternity and duty an indivisible law of the universe. Only when laws and ethics are combined indivisibly does a Jewish life become sacrosanct, endowed with a vitality sufficiently potent to glorify trivial duties until they are performed as nobly as deeds upon the battlefield. These *laws* and *ethics* must be wisely blended if Judaism is to achieve its purpose of perfecting human nature.

Take an example. In our philosophy, Mercy and Justice are not opposites. Mercy, if exercised without due consideration for the demands of justice, will hurt the recipient. Every sensible parent knows that in the training of the child, too much yielding to its petulant and querulous demands may result in effects that are undesirable and injurious. A sense of justice, that is, a knowledge of what, in the long run, will be good for the child must control the emotions flowing from parental love.

That is why our prayers for material blessings are not always answered. In fact, they *are* answered; for "No" itself is an answer. Only our Heavenly Father knows what is good for His children on earth. On the other hand, strict Justice unsoftened by the chastening effect of Mercy will be equally unbearable. In the second chapter of the Torah (Gen. ii. 4) God taught us this lesson of blending inextricably law and ethics. There the name *Adonai* is used of God before that of *Elohim*. The Rabbis deduced that the change of name was due to the fact that He saw that this world of ours could not be governed by the *norm* of rigid Justice (*Elohim*) untempered by Mercy (*Adonai*). The latter word means that He is Master over us, and makes allowances for shortcomings on our part. *Elohim* expresses the idea of a powerful Judge intent that Justice be done at all costs.

Here is an illustration. Suppose that God did not *"remember mercy in His anger"* (*berogez rahem tizkor*) but punished each man as soon as he sinned, how many would be alive to-day? Again, if He rewarded each of us as soon as we performed a noble deed, much, if not all of the ethical content of the *Mitzvah* joyfully performed, would be destroyed. Good would then be done, not for *goodness* sake, but for the thought of the material reward. One of the prime incentives of ethics (*lishmah*) would then be destroyed. With mercenary motives as the spurs to good deeds, a valuable tool in the carving of character would be blunted. In Judaism, the moral character of man is considered fundamental as a measure of the true value of his life. Salvation is not through *creed* but through *deed*. The character of the motive colours the value of the action.

Several other distinctions between *law* and *ethical*

doctrines might be considered. The latter consider man as created in the divine likeness and destined to undergo a process of perfection in this *"vale of tears"* in which *"man is born unto trouble, as the sparks fly upward"* (Job v. 7). Our *laws* stress that each man is a member of a large human society, the welfare of which should be his urgent concern. *Law* seeks to regulate our actions, while the moral code appeals to our reason, heart and will. Accordingly, whilst obedience to *ethical standards* is a matter left to our conscience, obedience to the *law* is enforced by penalties.

The punishment for violating the former is more severe than that meted out to the breaker of the civil law. Because ethical standards are uncompromising, protesting as they do against the evils of human society, telling man what he *ought* to be and how his relations ought to be ordered according to the will of God. Any infringement of this code, though not punishable in human courts, constitutes a violation of the holy principles by which our lives should be guided. It is in effect difficult to make any distinction in our teachings between laws that are purely ethical and those that are solely legal. The best proof for this contention is the study of the laws laid down in the Torah with their Rabbinical explanations.[1]

II. ETHICS OF MONOTHEISM

It must be borne in mind that Jews worship no abstract *"First Cause"*. To the Jew God is a *reality*, with whom there is personal relationship which inspires righteous and holy conduct. The insistence with which His Unity, as well as His Incorporeality and Holiness are stressed, is due to the protest made by Judaism against the immoral

[1] See Exodus xx-xxiii; xxv-xxxi; xxxiv-xxxv. Talmudic references will be advanced in the following pages.

practices which early contemporary religions associated with their local deities. What is now, more or less, accepted as theological doctrine was revolutionary when Judaism first proclaimed that there is only one God who is always approachable and nigh unto those who call upon Him in truth, who is at all times *"a gracious and merciful God"* desiring nothing more than their happiness.

To provide a further link between man and his Maker, man is described in the story of Creation as formed in the divine likeness.[2] Accordingly, our earthly life must be modelled on the heavenly pattern set out in the Bible. The Jew is asked to do what the Rabbis daringly, if poetically, picture God as doing in His ethereal abode. There He is pictured as wearing *Tephillin*[3]; as donning the *Tallit*;[4] as studying the Torah for three hours daily, besides praying for the welfare of all on earth.[5] God weeps over the short-sightedness of his children in eschewing the good and choosing the evil.[6] He was present at the marriage ceremony of Adam and Eve;[7] He visits the sick, consoles the mourner and assists at the burial of the dead.[8] In short, each good deed that man is asked to do is to ascend another rung on the ladder of perfection he is asked to scale if he is to reach heavenly heights.

This does not mean that God is corporeal. To borrow the words of Schechter:[9] "It is a way of humanizing the Deity and endowing Him with all the qualities and attributes which tend towards making God accessible to man." This principle of *"Imitatio Dei"* has been applied

[2] Gen. i. 26.
[3] Ber. 6ª.
[4] R. Hash. 17ᵇ.
[5] Ab. Zara 3ᵇ.
[6] Hag. 5ᵇ.
[7] Ber. 61ª.
[8] Gen. R. viii. 13.
[9] "Aspects of Jewish Theology", pp. 36ff.

in Judaism to every aspect of the higher life, to religious observance as well as to moral conduct. God is represented as Himself performing acts of grace He has commanded Israel to practise. For the *sine qua non* of our faith is "*first improve yourself, before you seek to correct others*".[10]

Lest such a conception of a monotheistic God, described both as immanent and transcendent, appear to the rational mind as contradictory or mutually exclusive, it is necessary to add that to the logic of the Rabbis these two sides of the divine character were considered as complementary. When they beheld in rapturous admiration the wonders of the universe, they described God as *transcendental;* when they witnessed the painful struggle with which human beings grappled with the problems of life, they pronounced Him to be *immanent*. This immanence was impressed upon the Jew by the teaching that His Presence (*Shechinah*) and His Holy Spirit (*Ruah Ha'kodesh*) fill the earth whenever sincere attempts are made to plant the sublime amidst the prosaic and the mundane. "*And let them make Me a sanctuary, that I may dwell among them*."[11] God is at once *above* the universe and, at the same time, the very *soul* of the universe. The link is the inflation of His Spirit and His abiding Presence, His *Ruah Ha'kodesh* and His *Shechinah*.

This must be remembered when discussing the duties Judaism has assigned to man in the worship of his Creator. Deeply interested and indirectly affected by the varying conceptions of faith and duty, the ancient teachers of Israel did not share the desire for metaphysical speculation which characterized the philosophers of Greece and Rome. In all probability, the theories of

[10]B. Bath 60ᵇ. קשוט עצמך ואח״כ קשוט אחרים
[11]Ex. xxv. 8. See J. Abelson "The Immanence of God in Rabbinical Literature".

Aristotle and Plato about the universe were known to some of the Talmudic Rabbis as they were known to Rabbi Yehudah Halevi and Maimonides, for example. But a study of the Talmud leaves us with the definite impression that in the Babylonian or Palestinian schools, the disciples were not encouraged to select natural science or metaphysics as a subject of study. On the contrary, such study received strong condemnation. This is clear from the famous story told of the four Rabbis who entered "Paradise" and sought to apprehend the Reality beyond the Universe.[12] Only Rabbi Akiba, we are told, emerged unscathed.[13] Of the others, Ben Azzai and Ben Zoma, one lost his life, the other his mind. The third, Elisha b. Abuya[14] lost his soul.

It may well be asked: *Why this aversion to speculative faith?* The answer lies, perhaps, in the belief of our Talmudic sages that theoretical speculation was a menace to faith. This must not be taken to mean that all religious enquiry was spurned. On the contrary, the Rabbis never urged a blind acceptance of Judaism but advocated a faith based upon reason. *"Let him that glorieth glory in this, that he understandeth and knoweth Me."*[15] Did not Rabbi Hillel warn us that *"the ignorant man cannot be pious"*?[16] Their attitude resulted from the logical approach they made in the realm of faith. Judaism, being a *practical* religion, considers that the daily problems which confront us are sufficient to occupy our minds. *"There are more things on earth, Horatio, than are dreamt of in your*

[12]Hagigah 14[b].
[13]In Hebrew, פ ר ד ס the first letters of the four words פשט, רמז, דרש, סוד "literally, *explanation, nuance, homiletic interpretation* and *esoteric meaning*"—the four keys before which a door closed on life's mysteries would burst open.
[14]Designated as *"Aher"* in the Talmud.
[15]Jer. ix. 23.
[16]Abot ii. 6.

philosophy." This advice of Hamlet well describes the attitude of mind of the Torah and the Talmud.

The consideration of transcendental theories, the contemplation of subjects which border on the *"other-worldly"*, are likely to divert attention from matters of more practical import. Life being short and uncertain, selection must be a guiding principle. The voice of Judaism says: *"Choose the practical, and avoid the theoretical".* The authoritative conclusion of Rabban Shimon b. Gamaliel[17] that *"Not learning but doing is the chief thing; and whoso is profuse of words causes sin"* is one that received universal acceptance.

This stress on *"good deeds"* is in keeping with Jewish teachings which describe God as the Father of His large human family. Rabbi Akiba used to say: *"Beloved is man, for he was created in the image of God: but it was by a special love that it was made known to him that he was created in the image of God: as it is said: 'For in the image of God made He man'."*[18] Believing in a holy and perfect Deity, the Jew was spurred on to noble thought and action. To act otherwise, is to prove unfaithful to God and His people, besides constituting a *Hillul Ha' Shem*—the most heinous of all sins for which death only can expiate.[19]

Especially to be censured was the act of defrauding one not of our own faith. Such a perpetration would lead to a defamation of Israel and his God. In the *"Ethical Will"* left by the Gaon of Wilna,[20] we are told that one of the questions to be asked after death will be: *"Hast thou lived in a friendly way with thy neighbour?"*[21] The Jew is inspired to acts of kindness in the last message left by another

[17]Abot i. 17.
[18]Ibid. iii. 18.
[19]Yoma 86ª.
[20]Rabbi Elijah b. Solomon (1720-1797), master of all Jewish learning.
[21]See "Ethical Wills", edited by Israel Abrahams.

great man, whose life was spent in pious deeds joyfully performed. *"Life is like a draught of salt water"*, wrote the Besht.[22] *"Its pleasures seem to quench, but actually they inflame thirst. The smile of to-day is the tear of to-morrow."* Judaism wishes its adherents to adopt the long-distance view of life; to act not on the spur of the moment, but to strive to emulate God *"in whose sight a thousand years are but as yesterday when it is past, and as a watch in the night"*.[23]

III. WHAT GOD MEANS TO THE JEW

When the mourner is greeted both during the *Shivah* and in his home and by the congregation on his entry into the synagogue during the service on *Shabbat* eve, it is significant that the word used for God is *Hammakom*, "the Place". *"May the Almighty (Hammakom) comfort you among the other mourners for Zion and Jerusalem."*[24] This designation is apposite, because of the stress that God is with us in our trials and sorrows wherever we chance to be. He is not a *local* deity whose power is cribbed, cabined and confined. The word is used to stress that the Jewish God is *omnipresent*, being especially near to those who are broken-hearted and who call upon Him for help in their trouble. Only a *finite* body is located in space; to the *Infinite*, space is meaningless. *"He hath neither bodily form nor substance: we can compare nought unto Him in His holiness"* (*Yigdal*).

Unlike the Greek deities who peopled the heights of Olympus, sipping nectar and feeding on ambrosia and indulging in pursuits immoral and unholy; unlike the

---

[22]Abbreviated for *Baal Shem-Tob* (1700-1760), the *"Master of the Good Name"*.

[23]Ps. xc. 4.

[24]Singer's Prayer Book, p. 112.

household gods (*penates and laertes*) of the Romans, whose sway did not extend beyond a tribe or a family, the Jewish God was *Hammakom, the* Place. That is, the Universe *"whose glory filled the whole earth"*. He encompasses all space, for no space can encompass Him.

It is obvious why Jewish Ethics lays such stress on God's *omnipresence*. When a man is impregnated with the consciousness that he is ever under the supervision of an *"All-seeing Eye"*, he will be armed with a strong deterrent to sin. *"Reflect upon three things"*, said Akabya b. Mahalalel, *"and thou wilt not come within the power of sin. Know whence thou comest, whither thou art going, and before whom thou wilt in future have to give account and reckoning"*.[25] When Rabbi Johanan b. Zakkai was breathing his last, his parting advice to the disciples who stood around him was: *"Fear God as you fear man."*[26] Few are those who sin when watchful eyes are upon them. Let man realize that all his actions, nay, his very thoughts, are under constant divine survey—a scrutiny far more penetrating than the *X-ray* which pierces the splint and bandage covering the broken limb—and he will be leading the life mapped out for him in Jewish ethics.

Another goad to right action was provided in the divine attribute of *Omnipotence*. Described in the Torah as *Shaddai* (the Almighty) to whom alone all *"strength and might"* belong[27] and by whom individual weal and woe are determined, it would be folly on the part of man to try to acquire unlawful possessions or to enjoy illegitimate pleasures, seeing that they are in direct contravention of His decrees. The Jew must have faith in this *Omnipotence* of *"the faithful God, who keepeth covenant and mercy with them that love Him and keep His commandments to a*

[25]Abot iii. 1.
[26]Ber. 28[b].
[27]כי לך לבדך הכח והגבורה

thousand generations".[28] He must ever be mindful of a God to whom faith is accounted as righteousness[29] and who has surrounded us with commandments in order to impregnate us with implicit trust in Him.[30] This faith must be blended with love and solemnity. With love— as tender as in the description *"As the hart panteth after the water brooks, so panteth my soul after Thee, O God: my soul thirsteth for God: for the living God"*.[31] With solemnity, as impressive as that felt by Jeremiah who, when forced by those who mocked and tortured him not to make any more mention of the God in whose name he constantly warned, protested: *"And if I say: 'I will not make mention of Him, nor speak any more in His name', then there is in my heart as it were a burning fire, shut up in my bones, and I weary myself to hold it in, but cannot."*[32]

The *Omnipotence* of God created in the heart of the Jew a sense of reverence for the life around him and a holy awe for its mysteries. The pages of Holy Writ reflect such longings and sensations.[33] When this attribute was combined with divine *omniscience*, the folly of sin was made all the more glaring. Since His knowledge is limitless, penetrating the innermost recesses of the heart, how can erring man hope to escape detection? The Midrash provides the answer.[34] "It can be compared with an architect who was appointed a collector of taxes. Is it not the height of futility for the evader of taxes to conceal

[28]Deut. vii. 9.
[29]Gen. xv. 6.
[30]Ps. xix. 8; cxix. 15, 67; II. Chron. xx. 20; Hab. ii. 4; Deut. xi. 1; xiii. 4; xix. 9; Is. lvi. 6.
[31]Ps. xlii. 2, 3.
[32]xx. 9.
[33]Gen. xx. 11; Ex. i. 17; iii. 6; Ps. ii. 11; viii; cxi. 5; Prov. i. 7; ix. 10; xv. 33; xvi. 6.
[34]Gen. R. xxiv. 1.

his wealth in some hidden crypt and underground cave? Did not the architect himself construct these secret hiding places? Similarly, foolish are the devices of the sinners who do evil in secret places. From whom do they seek to conceal their actions? *"Woe unto them that seek deep to hide their counsel from the Lord, and their works are in the dark, and they say: 'Who seeth us? and who knoweth us?'"*[35]

These three attributes of God have fortified the Jew in a hostile world. The need for an assuring faith in a Heavenly Father who endows each child with those faculties which constitute real personality[36] has been well put:[37] "In this seemingly friendless universe, where a bit of rock falling from a cliff can cut off the creative genius of a Shakespeare; silence the music in the heart of a Beethoven; and put out the light of the eyes of a Turner with an indifference that is appalling, man feels the need of a security that is at once final and absolute. . . . In all the chief matters of life, we are alone. We dream alone; we suffer alone; we die alone."

In the anguish of his heart, the Psalmist cries: *"Look on my right hand, and see, for there is no man that knoweth me. I have no way to flee; no man careth for my soul."*[38] To cheer man in his loneliness, God was depicted as a loving Father. Even in His anger he doth remember mercy, assuring all who pulsate with the breath of life which He has infused into them that none need feel alone in this apparently friendless universe. He is with us in our troubles, loving us and deeply concerned with our destiny. He made Adam a co-partner with Him in the act of Creation. For did not God use the plural *"Let us*

[35] Is. xxix. 15.
[36] See Niddah 31[a].
[37] In "Man and His Creator", by I. Epstein.
[38] cxlii. 5.

make"[39]—thus hinting at man's share in the making of himself and in omnipotent creativeness?

Such a belief gave meaning to Jewish life and a sense of direction to human destiny. Freedom of choice is further a sign of the Divine origin of man who can either partake in an ever-increasing degree in the divine work of perfecting himself and the world around him; or being foolhardy and *"smitten with blindness"*, may decide to rank himself with those *"children of darkness"* who oppose the Divine Will, and in so doing forfeit life itself. To help him to make the wise choice, the six hundred and thirteen *Mitzvot* were given, divinely designed as the most effective instruments for the formation of character. They have the power to make each Jew *"a witness of God"*,[40] capable and willing to do what is right and good in the eyes of God and man.

Never do these commandments force us to violate reason and act out of blind belief. Our religion does not minimize the approach of the scientist. It merely stresses the limitations of the human mind. "While including matters which cannot be apprehended unaided by human reason, it does not admit aught which is opposed or does violence to reason."[41] The fact that the teaching of retribution is one of the principal dogmas of the Creed of Maimonides[42] does not imply that our God is zealous to avenge those who do wrong. It simply emphasizes a cardinal belief in Jewish ethics: that God is not indifferent to human conduct. God does care for each one of us and in so caring, shows that He loves us all.

[39]Gen. i. 26.
[40]Is. xliii. 12.
[41]I. Epstein: "Man and His Creator".
[42]Creed XI: "*I believe with perfect faith that the Creator, blessed be His name, rewards those that keep His commandments, and punishes those that transgress them.*"

IV. OUR LINK WITH GOD—THE SOUL

Judaism is emphatic that man was created pure, untainted by *"original sin"*. This is the profession he makes at the commencement of the daily morning prayers when he exclaims: *"O my God, the soul which Thou gavest me is pure."*[43] It is this soul, the spark of divine fire which man carries with him, that links him to God. In some, this celestial light may be dimmed by sin; in others, almost extinguished by depravity of outlook or corruption of deed. Realizing that the character of a life largely depends on the care bestowed by the individual to keep his soul unstained; knowing that it is of man's own freewill that he becomes a sinner, Jewish ethics are tireless in insisting that it is the *soul*, of all forces the mainspring, that raises man above mere animal existence. It is the soul which reasons with man: "Of what use toiling all one's life for *material* possessions, when such wealth has a transitory value only, since *'at his death, he shall carry nothing away; his glory shall not descend after him'?*"[44] What man should strive for, pleads the soul, is the acquisition of a good name and as the doer of good deeds. Only these acts of kindness shall precede him before the Heavenly Tribunal when his race on earth has been run.

Since it is the soul that raises man from earth to heaven, Judaism has invested the Sabbath with an *"additional soul"* (*Neshamah Yeterah*). This day, hallowed by God Himself at Creation, becomes a spiritualizing force in human life if correctly observed *"in love"*. It must not be concluded that because the stress is on the spiritual nature of man that our ethical code belittles the

[43] Ber. 60[b]. See the paragraph in Singer's Prayer Book, p. 5; cf. Ps. viii. 6, 7.
[44] Ps. xlix. 18.

importance of the bodily elements in man. The earthly body, given to us as the abode of the spirit, is God's masterpiece. By its elaborate organism it proves that there is no creator like our Creator.[45] It also reveals His infinite goodness and boundless wisdom. No two men have been created exactly alike. Each of us differs in those essentials that make up personality. Why has this distinction between man and man been made? To teach independence and freedom of will, faculties not to be dragooned by unscrupulous taskmasters but to be used in the task of making our lives *replicas* of the heavenly pattern.

Freedom of Will rejects the doctrine of *"original sin"*. That is the crown of Jewish ethical thought. The disobedience of Adam (recorded in Genesis iii), must not be confused with the doctrine just mentioned. On the contrary, the very narration proves the supremacy of Judaism as *"a way of life"*. It takes full cognizance of the frailty of man, composed of earth and heaven. The Torah is adamant in the contention that despite the sensuous nature of man, he should be able to subdue his evil inclination. Far from being harsh, such a demand is virtually a compliment. Just because Judaism credits its adherents with the moral strength required to master their sinful disposition is temptation oft placed their way. Should this at first be difficult of achievement, it will fill him with the resolve to make amends and vow never to fall again.

To obtain such forgiveness, the Jew makes a direct approach to God. There is no *"iron curtain"* between him and his Heavenly Father. As the erring child is received with open arms by the father whose mercy he seeks to obtain and whose forgiveness is always his for the asking, so God is ever ready to welcome back those who have

---

[45]A Rabbinic play on the word *tzur* (rock) which is made to read *tzayar* (Painter, or Creator).

strayed.[46] To be sure, *"the imagination (inclination) of man's heart is evil from his youth"*;[47] but when canalized towards righteous paths, this propensity to evil can be curbed by good example and constant reminder of the true moral standard. Our evaluation of the divine soul within us saves us from the belief in the depravity of human nature, a state of mind responsible for much that is harmful around us.

Why should one strive towards perfection when tainted by *"original sin"*? Why practise restraint when one is credited with descent from an anthropoid ape? Robbed of the ethical incentive of *noblesse oblige*, man will behave as befits one springing from lowly origins. Judaism warns us that human nature is susceptible to sin and emphasizes that the soul was given to us in a pure condition and it is our bounden duty to keep it pure. *"Behold"*, says the wisest of all men,[48] *"this only have I found, that God made man upright; but they have sought out many inventions."* Once we admit moral *freedom*, we must automatically admit moral *responsibility*. One is a corollary of the other. Freedom of will is not negatived by a staunch belief in divine Providence. Both are correlative and complementary.[49] Not all who mock their chains are free. To possess freedom without moral responsibility is to be forced often to place manacles on our hands to keep them from trembling.

V. OUR PRACTICAL OUTLOOK ON LIFE

To speak of a *realistic* and *practical* approach to God may seem to the uninitiated to use wrong terms when

[46]Ezekiel xviii. 2-32; Ps. cxxx. 7-8.
[47]Gen. viii. 21.
[48]Eccl. vii. 29.
[49]For further references on this subject see: Deut. xxx. 19; Jer. xviii. 7-11; Prov. v. 22; Abot iii. 19; iv. 1.

applied to the eternal verities of life. Yet realism and tangibility are not associated only with those things which can be touched or handled. Judaism has one grand purpose: to extract from life the beauty inherent in all things created by God.[50] To do so, it has pictured the world not as a torture chamber, in which our food is mixed with tears and our blessings with delusion; but as a field made glorious by opportunities ever before us, or by misery and pain which prove often the gateways to a better life. *"That thou mayest live and rejoice with all the good things God has given thee"*[51] is the incentive behind many a command made by the Torah.

The prohibitions governing the Jewish life have no other aim than to cultivate within us a conscious will to self-discipline, able to enlist even our waywardness in His service.[52] It is these *"Thou shalt nots"* that have contributed towards the longevity of our nation.[53] It is these divine checks to human frailty that have taught each member of the *"Kingdom of priests and a holy nation"* the value of moderation and the necessity to rise above mere desire and to be stronger in his religious affirmations if his nation were to survive. *"And thou shalt choose life"* is the cry of our Torah; but it must be a life rich in content, cognizant of the duties we owe not only to our Father in Heaven but to our fellow-men on earth. Unless our life on earth has been worthy, the gates of heaven will be barred at our approach when life's sad tale is over. The view of Rabba deserves quotation.[54] "When a man is brought before the Heavenly Tribunal, he is asked: '*Did*

---

[50]Hence the blessings to be recited on all occasions.
[51]Deut. xxvi. 11.
[52]See Ber. 54[a]: ואהבת את י׳ אלהיך בכל־לבבך—בשני יצריך, ביצר טוב וביצר הרע
[53]The source of Jewish nationalism is Judaism.
[54]Sabb. 31[a].

you conduct your affairs in all faith and honesty? (באמונה).
Did you fix regular periods for the study of the Torah?
(קבעת עתים לתורה). *Did you confidently await salvation?*
(צפית לישועה). *Did you study with your best faculties?*
(פלפלת בחכמה). *And did you understand the implications
of your studies to translate their lessons into life?'* "[55]
(הבנת דבר מתוך דבר)

The practical approach of Judaism to life is made
further manifest by its conception of God and the
teaching of the equality of all mankind. By attributing
Omnipresence to Him, we declare that He is linked with
Eternity. *"There is no place or time that is without Him"*
is a fundamental tenet of Judaism. His *omnipotence* is
another reminder that His purpose and intervention in
the lives of men cannot be frustrated. It is also an
assurance of a divine, overruling power, a power which
rewards and punishes according to our actions.[56] This
consciousness will endow life with purpose and content
instead of reducing it to a series of blind chance happenings. Remove this Omnipotence and you destroy with it
the guarantee of our faith that no machination, whether
it be in thought, word or deed can circumvent the
ultimate realization of His purpose.

Our ethical concepts are philosophic and practical,
impressing upon us that without religion man lives
selfishly and badly. Our knowledge of God is based on
the Exodus and the Revelation at Sinai, the two great

---

[55]This quotation, though cited before in this work, is repeated
on account of its importance.
[56]We cite some Biblical references to Reward and Punishment,
a teaching contingent on the doctrine of man's Freewill.
Ex. xx. 5-6; xxxiv. 6-7; Lev. xxvi. 3-9; 14-16; Deut. vii. 9;
xi. 13-17; 28-28; xxviii. 1; Is. iii. 10-11; xxvi. 21; Jer. xxxi.
29-30; Ezek. xviii. 1-32; Ps. xxxi. 24; lxii. 12; cxlv. 20; Prov.
v. 22; x. 29; xi. 31; xiii. 21; xvi. 4; xxi. 7; xxii. 8; Ecc. vii. 15;
xii. 13-14. Cf. Kidd. 39ᵃ: שכרא בהאי עלמא ליכא—"There is no
reward in this world." Abot i. 3; iv. 2.

national experiences of Israel. Both these approaches, historical and supernatural, are complementary and help to explain each other. A chemical analysis of man will inform us only of his physical components, without making us any the wiser about his character and moral conduct. Natural science and metaphysics, similarly, will only help to unfold His glory, wisdom and might. They will *not* bring home to us the reassuring conviction that *"not even a finger is bruised by man here below without this movement having been previously determined in heaven"* (Hullin 7b).

It is not to philosophy and science that one must turn for the meaning of life and its perplexities, as well as for a fuller understanding of Him, but to our Bible, our literature and our history. A study of these sources will gradually reveal that behind all our planning and action, behind the daily recurrent scene, there is a constant unfolding of a divine purpose, a determined approach towards a destined goal. Without this divine flash of truth, our days would be purposeless, *"a tale told by an idiot, full of sound and fury, signifying nothing"*.

Underlying our relationship to God is the dominating and pervasive principle that the moral code makes no distinction between Jew and Gentile. All being His children, all are included in the protection afforded by the regulations of the Torah. Meaningless and pernicious to Judaism is the cleavage between man and man on account of descent or belief, race or faith, class or nationality. The absence of all missionary activity in Judaism must not be construed as a want of confidence in its power to win converts. On the contrary, it is in keeping with its conviction that the fulfilment of the ethical requirements of our Torah is possible of achievement also outside its own immediate circle. The pious of all creeds are heirs to the eternal life.

Proofs for this statement are numerous. A few will suffice. The Torah proclaims this equality almost on every page. The Prophets re-echo it in solemn utterance.[57] The Talmudic Rabbis continue in this vein, emphasizing this teaching with their characteristic form of hyperbole and love of exaggeration.[58] It is because of this equality of all fellow-beings that our moral code considers the outraging of the feelings of another as a cardinal sin, tantamount to *Hillul Ha'shem*, that is, to profaning the majesty of God Himself. When such lack of consideration occurs, denunciation should not be withheld even if the perpetrator be a scholar. Commenting on the verse *"There is no wisdom or understanding or counsel before the Lord"* (Prov. xxi. 30), a Rabbi says: "Wherever there is a *Hillul Ha'shem*, no respecting of persons may be allowed."[59]

VI. THE ETHICS OF HOLINESS

It is remarkable that whenever the command to be holy appears in the Torah it is addressed to the *whole* nation, rather than to the individual. Thus at Revelation the entire congregation of Israel is urged to be *"a kingdom of priests and a holy nation"* (Ex. xix. 6); the Dietary Laws (Leviticus xi) are sealed with the words *"And YE shall sanctify yourselves and become holy, for I the Lord am holy"* (v. 44); and in Exodus xx. 30, we are told: *"And holy men*

[57]Is. ii. 2-3; lvi. 6; lxvi. 20-21; Jer. iii. 17; Mic. iv. 1-2; Zeph. iii. 9.
[58]Vid. Ber. 6[b], which quotes the views of Rabbi Eleazar, Rabbi Abba bar Kahana and Shimon b. Azzai on the love God has for *all* his creatures. Cf. Sukk. 49[a], which quotes Rabbi Hama bar Papa's belief that the gracious man (of all creeds) is also one who can be described as a fearer of God. Also Sot. 31[a], where Rabbi Shimon b. Eleazar praises an action performed from the *love* of fellow-man more than one performed on account of a *fear* of God. See also Abot iv. 3; Ab. Zara 3[a]; 10[b].
[59]Shevuot 30[b].

shall ye be unto Me". The remarkable chapter, to which attention has already been called (Lev. xix) begins: "*YE shall be holy*". Why? To emphasize that to achieve perfection and to model our lives on the Deity, we must work *collectively*, regarding the welfare of the individual as a public concern.

The word "*Kadosh*" (Holy One) as applied to God means "*One set apart*" and stresses His transcendence and independence of all besides Himself. In other words, to be *holy* means to be master over one's life and nature, able to lead an existence separate and independent. Jewish ethics stress that not only is He the Holy One but that He also summons man to this task of holiness. For man this task has a twofold connotation, negative and positive. On its negative side, it implies a breaking-away from whatever urge of nature that makes self-gratification the purpose of existence. This does not mean the ignoring of the legitimate calls of nature or the practice of rigid asceticism. All it means is a severance from lust and passion that drag man down to the level of an animal.

In pondering the ethical implications of holiness, one realizes how false is the classification of most historians of civilization that whereas Rome contributed Law and Political Administration and Greece Beauty and Philosophy, the contribution of Judea was solely in the field of religion. This is not strictly true. Judaism has enriched the world from *every* aspect, just as the diamond sparkles from each of its facets. By directing attention to the manifestation of beauty and order in the universe; by ordaining that blessings be pronounced at every sensation enjoyed; by its insistence that the whole universe is sustained and controlled by spiritual principles, Judaism has taught the sense of Law and Beauty, making man appreciative of the starry heavens[60] and the mysteries of

[60]Ps. xix. 2; Is. xl. 26.

this beautiful earth, with its pageant of seasons and endless cycles of dynamic, resurgent creation.

Science, far from robbing thoughtful man of this eternal source of wonder and trust, has added a deeper faith in God. It has proved that to regard the world as a product of chance is inconceivable. Blind chance could not have arranged everything so harmoniously. The controlling power is not a mathematical machine but a personal God who takes compassion on us as a father does upon his children.[61] Without this sense of security, the universe would be a friendless and lonely place. Our concept of holiness is *social* in character and forms the basis of our approach to God and our relationship with man. The Torah was not given to the cloistered saint or the veiled nun, but to the farmer, the labourer and to the employer. Accordingly, it includes the exercise of charity and love towards all men. Holiness (*Kedushah*) expresses itself in service and duty to others.

Let us pause for a moment upon a differentiation between *Kedushah* and *Taharah*. The first is *ethical;* the other, spiritual and levitical. *Holiness* is dynamic; purity, static. To be *holy*, is to possess a stimulus, "*a call*", a consecration to service and action. It is to be armed with self-control, the basic motive of many of our practices. As a *practical* faith, Judaism has from the outset realized that without self-control there can be no mercy, no righteousness, no holiness, no imitation of God.

To investigate and to declare, as the Greeks were fond of doing, *what* is virtue; to extol beauty without seeing that those at the head or in the ranks *lived up* to their teachings, was not good enough. The "*something more*" which was needed could not be supplied by the Roman lawgiver and Greek philosopher. The gap could only be filled by Judaism with its doctrine of "*Salvation by Deeds*".

[61]Isa. lviii. 9.

Faith is of value only if it leads to rightful action, if it makes us humbly appreciative of what we have.

A Rabbi has beautifully described this feeling. Commenting on the words *"Honour the Lord with thy substance and with the first-fruits of all thine increase; so shall thy barns be filled with plenty and thy vats shall overflow with new wine"*,[62] he remarks: "Honour Him with what He has given thee. If thou possessest beauty, praise Him for the beauty He has given thee. If thy voice be pleasant, use it to beautify the service in the synagogue."[63] Judaism submits all beliefs to this practical test: *Do they serve as a means of fostering righteous conduct and the moral life?* That is the criterion by which all our professions of faith stand or fall.

Judaism has not yielded to the temptation of drawing any systematization of doctrines or Articles of Faith. Our history shows that when these attempts were made by highest authority such as Maimonides, all the batteries of opposition were launched against him. To dogmatize about Immortality or Reward and Punishment was never considered of practical moment in Jewish life. The performance of good deeds and the dispensation of lovingkindness—these were the essentials. Judaism begins by accepting Revelation, Good and Evil, Immortality (and other matters, which are problems of philosophy) as axiomatic. No attempt is made to define what these terms mean. We are taught that God is a *reality;* that is the *end* of the matter. Let philosophers indulge in the pastime of theorizing and generalizing to their hearts' content. Our task is to wed the imperatives of Judaism to our daily deed.

Is this attitude unreasonable? Not when we bear in mind that modern physical science has demonstrated the

[62]Prov. iii. 9.
[63]Pesikta Rabbati xxv.

difficulty of explaining what is apparently the simplest particle of matter, even being compelled to admit a degree of supernaturalism. To quote Sir Arthur Eddington:[64] "*Something unknown that makes the electron do something we know not what.*" Judaism realizes the limitations of human reasoning and is content to repeat with the Lawgiver: "*The secret things belong unto the Lord our God; but the things that are revealed belong unto us and to our children for ever, that we may do all the words of this Law.*"[65] This does not mean that we subscribe to the theory that "*Credo quia absurdum*", "*I believe because it is absurd*", a statement which involves the surrender of reason.[66] Judaism has more respect for human intelligence than had some scientists and philosophers, be they Descartes or others. What it does proclaim is logical, natural and rational. True faith proclaims: "*I believe, even if it is beyond my understanding*"—on the contrary "if I could understand everything, I would be God Himself".

In his introduction to the "*Duties of the Heart*", Bahyah ibn Pakuda points out that though reason may not agree with *all* our *Mitzvot*, it does not reject any of them. There is nothing, for instance, irrational in the teaching that man is a co-partner with God[67] in creation; that the earth will yield its produce if man ploughs and sows and that the whole of Nature will administer to his needs if he collaborates with it diligently. This absence of dogmatic formulation, far from being a weakness, is in reality a source of strength to Judaism. It allowed, from the earliest times, for the adaptation of all systems of philosophy.

[64] In his "The Nature of the Physical World", p. 291. Eddington, by belief, was a Quaker.

[65] Deut. xxix. 28.

[66] So Tertullian; see also R. Burton's "Anatomy of Melancholy" (1621).

[67] שותף במעשה בראשית is the Hebrew expression.

Though attempts at the formulation of our creeds were already made in Talmudic times,[68] it was not till the ninth century of the present era that their impact was first felt. The new intellectual thought then stirring the Moslem world in Spain had its strong repercussions on the Jews who in that Golden Age enjoyed economic, social and cultural freedom. The *apogee* of such systematization was reached in the works and codes of Maimonides,[69] representing a view of life and of man which embraced the following phases: true beliefs concerning God; observance of precepts leading to right conduct; the inculcation of these beliefs; and the conception of the purpose and the goal of human existence leading to the attainment of eternal life.

[68] See Sanhed. x. 1.
[69] For his Thirteen Creeds, see Singer's Prayer Book, pp. 89-90.

CHAPTER EIGHT

WHAT HIS FAITH MEANS TO THE JEW

WE have already shown that our idea of God is an *ethical* monotheism. The Jewish God is *One* because He sums up within Himself all perfection and holiness. Beside such faultless excellence all else must pale. This monotheism was born of the ceaseless urge in the Torah to love and obey God with all our heart, soul and might. To *love* and *obey* are two commands in Judaism which are indivisible and indissoluble. To Him who is One we must surrender our *all*, becoming ourselves united in fellowship in emulation of this Divine unity.

This conception of godliness does not imply an understanding of the nature of His being. All it means is that Judaism provides us with a knowledge of His government and with an urge to follow the right way God laid down for us in the Torah.

It is incumbent on each one of us to seek to know His ways and, having found them, to walk in them all the days of our life. An infallible aid in the acquisition of such peace of mind is an unswerving loyalty to the ethical teachings of Judaism and a translation of our creed into deeds of helpfulness towards all, including a helpful consideration towards the dumb animal. Our *own* actions make God either near to us or very remote from us. The more resolute our determination to be true "*sons of God*", the nearer we will be to Him. Obedience to the Torah means His accessibility by us at all times. It means the acquisition of purpose in a life otherwise meaningless and frustrating.

Is this an impossible aim, a phantom, an illusion of a God-intoxicated brain? No, says Judaism. As a being coined in His divine likeness, man has been endowed from birth with the power of moral realization, though it is only the courageous who is powerful to triumph over those passions that seek to weigh him down. Not only by *being* good but by *doing* good does man create his real life on earth.

We are taught that the reward of a *Mitzvah* is the *Mitzvah*.[1] This means, by the performance of good deeds man becomes conscious of the power latent within him to decide what he should do and what to avoid. Freedom to shape his own life is the demand made of the Jew by his religion. Man is not crushed by an ineluctable and inexorable Fate ordained for him before he came into the world a crying infant. True, his ways are mapped out for him; but his is the glory and the power to choose to walk in them, or in stubbornness to decide to glide down to *Avernus*. Moreover, and this is perhaps the greatest comfort of faith, his is the opportunity to turn back penitently to a loving and forgiving Father after he has tasted the error of his backsliding.

"*Atonement by Repentance*" is a cardinal teaching. An important day in the year (*Yom Kippur*) is dedicated to this belief. No vicarious saviour, no miracle or sacrament can achieve for him what only his own life and conduct can do. This goal is advocated for the whole of mankind as well as for each individual. The true purpose of existence and the real nature of faith are to be found only in the dispensation of goodness and in the amelioration of suffering. To spur the Jew on this Elijah-like task of succour and reconciliation, the moral commandments have been given—sign-posts at every turn of his path, admonishing, encouraging the pilgrim on his progress.

[1] Abot iv. 2.

This is what Judaism means to the thoughtful Jew—
a task to be fulfilled and a mission to be borne. As a nation,
Israel will survive on its own land if it displays a
readiness to serve mankind and a determination to fulfil
itself through ethical conduct in diplomacy and statecraft.
No other guarantee for the survival of our nation is valid;
no other *raison d'être* of our individual lives is deserving
of consideration.[2]

I. OUR DUTY AS JEWS

To be a faithful Jew means so to conduct oneself as to
have placed God before him in all his ways. "*To know
God*"—the main target of the Jewish life—does not mean
trying to fathom the unfathomable but to learn to
understand ourselves. When God revealed Himself on
Sinai, it was to show us what He requires of us for the
sake of the true life and to tell us that the nearer we are
to Him, the nearer He will be to us. "*The Lord is nigh
unto all them that call upon Him, to all that call upon Him
in truth.*"[3] To call upon Him means to strive after the
good; to find Him, means to *do* good.

It is in the obedience to His commands that our fleeting
glimpse of His nature can become an abiding vision.
Micah, in a deathless utterance, proclaimed that Judaism
is an ethical faith and that ethical conduct constitutes its
pith and marrow, its essence and nature: "*It hath been
told thee, O man, what is good, and what the Lord doth
require of thee: only to do justly, to love mercy, and to walk*

---

[2] The thoughts above have been inspired by Dr. Simon
Bernfeld's compilation "The Foundations of Jewish Ethics",
Macmillans, New York, 1929. See also Gen. xviii. 19; Isa. i.
16-17; lvi. 1; Jer. xxxi. 31-33; Mic. vi. 8; Ps. xv; xxiv. 3-5;
Prov. viii. 13; Job xxviii.

[3] Ps. cxlv. 18.

humbly with thy God."[4] Dr. Bernfeld observes that "Judaism did not launch upon the world a new conception of religion, but sought to illumine and ennoble all human effort and relationship, thereby teaching the proper task of man on this earth".[5]

Our religious mode of life was the first to give humanity a God who, within Himself, incorporated all that was ideal and who demanded the same combination of virtues in those who followed Him. Those who spoke in the name of the Jewish God made it clear from the outset that to serve Him was not to indulge in theoretical discussions of ethical tracts but to translate His moral demands into a life of good deeds.[6] Jewish authorities never compiled an "*Index Expurgatorius*", before the people. The only recorded instance in the Talmud of an attempt being made to exclude the Song of Songs, Ecclesiastes and Esther was triumphantly frustrated by an authority no less eminent than R. Akiba.[7] Man was to be judged by his actions, the only true criterion of godliness.[8]

Our duty as Jews is clear: to hallow God before all men by doing good. To act otherwise, is to profane the conception of Jewish divinity. Judaism has set its face sternly against any manifestation of extremism, whether religious asceticism or pagan hedonism. Any lip-service to a cause was denounced, and formal action when divorced from moral content received the lash of condemnation. Our prayers were called by the Rabbis "*the service of the heart*" (*avodah she'ballev*).[9]

---

[4] vi. 8.
[5] *loc. cit.* pp. 34ff.
[6] Ibid. p. 41 for H. Cornill's testimony.
[7] See Meg. 7[a].
[8] See Lev. xviii. 5; Deut. v. 1; Jer. vii. 3-7; Amos v. 14-15; Ps. xxxiv. 12-15; xxxvii. 27; cf: Kiddushin 40[b].
[9] Sot. 31[a].

Torah, wrongly translated by the Greeks as *nomos* (Law), literally means *ethical* teaching upon all the relations of life. To do one pious act out of *love* for God was considered more meritorious than to perform many out of *fear*, declared one Rabbi. Similarly, it is not the number of precepts a Jew fulfils that matters as much as *how* he performs them.[10] The Torah is clear upon the responsibilities that devolve upon the Jewish life.[11] Man is *not* born a sinner; he descends to that state of his *own* volition. He can ascend again to the godly life by his resolve to break from evil. "*Behold, this only have I found, that God made man upright; but they have sought out many inventions.*"[12]

Before the impact of Greek-Arabic thought in the Middle Ages, Jewish philosophers concerned themselves little with the problem how to reconcile Freedom of Will with the conflicting idea of divine Providence and Omniscience. When this difficulty began to stir the conscience of Jewish thinkers, they were forced to come to the conclusion that one does not exclude the other. Corroboration for this they found in Sacred Writ[13] and in the cardinal belief of Reward and Punishment. What sense is there in rewarding an act which *must* be done, or in punishing an act performed by an automaton when constrained to do so at the pulling of strings by a hidden Power?

It should be noted that Biblical reward is not material and personal but the survival of the nation under ideal conditions. These conditions were undisturbed peace, public welfare and social harmony in which all could freely participate and through which alone man could

[10]Ber. 5[b].
[11]Gen. xvii. 1; Jer. xxxi. 33.
[12]Eccl. vii. 29.
[13]Deut. xxx. 19; Jer. xviii. 7-11; Prov. v. 22; Ezek. xviii. 30.

attain moral perfection. The best reward is the feeling of satisfaction experienced when something noble is done; the worst punishment is the feeling of guilt accompanying an offence against the better nature of man.

The Talmud is emphatic: pious deeds are not rewarded in this world. The Reward and Punishment mentioned in Lev. xxvi and Deut. xxviii are to be viewed merely as attractions or deterrents to obedience or infidelity. Here below, we have a task to do; the reward for its fulfilment will come later.[14] What greater punishment can man have for an act spelling a *Hillul Ha'shem* than to be told that he has polluted the soul which God has put within him pure and unsullied at his birth?[15]

II. ALL MEN ARE EQUAL

Jewish Ethics are dominated by the equality of all human beings. "*One law shall be to him that is home-born, and unto the stranger that sojourneth among you*" (Exodus xii. 49). To countenance any distinction would be inconsistent with the quintessence of our teachings. Since One God created us and since He reveals Himself as a loving Father, it follows as a corollary that we are *all* his children. "*Have we not all one father*", pleads Malachi (ii. 10), "*and hath not one God created us? Then why do we deal treacherously every man against his brother, profaning the covenant of our fathers?*"

Nor must it be thought that the belief of the Election of Israel negatives a belief in the equality of *all* peoples

[14]Kidd. 39[a]. See also Luzzatto's Introduction to his *Messillat Yesharim.*
[15]See Lev. xxvi. 3-9; Deut. v. 9-10; xi. 13-17; Isa. iii. 10-11; xxvi. 21; Ezek. xviii; Ps. xxxi. 24; cxlv. 20; Prov. v. 22; x. 29; xiii. 21; *Talmud: Abot* 1, 3; *Sotah* 3[b]; *Makkot* 24[a].

in His eyes. What the phrase "*Chosen People*" stresses is that Israel, as the depository of divine truths, must not keep to itself truths for which they have been chosen to communicate unto the world at large. Israel has been chosen, not to inherit the pleasures of this world for themselves but to point out to others also the glories of the higher life, here and in the Hereafter.

The pious of all creeds will share the Life to Come. Consequently, the Jew has studiously avoided converting others to his outlook on life. He has only welcomed those into his fold, and even then reluctantly, who sought admission of their *own* volition and freewill and who were urged to do so by disinterested motives, by the desire to embrace the faith of Israel. Not *exclusion* is our aim, but tolerance and consideration for all; above all, a genuine respect for the sincere faith of another.

Judaism has never entertained pretensions to be the sole depository of the means of grace. It has neither claimed membership of our faith as a guarantee of the salvation of soul, nor has it denied salvation of soul to anyone not born a Jew. According to the Talmud,[16] a man who renounces idolatory automatically ranges himself on the side of Judaism. All he needs for salvation is the exercise of his moral powers for doing good.

The *Pesikta* quotes a striking thought. The reason why the Torah was given in the month of *Sivan*, when the Zodiac sign is *Gemini* ("*the twins*") was to emphasize that its laws are applicable to all nations. Those stemming from Esau, as well as to those descending from Jacob, his twin brother, are equally bound to follow the golden path of the Torah. Characteristic of the Jewish faith is this sense of reality, a reality which does not attach prime importance to material or tangible things which are ephemeral, but which concentrates rather on the moral

[16]Meg. 13[a].

life as expressed in noble conduct and the will to create and shape, to labour and perform. Every page of the Torah is shot through with this desire to love and to be loved, to be happy and to rejoice the hearts of others.[17]

This sense of reality is fostered by the consciousness of a personal, omnipresent God who revealed Himself at Sinai not as the Creator aloof from the universe but as One *"who brought thee out of the land of Egypt, out of the house of bondage"*.[18] His first revelation to His people at Sinai, as to His Lawgiver Moses[19] at the thorn-bush (*Sneh*), was prompted by the suffering and loneliness which, as a just and merciful Father, He could no longer tolerate. It was by such a series of revelations that God made His teachings known, teachings which form the essential doctrines of Judaism and which have become the national constitution of Israel. This constitution sealed the work of Moses by helping him to make an intractable horde of slaves into a chosen people. The effect was that the Torah was declared infallible and immutable and of divine authorship. To violate a religious command was considered an act of treason not only because it was breaking a constitutional clause, but also because of its direct disobedience of a Torah whose efficacy had been proved time and again.

III. JUDAISM AND REVELATION

Judaism means a series of revelations made by God to those selected by Him for the propagation of truths that all men should cherish. The prophets were not the only

---

[17]See Deut. xvi. 11-14; xxvi. 11.
[18]Ex. xx. 2. Note the *singular* person throughout the Decalogue. God brought *each one of us* out of slavery and bondage. At the *Seder* table, each Jew is asked to consider himself *"as if he himself departed from Egypt"*.
[19]Ibid. iii.

oracles of divine communications. All who, putting aside the clamour of routine and materialism, turn, like Moses, to the quiet places of life, may behold the sacred flame and listen to *"the still small voice of God"*. On *Shavuot*, the Reading from the Torah is the chapter describing the Revelation to the whole people;[20] while the *Haftara*[21] describes the revelation that came to the exiled prophet, a lonely figure beside the River Chebar. May not this be indicative of the assurance that God reveals Himself not only in Nature but also in human experience, especially in moments of religious ecstasy or when the spirit of man has completely mastered the demands of the body? When one is in tune with the Infinite, one becomes conscious of His presence and is worthy to receive the divine message.

The prophets were essentially bearers of heavenly messages, chosen for their *rôle* because of some superior human qualities they possessed and because of more sensitive spiritual powers that appeared characteristically theirs. But withal, they are described as fallible beings; so that it should not prove impossible for ordinary people to emulate them. They began with warnings against impending danger and they hurled their castigation at kings and princes. Often they uttered consolation to a distraught people and prefaced their statements with the introduction *"Thus saith the Lord"*.

That not all prophets spoke alike is a further demonstration of the universal nature of our faith, which selects its men of vision from all ranks of men. The quality of their message differed according to the measure of their individual approach to life and their breadth of vision as well as the picturesqueness of their style. Their messages came from the same divine source but were presented to the people in accordance with the style and temperament

[20]Ex. xix-xx.
[21]Ezek. i.

of the prophet. The sun remains the same, despite the variety of coloured lenses through which it may be beheld. The various letters of the alphabet can be so conjoined as to make them yield sublime poetry, or indecent epithets. It all depends on the mind that employs their aid in the expression of its thought.

Towering over all is Moses, selected as the Lawgiver not only because of his outstanding personality but on account of the nature of the message he was asked to deliver. All other divine communications are so many points of emphasis of the laws that should be the immutable standard of living to Jews of all times. If other prophets spoke primarily to their own generation (being concerned with the ills and hopes of their times), Moses addressed himself to *all* generations, born and unborn. He spoke of the eternal good and evil things of life. *"Neither with you only do I make this covenant and this oath; but with him that standeth here with us this day before the Lord our God, and also with him that is not here with us this day."*[22]

The actual details of the Revelation at Sinai, when our forefathers became conscious of the Voice of God speaking to each one *in particular* yet addressing the world *in general*, were regarded by the Rabbis as a matter of speculation. They were of little moment beside the tremendous fact that Israel was receiving authoritative beliefs and doctrines that were to form the basis of human conduct for all time.[23]

To this text-book of the ethical life—the Torah—we turn not for scientific knowledge but for guidance and solace in the crises of life. It is an expression of little faith in the Bible if an attempt be made to harmonize the latest speculative theories of scientists with the deathless

[22]Deut. xxix. 13-14. See also *Ibid.* xxxiv. 10; Num. xii. 6-8.
[23]Cf. Sanhed. x. 1.

pronouncements of the Torah. The value of our Bible is not contingent on such reconciliations, for it speaks in a different accent and on different problems. Science deals mainly with the *"Why"* of things; the Torah is concerned more with *"How"* things came into being.

From this it will be seen that the domain of faith has the whole world as its territory, while that of science is bounded by reason and established data. Israel, because it has made obedience to the Torah its cardinal principle (making it embrace the whole of human conduct and making future life depend on its acceptance), has become the instrument through which this divine agency exerts its power. *"Israel"*, wrote Yehudah Halevi, *"is to the nations as the heart is to man."*[24] When Israel will cease to function as *"the witness of God"* among *"the families of the earth"*, civilization will be heading for the crack of doom.

IV. THE WORLD OF THE BIBLE

In writing of what his faith means to the Jew, something must be said of what his Bible means to him. One depends on the other. The Bible to the Jew is the crown of religious writings, the record of those times when God spoke direct to man. True, the Biblical books greatly vary in form and content; much appears to have little or no relevance to religious life as understood by modern men. Closer study, however, shows that any isolation of its component parts diminishes one of its great values; namely, the demonstration that religion emerges in and through the ordinary experiences of human life. "The Law of the Lord is whole, restoring the soul" (Ps. xix. 8). Multitudes of thoughtful people have throughout the ages added their testimony to the unique value attributed by the Jew to his

[24] Cuzari ii. 36.

Torah. All types of men, of every degree of intelligence, at every stage of culture and in every condition of life, have found in our Scriptures the divine guidance and comfort they needed.

Jewish history has shown the close connection between ignorance of the Torah and assimilative tendencies. The best assurance for the flowering of the Jewish spirit is constant reference to its inspired literature. "*For they* (the *Torah* and *Mitzvot*) *are our life and the length of our days*" (Liturgy). The Jew has never faltered in his belief, despite the taunts hurled against the Bible by the Biblical "*Higher Critics*" during their short-lived triumph—a criticism which, in the long run, even proved an aid to faith. For the careful study applied, as a result, to the Bible yielded fruitful explanations of difficulties which used to be evaded rather than answered.

To the Jew, his Torah has no peer as a source of instruction in the art of right living. For him, it combines the loftiest teaching with abundant illustrations to show how its ideals can be lived. The Bible will always be the *divine* Book because it is, at the same time, so intensely *human*. Its uniqueness consists in that while it contains not a little which is within the understanding of an intelligent child, it is also so profound that the studies of two thousand years have not exhausted its significance for scholars and philosophers.[25] "*And the voice of the Shophar waxed louder and louder*" (Ex. xix. 19). Unlike the human voice which gets weaker after much use, the "*Voice of God*" assumes more force with time.

The Bible by no means exhausts the *sources* of Jewish faith. The Jew has preserved, in addition, a treasury of doctrines and sayings transmitted from father to son. This traditional literature, the Oral Law (*Torah she'be'al*

[25]The writer once attended a Hebrew lecture lasting two hours in which Prof. Martin Buber explained three Biblical words.

Peh) constitutes the largest part of Judaism. Many *Halachic* doctrines not mentioned in the Torah have been, explicitly or implicitly, traced to the forty days Moses spent with God prior to communicating them orally to Israel.[26] So have many well-known *haggadic* illustrations been connected with Sinaitic teachings. This Oral Law comprises all the interpretations and conclusions which our scribes have deduced from the written Torah,[27] together with the regulations instituted by them.

These are to be found in the *Mishnah*, *Gemara*, *Tosefta* and *Halachic Midrashim*, all of which were originally not committed to writing but transmitted and taught orally. In these sources, the claim is often repeated that a complete body of Rabbinical doctrines had been revealed unto Moses on Sinai, together with the hermeneutical rules according to which they might be developed. An example of such exegetical principles is the thirteen rules of R. Ishmael.[28] These rules are indispensable, in view of the terse utterances of the Torah. May not the very brevity of the Scriptures be a further proof that, side by side with the Bible, there existed a vigorous body of tradition?

Let one illustration suffice. In Deut. xii. 21, the commandment of slaughtering the sacrifice is given with the addition "*as I have commanded thee*". We will search in vain for a command in the Torah advising us *how* to slaughter the animal in the prescribed way. It is when we turn to the Talmudic Tractate *Hullin* that we find the laws of *Shechitah* enumerated in detail. These are invested with Divine authority because they are believed

---

[26] These traditional observances are described in the Talmud as הלכה למשה מסיני

[27] For which they claimed Biblical support (אסמכתא דקרא).

[28] See Singer's Prayer Book, pp. 13-14. These are included in the Siddur, in order to enable the Jew to study, as well as pray, each day.

to form part of the instruction given to Moses by
God on Mount Sinai. We can understand the opinion
expressed in the Talmud that customs and ceremonies
observed by the rank and file of the people are to be
regarded as sacrosanct as the Torah itself.[29]

V. THE ETHICS OF TRADITION

It would be wrong to regard the many customs and
observances that have been derived from Biblical commands as illegal additions coming under the ban of not
adding to or subtracting from that which is written in the
Torah.[30] This interdiction, as is plain from its context,
applied only to individuals, not to the *Sanhedrin* or judges
who were authorized to expand existing laws and to frame
new ones, after they had carefully examined the changing
conditions of the times. The stipulation was that they
must conform to logical rules in harmony with the spirit
of the Torah. R. Johanan b. Zakkai made new decrees
after the fall of Jerusalem in 70 C.E. Basing himself on
Deut. xvii. 8-11, he vested the *Sanhedrin* he established
with supreme authority to present to the perplexed and
despairing people a Judaism reinterpreted and adapted
to the catastrophic change that had taken place in their
national life. Furthermore, the Talmudic sages themselves
declare that so decisive should the decrees of a *Beth Din*
be that even when they inform us *"that our right hand is
our left, and our left our right"*, we must listen to them.

Has not the Biblical command to take the *Shophar* and
the *Lulav* been forbidden if *Rosh Hashanah* or *Sukkot*
occurs on a *Shabbat* because their use on that day was
considered likely to weaken its rigid observance? Did not

[29] מנהג ישראל תורה היא
[30] Deut. iv. 2.

13

Hillel reinterpret the laws of the *Shemitah*[31] with its remission of debts by introducing the Prozbul, when he saw the spirit of this humane institution thwarted by cunning and deceit? This document, drawn up by the *Beth Din*, made it possible for the lender to reclaim the debt from a fraudulent borrower even after the seventh year of Release had passed. When the aim of a Rabbinic command is to enforce Biblical ruling in monetary assessments of damage, or to strengthen the claims of a hired servant, the Rabbis are vested with full authority to read a new meaning into the command, as in the case of the *Lex Talionis*.[32]

Even in matters not strictly monetary such Rabbinic power was made manifest. Take the case of the *Agunah*, the anxious widow, whose remarriage was allowed on the corroboration of *one* witness only testifying that her lost husband was found dead. Even if that witness be a woman who elsewhere was incompetent in the eyes of the law to act as a witness, her evidence here was considered valid. The plight of such hard examples forced the Rabbis to reinterpret some of the Biblical laws on the grounds of the humanitarian reasons advocated by the Torah.[33]

The Rabbis did not go beyond their constituted authority by their adjustments and correlation of life to Torah. They had as rooted an objection to reform as the most conservative in our ranks at any time. They felt no compunction, however, in adding new regulations and

---

[31]Ibid. xv. 1-6; Lev. xxv. 1-7.

[32]Ex. xxi. 22-25. The compensation for an injured limb was an assessment in money, amounting to the difference between a man possessed of all his limbs and one bereft of the part of the body which had been injured. This difference in value was ascertained by the market value of a slave, possessed of that limb, or not.

[33]The Talmudic phrase is משום עגונה הקילו בה רבנן; Yeb. 88[a]; Gitt. 3[a].

setting aside existing ones if these helped to clarify the
Biblical injunctions and to foster the spirit intended, to
a generation far removed from the period in which the
commandment was first given. When R. Johanan b.
Zakkai abolished the laws governing the *Sotah*[34] on
account of the spread of immorality in his day,[35] he followed a natural process of growth and expansion whereby
Judaism developed into a living religion that aimed to
regulate all the details of daily life. When this renowned
Rabbi saw that murder was raising its head among the
dissident groups (*sicarii*) embittered by the fall of the
Second Jewish State, he abolished the laws of the Red
Heifer.[36] His aim was to show that Jewish law is elastic
and pliable; but he made one important *caveat*.

This was: provided such changes were undertaken by a
trusted Rabbinical Court ever mindful of the original purpose of the Torah and eager to adapt the divine principles
to the fluctuating circumstances of the age. Such changes
were made from time to time and were due to two factors:
one, because Rabbinic authority was derived from the confidence placed by the people in their accredited teachers;
two, because of the affectionate regard for the needs of
the people which these ancient teachers possessed. Many
of our traditional laws and customs had their origin in
popular practice (*mores*) before they became the *law* (*lex*)
of the nation.[37]

There should be no need at this stage of our enquiry to

---

[34]The unfaithful woman whose Ordeal by the Bitter Waters is
described in Num. v.

[35]Sot. 47ª.

[36]Deut. xxi. 1-9.

[37]Many a seemingly interminable discussion is sealed with the
presiding Rabbi's advice "go and see how the people behave
in such circumstances" (פוק חזי מאי עמא דבר). Also אם קבלה
נקבל ,היא—"if it is accepted by tradition, then nothing more
is to be said".

point out the loftiness of moral purpose found even in legal enactments. This knowledge inspired the people to exhibit a readiness to comply with the demands of orthodoxy. Next to the Bible, the Talmud became the main study of Jews, perhaps on account of the comprehensive collection of traditions it contained. Being so numerous, and scattered unsystematically over the sixty-three tractates of the Babylonian Talmud, this collection was afterwards codified and systematized under appropriate subject headings. This systematization began immediately after the redaction of the Talmud at the end of the sixth century; the most famous of such collections being the *Mishneh Torah* of Maimonides (1180) and the *Shulchan Aruch* of Joseph Caro (1564). Subsequent literary endeavour in this field centres around these two great Codes, both regarded to this day as the authoritative sources of Jewish religious life and practice.

Traditional Jews do not yield to others in broad-mindedness; if anything, they are more logical and humane than those who consider themselves rationalists and humanitarian cosmopolitans. They realize, however, that since the Bible is terse in utterance and since they are so far removed from the age of the Lawgiver, they are in greater need of that vast collection of explanations of Biblical precepts which developed orally alongside the Written Law. They realize that many of the most important commandments like the Sabbath, *Tsitsit, Tephillin, Mezuzah, Sukkot*, to name only a few, would be impossible of correct fulfilment were it not for the guidance offered in the Talmud. So loyal to Biblical authority was tradition that it had recourse on occasion to some ingenious interpretation of the ordinary meaning of the text in order to derive from it the necessary support for popular usage and custom.

The man who strove hard, not always correctly, to

trace the philosophic development of tradition was Isaac Hirsch Weiss (1815-1905), a scholar who taught at the Bet Hamidrash in Vienna. In his *Dor Dor Ve-Doreshav* (1891), he presents us with a history of the development of the Oral Law from the earliest times to the end of the Middle Ages. Though in many respects open to criticism, this work remains the standard account of the origin of the structure of the Talmud. Weiss does not consider the *Halachah* as fixed for all time; contending that it, like all other things, is constantly liable to variation. Not every law could be regarded as having been *"given from heaven"*.[38] Were this so, R. Johanan b. Zakkai would not have set them aside before the exigencies of the moment.

A liberal spirit always existed in the elucidation of the Scriptures. Behind all Rabbinic reinterpretations was the consciousness that every enactment of the Torah was good and wise, requiring mainly an earnest and religious mind to discover its aim. Those who approach tradition in this spirit cannot be classed in the same rank as the modern *"reformers"* who have displayed a readiness to drain the spirit from Judaism and reduce it to a minimum of faith. To emphasize their loyalty to tradition, these Talmudic teachers declared that *"everything which any student will teach at any future time was already communicated to Moses on Mount Sinai"*.[39]

Viewed in this light, greater respect for traditional observances will be engendered. Far from being unnecessarily prolific or indulging in hair-splitting dialectics, traditional Judaism is in possession of a varied and remarkable *"Corpus Juris"*. Such an obvious command as *"thou shalt teach them diligently to thy children"*[40] gave birth to a complete school system of Jewish education

[38] הלכה למשה מסיני
[39] Erubin.
[40] Deut. vi. 7.

long before the education of children became the concern of the State.

Since the Torah was given in the presence of all Israel, the Rabbis ruled that only the majority and not the individual, however eminent he may be, can decide on its interpretation and application.[41] When R. Eleazar refused to be guided by "a heavenly voice" in an Halachic matter, a voice from heaven pronounced him to be correct. Only in extreme cases was permission granted to act not in strict accordance with the dictates of the Torah.[42] Similar relaxation was afforded when an observance of certain traditional laws involved loss of property, the sacrifice of man's dignity, or when their fulfilment would involve too heavy a burden on the majority of the community.[43]

Such consideration was not intended to minimize the important part played by religious customs which the Rabbis regarded as equivalent to Biblical precepts.[44] But if the practice of any observance was proved to stem from some popular fallacy it was put aside, albeit reluctantly. Their love of continuity caused the Rabbis to make a *proviso* that no *Beth Din* can abolish a decree of another Court of Law unless it be considered greater in numbers and wisdom; a condition which will be better understood

---

[41]To stress this more vividly, the Rabbis have coined the phrase אין משגיחין בבת קול; which means that, once a custom has been established by popular usage, even supernatural intervention is not allowed to abrogate it lightly.

[42]Sanction for this was found in the words of the Psalmist: (עת לעשות לי' הפרו תורתך—cxix. 126) which, freely translated, means that when *action* is needed, *theory* is set aside.

[43]The Talmudic principle is (B. Bath. 60ᵇ): אין גוזרין גזרה על־הצבור שאין רוב הצבור יכולין לעמד בה "One should not burden a community with decrees, to observe, which would be well-nigh impossible for the majority of that community."

[44]מנהג ישראל תורה היא "Jewish established customs have the validity of Law."

when it is recalled that wisdom was on the down-grade. This view was not due to a false "inferiority complex" but to the respect they had for the wisdom of past generations. Their reluctance to modify a religious custom was not due to the belief that the observance had the divine sanction of a Biblical command. It meant that even a body of learned Rabbis should not be too quick to abolish any usage unless they could furnish adequate reason for its abrogation.

That the Talmud was wise in making this stipulation, who can gainsay? Has not our history brought to the fore two types of religious leader? One who possesses a kind of gramophone fidelity of reproducing faithfully the views of others, without having himself the originality or *savoir-faire* to see whether the decision arrived at is in the best interests either of the Torah or the community. The other, deriving his authority and inspiration from the past, has the tact and knowledge required to reconcile the doubting mind with the purpose of the command, thus ensuring the survival of Judaism for future generations. A study of our literature and of history leads to the conclusion that it was this second type that ultimately turned out to be the true defenders of the faith.

VI. JUDAISM AND CURRENT PROBLEMS

Towards the end of our present survey, evidence will be adduced to show that those who expounded our faith sought to correlate their approach to God with their approach to man. They taught that to be God-fearing means not to do anything to their fellow-man likely to cause displeasure to their Maker and thus render them unworthy of Divine love. This *"Fear of God"* does not mean a fear that terrifies and drives us haunted from His presence. It may be more true to say that the term *Yir'at Ha'shem* means a solemn respect that draws us nearer to Him, making us more deserving of His love. Such an approach to Judaism means a constant longing for communion with Him and a feeling of joy when performing a religious command.[45]

The true Jew not only obeys the *letter* of the law; he is anxious for the opportunity to do even more than the strict law demands of him.[46] "*Fear of God*" is the beginning of knowledge; the end of religious teaching is to love God and serve our fellow-men. It means to be conscious that we owe Him a debt of gratitude which we can never adequately repay. One of the ways in which we can express our gratitude is to find pleasure in the performance of the duties devolving upon us, as well as to be possessed of an implicit trust that all that happens to us is, in the long run, for the best.

Filled with this belief, we can safely entrust ourselves to Him everywhere and at all times, confident in His guidance, glorying in His salvation. Real faith, though it inspires resignation, does not mean a heartless indifference, a kind of "*could not care less*" attitude. It must be dynamic and ready to inspire heroism and self-sacrifice. "*The Lord is a man of battle*";[47] so must a faith that is worth while be militant for its convictions. Especially courageous must faith be against evil inclinations, against the *Yetser Ha'ra*, placed in us in accordance with the Divine scheme of things as an essential constituent in human nature without which the march of civilization, chequered as it is, would be impossible.

The religious Jew of to-day need not turn for guidance

---

[45]The phrase coined by the Talmud is שמחה של מצוה; see Shabb. 31[b]; Ber. 33[b].

[46]Cf. B. Metz. 30[b]: לפנים משורת הדין—"inside the line of the law", equity.

[47]Ex. xv. 3.

in the perplexities of his age to contemporary secularist philosophy, psychology or sociology. Judaism can answer all his doubts and problems. To understand those answers, however, one must alter one's approach to faith and tradition. This statement should not appear dogmatic. It is folly to regard every move at a reinterpretation of our eternal values with suspicion, as if a longing for reform was in the air. Our history is dotted with examples of such "suspicious" moves which finally have been the gateways to salvation. Zionism, originally regarded as an anti-religious movement because it sought to hasten our redemption, has in our day become an important factor in keeping many within the fold of Jewry. Now that we have the State of Israel, it should be our task to show the world how a modern country can be built in accordance with the "*blue-prints*" drawn up by the Divine Architect Himself. Through the Torah-plan, Israel can provide safety, peace and plenty for all those who dwell within its borders.

Of course, in the building of *Medinat Israel*, certain adjustments will have to be made in the *Halachah* in order to make it relevant to the issues of the day. This does not mean joining the ranks of those who euphemistically style themselves "*progressive*" Jews. Our approach is antipodic to theirs; for whereas they reject outright any part of the *Halachah* which does not appeal to them, we regard the Oral Law with its mass of tradition a vital part of Judaism. We must develop our legal codes so as to make them pronounce as authoritatively on vital issues of to-day as they did to the generations of Maimonides and Caro when they were finally systematized and codified. To invest them with this renewed authority, certain reinterpretations and readjustments will have to be made.

Lest these words appear to some as pandering to the

popular demand for revision of our laws, it may not be out of place to quote the words of the late Rabbi A. I. Kook[48] against whom the breath of suspicion cannot be uttered. Far from being nervous of *halachic* adjustment, this great authority believed that "*the more worldly life is, the more holiness there can be. We have occupied ourselves much with the soul, but we have forgotten that we have a sacred body, as well as a sacred soul. Our repentance will be successful only if with our spiritual repentance there will be combined physical repentance. Such repentance means healthy blood in a healthy body and in firm limbs. It is our duty to work with the living for the living in order to sanctify life.*"

Rabbi Kook was every inch alive to the problems of our time, as can be seen from this further quotation:[49] "*Without formulating precisely what character a society organized according to the laws of the Torah would bear, we may say with assurance that a consistent application of the Torah in the spheres of economics and social life, without yielding or compromise, would not permit the capitalist system to exist.*" It is a pity that the theology of Rabbi Kook, a man so potent in his generation, does not find in our own days worthy and valiant protagonists, equally stimulated to creative religious interpretation. Yet no *desideratum* is greater at the present moment, especially in the Jewish State, than introducing into the life of the nation all those branches of the *Halachah* affecting law,

[48] Born in 1865, died in 1935. He became Rabbi at the age of 20, and served as Rav in Lithuania till he became Rabbi in Jaffa in 1903. During the 1914-1918 World War, he was Rav of the *Mahazike Hadat* in London, and returned to Palestine in 1919 to become Chief Rabbi of the whole country. All his published writings breathe a love for God and man.

[49] See a thoughtful, though brief, article "The Religious Outlook of the Modern Orthodox Jew", by Hershel Zinger in the Bachad monthly "Chayenu", 1949.

economics and social affairs which have, of necessity, fallen into disuse in the *Galut*.

VII. OUR TASK THESE DAYS

Our paramount task these days is to make Judaism once again the all-embracing "Way of Life" of the Jewish people in its own land. To the Jew, his faith means a conviction of the supremacy and the priority of spirit over matter, of the unseen over the seen. This priority of spirit over matter means to him the Unity and the Omnipresence of God, besides which men and events dwarf into the background. That man—a frail and transitory dweller on earth, a pendulum "twixt a smile and a tear"—can have these thoughts is proof that he is not merely matter and of ephemeral worth but that he is also possessed of a spiritual mind which is linked to eternity. Only fire can kindle fire, so can only spirit beget spirit; only the *divine* in man can sense the divine in the universe. In the knowledge of our smallness, lies our greatness; in the measure of our restlessness, is to be found the possibility of our rest. "*A spark disturbs our clod.*" What our faith tries to do for the Jew is to make his inherent goodness overmatch his inherent evil and his greatness outweigh his littleness.

Not all will understand this philosophy of the Jewish outlook on life. But is it necessary to *understand* the problems of life in order to be happy? A great thinker once voiced the opinion that "*though the failing heart cries out for evidence, at the worst live as if there were God and duty and they will prove themselves to you in your life*". To the duties of thinking and praying, Judaism adds those of *doing* and *living*, advising us to *live* the life of love and assuring us of moral victories. In more senses than one, the wise words of Goethe are true: *"Wer immer strebend sich bemuht, den können wir erlösen"*,[50] "Whoever aspires unweariedly, is not beyond redeeming". He will be redeemed from the burden and the agony of doubt. When he has found faith at last it will be a strengthening faith, one that has been deepened by trial, purified by suffering, intensified by love.

It is due to this all-embracing and stimulating faith that Jews, as a nation, have *"encroached upon Time and exhausted Eternity"*. Other nations, springing from obscurity, rose and achieved greatness; but their downfall was as sudden and as unexpected as was their triumph. Their temples and shrines have become ruins; their monuments and obelisks have mingled with the dust and their grandeur and pomp have disappeared. The Jew survives them all. He has seen nations totter and crumble and despotic upstarts, first rising to giddy heights, later falling to abysmal depths.

Turning the pages of his glorious, blood-soaked history, he sees his people exiled, plundered, tortured, massacred. But he sees also how his ancestors outlived all the persecutions of a hostile world, deriving new vitality from their sufferings and becoming *"born again"* after the baptism of pogrom and massacre. Driven hither and thither about the four corners of the globe; here tolerated, there banished; here recalled, there driven out again into exile, the Jew has left his trace everywhere. Like the wandering thistle-down, blown about from field to field at the sport of winds, the Jew, driven by persecution, has taken root in every land and clime. The result of this suffering and dispersal? God is worshipped all over the globe by the Jew. The four corners of the earth resound with the proclamation *"Hear O Israel, the Lord our God, the Lord is One"*.

[50] See "The Greatness of Man", by C. G. Montefiore, "The Jewish Guardian", Feb. 22nd, 1929.

In our day, thanks to Divine Providence, over a million Jews have found a haven in the Third Jewish Commonwealth, and more are entering the ever-open door. But our mission to the world has not ended; it has simply begun again. Standing on the lofty eminence of Sinai's peak, the Jew can philosophically look down upon the battle of creeds and the hostility of nations with a heart stirred with pity for the combatants. He sees them grappling with the shadows of real things, while the *real* substance of life and endeavour, the Torah, is held firmly in his possession. From the arid ruins of two World Wars in one generation, with rumblings of worse to come; from the shattered ideologies, exploded creeds, ashes of burnt-out beliefs, and the hatred of nations, the Jew has once again arisen, Phoenix-like, to new life from the tomb of suffering and the womb of Time.

This third historic attempt to be on the map of the world offers mankind a new way of life and a burning faith which can become a light in its darkness and a panacea for all its ills. *"Arise, shine, for thy light is come, and the glory of the Lord is risen upon thee. For behold, darkness covers the earth, and gross darkness the peoples; but upon thee the Lord will arise and His glory shall be seen upon thee. And nations shall walk at thy light, and kings at the brightness of thy rising"* (Isa. lx. 1-3).

What is the Jewish prescription for the ills of to-day? The creation of a civilization based on the conception of Social Justice expressed by the Torah and the existence of a democratic socialism in which all will be given their due and the labourer made worthy of his hire. This must not be taken to mean the reintroduction into life of an intellectual Ghetto in which all action is regulated by tradition and law. The ethics of our *Halachah*, far from limiting cultural activity, in fact stimulates idealism and infuses every aspect of life with the spirit of the Torah.

Based on sound Jewish principles, the Third Jewish Commonwealth will be like the rock at the edge of the sea against which the tempestuous waves beat their fury in vain. *"The grass withereth, the flower fadeth, but the word of our God shall stand for ever"* (Isa. xl. 7-8).

CHAPTER NINE

OUR SOCIAL ETHICS

I. WHAT ARE SOCIAL ETHICS?

THE history of Judaism is that of the emergence of ethical ideas from the legalities of ritual and ceremony into the social and universal sphere. One illustration will serve. The erroneous translation of *Tephillin* (literally, aids to *"prayer"*) by the word *"phylacteries"* (derived from the Greek *"Phylax"*, *"a guardian"*), is indicative of those times when to wear them was considered by others, like the Greeks, a *prophylactic*, a defence against demons and evil spirits whose number in those ages of superstition was legion. It says much for the onward march of Judaism, as an ethical faith, when it is recalled that, beginning at a time when the rest of the world was swamped by superstition, magic and necromancy—all claiming myriads of adherents —it was the first to throw aside witchcraft and paganism, stressing that beside nobility of conduct, everything paled.

Already in prophetic times,[1] Social Ethics were preferred to sacrifice, the emphasis being that it was in the service of mankind that true worship of God consisted. This teaching was later crystallized by Rabbi Hanina b. Dosa in the Mishnah thus: *"He in whom the spirit of his fellow-men takes delight, in him the Spirit of the All-present takes delight: and he in whom the spirit of his fellow-creatures takes not delight, in him the Spirit of the All-present takes no delight."*[2] The order (in which *"the spirit of man"*

[1] 1 Sam. xv. 22-23. See Isa. i. 11-17; Jer. vii. 22-28, to cite only three passages.
[2] Abot iii. 13.

precedes that of the All-present) is significant. It cannot
be emphasized too much that love for all, as expressed in
such commands as "*Love thy neighbour as thyself,*"[3] is the
alpha and the *omega* of Judaism.

By Social Ethics, Judaism means a power of expressing
in a *practical* manner our sympathy in another's plight, our
humanity and self-denying generosity and our endeavour
to render less the sum of human wretchedness. The Torah
expects something more of us than an outward obedience
to the *letter* of its precepts. To help the poor; to befriend
the stranger; to strengthen the weak; to defend the helpless;
to protect the widow; to plead for the orphan; yes, even to
help our enemy and to be considerate towards the dumb
beast—these are *some* of the flowerings of our legislation.

Prophetic teaching echoes this abiding love for all
mankind, this zeal for all human causes, as the truest
manifestation of the will of God.[4] It was Judaism that
was the first to exhort its adherents at a time when such
views were almost incomprehensible, that "*If thine
enemy be hungry, give him bread to eat: if he be thirsty,
water to drink*".[5] It was the Talmud, a work maligned by
its detractors, that warned the Jew that "*He who shames
his friend in public, has thereby forfeited his share in the
World to Come*";[6] that "*he who honours himself through the
shame of another will have no portion in the World to
Come*";[7] that "*it is better for a man to cast himself into a
flaming oven than to shame his comrade in public*".[8]

[3] Lev. xix. 18.
[4] See especially Mic. vi. 8.
[5] Prov. xxv. 21.
[6] B.M. 59.
[7] Yer. Hag. ii. 1.
[8] Ber. 43. In Ta'an. 30[a], we read that on the 15th Av, Jewish
maidens danced in the Judean vineyards in borrowed dress,
so as not to shame those who had none to wear. Consideration
for the feelings of another was developed into a fine art in
ancient Judea.

The prejudice in which Judaism is held by many spiritual leaders of other faiths is due to their lack of understanding that it was just by such means of conduct that the rare human virtues—charity and sympathy, modesty and mercy, patience and pity—were preserved and promoted throughout the Dark Ages. Jewish life, organized under such a system of regulations, far from obscuring or minimizing social responsibility on the part of the individual has, on the contrary, ranged the Jew as a protagonist for the defence of the wronged against the oppressor. This legalism it was that impressed upon the Jew even more than did his suffering for the beliefs held by his nation, that he is a member of one large family in which the honour of *all* is in the keeping of *each*. It was his *Halachah* that cautioned him to exercise the greatest watchfulness that no action or word of his might bring to others shame or suffering.[9]

Social Ethics, then, means right conduct (*ortho-praxia*), sincerity of belief and a *total* submission to the demands made by our bi-partite Decalogue with its equal stress on duties to God and duties to man. Our Codes are exercises in spiritual discipline which may only be set aside in the Messianic Age when mankind has attained to perfection, but the Torah and the Social Ethics of our religion developed from it are as eternal as their Author. Being eternal, they are perfect; only imperfection can eventually give way to excellence. They are universal, because they apply to every one of God's children equally, be they Jews or Gentiles.

The essential teaching of Judaism is that its believers must have love and kindness for *all*, malice and prejudice towards *none*. When first created, man was told that "*it*

[9] So Rabbi Huna's teaching in B.Bath 22; Rabban Gamaliel's address to his court in Sanhed. ii; also Rabbi Tanhuma's statement in Genesis R. xxiv. 7.

is not good for man to be alone".[10] He must regard himself as a member of a large family, a limb in a body known as humanity. This consciousness creates many responsibilities and solemn duties towards those with whom he is a fellow-pilgrim on earth. His life is no longer to be considered as his own to do with it as he pleases. He will now realize that just as *their* conduct affects him, so will *his* conduct affect them.

The story of the man in the boat who, having nothing to do while his friend was strenuously rowing, idly occupies his leisure in drilling a hole under his seat and answers his friend's complaint of his dangerous action with the retort that the hole is under *his* seat *only*—forgetting that the water would flood the whole boat—is at the very essence of social ethics.[11] One of our teachings in the Torah is that the indiscretions of one man may cause the misery of a community.[12] This is especially true when applied to the attitude the world adopts towards the Jew. Instead of judging him by the *best* representative, he is judged by the *worst* type.

Our ethics teach us to be considerate and pleasant towards others.[13] Such consideration for the safety of others was shown by one saintly character[14] who, after the ceremony at his wedding, picked up the pieces of the glass he had just broken lest one trod upon them to his hurt. It is not enough for the pious Jew not to cause injury directly; he must go out of his way to prevent the occurrence of any such damage. It is told of many Rabbis that on perceiving any obstacle on the ground likely to cause injury, they would remove it. "*He who wishes to be*

[10]Gen. ii. 18.
[11]Lev. R. iv. 6.
[12]See Num. xvi. 22, in connection with the rebellion of Korah.
[13]Ket. 17ᵃ: לעולם תהא דעתו של־אדם מעורבת עם־הבריות
[14]Rabbi Leib Hassid of Kelm.

*regarded as pious, must fulfil the words laid down concerning
damage*" (B. Kam. 30ᵃ: הַאי מַאן דְבָעֵי לְמֶהֱוֵי חֲסִידָא לִיקַיֵים
(מִילֵי דְאָבוֹת

II. RESPECT FOR OTHERS

"*Who is honoured?*" asked Ben Zoma.[15] It was a
rhetorical question, for he himself knew the only true
answer. "*He who honours others; as it is said:*[16] '*For I will
honour them that honour Me, but those that despise Me
shall be held in contempt*'.*" The Talmud is emphatic that
the honour of others should be a prime concern.[17] One
is absolved of a command of the Torah if its fulfilment be
at the expense of one's own prestige. For though we are
told:[18] "*Thou shalt not see thy brother's ox or his sheep driven
away, and hide thyself from them; thou shalt surely bring
them back unto thy brother*", yet in the case of an old man,
a scholar or a woman, the fulfilment of such a command,
involving effort and loss of dignity, is not expected.[19]
Far better that a man throw himself into a burning furnace
than put his friend to shame. This opinion is expressed
several times in the Talmud.[20] A proverb current in those
days was: "*Do not shame others, that you yourself be not
put to shame.*"[21] When Rabbi Nehuniah b. Ha'Kanah was
asked to account for his longevity, his reply was: "*Never
have I acquired honour at the expense of another's shame;
neither have I ever gone to sleep reviling others.*"[22] God is
thought of as saying to Israel: "*My children! What do*

[15]Abot iv. 1.
[16]I Sam. ii. 30.
[17]Ber. 28ᵇ.
[18]Deut. xxii. 1.
[19]B.Metz. 30ᵃ. Cf. Hoshen Mishpat 263. Ber. 43ᵇ.
[20]B.M. 59ᵃ; Sot. 6ᵃ.
[21]M.K. 9ᵇ.
[22]Meg. 28ᵃ: לֹא חֲבֵישׁ וְלֹא חֲתַבֵּישׁ

*I ask of you? Only that you love one another and respect
one another.*"

One can see how high the respect for others is regarded
from the law of Exodus xxi. 37: "*If a man steal an ox, or
a sheep and kill it, or sell it, he shall pay* five *oxen for an ox,
and* four *sheep for a sheep*", said Rabbi Johanan b. Zakkai;[23]
"for since he has to carry the sheep away on his shoulder,
an act unbecoming to any man, his fine is less than that
of an ox which he needs only to lead away." Of this Rabbi
it was told that none ever preceded him in greeting
anybody, Jew or non-Jew alike. (Ber. 17[a]). Shammai, the
forensic antagonist of the gentle Hillel, is recorded to have
said: "Receive *all* men gladly, for God will only forgive
such sins that are perpetrated against Him. Those you
have committed against your neighbour, not even Yom
Kippur has the power to atone for. You must first obtain
the forgiveness of your neighbour before you ask God to
forgive you."

When the question "What constitutes a *Hillul Ha'*
shem?" was posed in the academies, the Rabbis capped
each other in their citation of examples. The thread that
linked all their replies was "*a desecration of God's name*"
is caused by any act that causes another shame or hardship.
For such an act, only death can compensate.[24] Does it
not say:[25] '*And the Lord of Hosts revealed Himself in mine
ears: 'Surely this iniquity*[26] *shall not be expiated by you till
ye die*', *saith the Lord, the God of Hosts.*" Correct weights
and measures are the subject of many regulations in our
Codes, because they are practical illustrations of the
Biblical command "*And thy brother shall live with thee*".

---

[23]B.K. 79[b]. Though this point has already received mention, its
fine ethical nature bears repetition.

[24]Yoma 86[a].

[25]Isa. xxii. 14.

[26]Read what precedes in this chapter of Isaiah describing the
Hillul Ha'shem of his contemporaries.

To cause pain to man or beast is to forfeit membership of the Jewish brotherhood whose claim to holiness is its moral Codes with their stress on sympathy, hospitality, consideration and justice. Hospitality is said to be greater than divine worship.[27] It is included in the list which reads: honouring parents; practising charity; studying Torah; visiting the sick; dowering the bride; attending to the dead; devotion in prayer, and making peace between man and his fellow, of which a man enjoys the interest in this world while the capital remains in the world to come.[28] In ancient Jerusalem, the custom prevailed of hanging a table-cloth on the door facing the street when a meal was in progress; an invitation to the wayfarer to join in the meal within.[29] Of this daily custom, the invitation at the commencement of the Seder on the first two eves of *Pesah* is reminiscent.

Respect for others was fostered by the teaching that man was created alone. The world should be reminded that to save the soul of *one* person is equivalent to preserving humanity. Did not all *"the families of the earth"* proceed from Adam? We mourn the dead with such customs as *Keriah, Shivah, Kaddish, Yahrzeit* and *Yizkor*,[30] for these emphasize the importance of the soul that has winged its flight heavenwards. When a man was found slain outside the boundaries of the nearest city, the elders thereof had to declare in all solemnity: *"Our hands have not shed this blood, neither have our eyes seen it."*[31] This was not because they were suspected of being directly concerned with the murder, but because they must clear their conscience before the entire assembly

---

[27] Shabb. 127[a].
[28] Peah. i. 1; see Singer's Prayer Book, p. 5.
[29] B.B. 93[b].
[30] See the writer's "Jewish Customs", Chapter x.
[31] Deut. xxi. 7 (see the whole passage vv. 1-9).

that the death was not the direct consequence of a failure on their part to provide shelter and hospitality for the wayfarer.

Abraham was the pattern of hospitality, given readily. When such respect was shown to a needy scholar, the reward was even greater; then it was as if he had offered sacrifices at the time when the Temple still existed.[32] The Midrash records that the daughter of Rabbi Akiba was saved from death on her wedding-night because she had offered her meal to a poor, uninvited guest. A Jewish community is not complete without its Shelters and Hostels for the orphan and the needy and its institutions providing for every range of human wants and needs.

High on the list of Social Ethics is the care of the sick. God Himself is described as visiting those who are infirm and wracked by illness.[33] When Rabbi Joseph once preached on Exodus xviii. 20: "*And thou shalt teach them the statutes and the laws, and shalt show them the way wherein they must walk and the work that they must do*", he explained the latter half of the verse to mean that they must be taught the importance of kindly deeds (*hadderech*) and the urgency of visiting the sick (*yelechu bah*). The story is told of Rabbi Akiba who, visiting a disciple when he was gravely ill, personally attended to his wants. On his recovery, he came to the Rabbi, transfigured by gratitude, assuring him that *his* visit it was that put new life and hope into him. Whereupon Rabbi Akiba taught that "*he who does not visit the sick is guilty of shedding blood; the reward of such a visit is that one is saved from Gehinnom, from the Evil Inclination and from all kinds of suffering*".[34]

Great, especially, must be the respect to be shown to

[32]Ket. 105b.
[33]See Midrash Rabba to Gen. xviii.
[34]Cf. Ned. 40a.

the dead. Even a High Priest who is a Nazirite may attend to the burial of one who has no immediate relatives or friends to do so.[35] The study of the Torah may be interrupted if thereby a person be brought with greater respect to his final resting-place.[36] Such consideration for the living and the dead reflects the ideal human relationship advocated in the Torah.

The word "*thy neighbour*" (*re'acha*) in Leviticus xix. 18 includes the non-Jew. The occasional derogatory remarks made by individual Rabbis in the Talmud against those who serve idols are due to some bitter experience which still rankled. An unbiased survey of such hostile expressions will convince all but the prejudiced that these were wrung from anguished lips under extreme provocation. In general, the Rabbinic outlook in the sphere of social ethics is *universal* rather than *national*. It is certainly never parochial in outlook. In most of the ethical maxims, the term employed for men is *beriot* (creatures). Perhaps the most characteristic of such teachings are that "*one may not steal the mind of his fellow-creature, be he even a Gentile*".[37] "*It is more serious to steal from a Gentile than from a Jew, for this involves a Hillul Ha'shem*"[38] and that "*it is meritorious to dispense kindness to Gentile as well as to Jew*".[39]

Then how account for the outburst of Rabbi Simeon b. Yohai that "*the best of the heathen deserves death*"?[40] The history of his times supplies the answer. The author of this harsh opinion was a victim of the Hadrianic persecutions. He had seen his beloved teacher Rabbi Akiba, together with the nine other illustrious martyrs, subjected first to the most cruel persecutions following

---

[35]Such a corpse is called מת מצוה
[36]Meg. 3[b].
[37]Hull. 94[a].
[38]Tosefta B.K. x. 8: חמור גזל הנכרי מגזל ישראל, מפני חלול השם
[39]Gittin 61[a].
[40]Mechilta Ex. xiv. 7.

the defeat of Bar Cochba's revolt (135 c.e.) and then undergoing deaths the most diabolical. He had been compelled with his son to hide in a cave for thirteen years to escape death at the hands of the Romans. Are his words to be wondered at when ultimately he was allowed to emerge from his enforced hiding? To say, however, that his view is representative of Jewish social ethics is as untrue as it is unjust.

The real voice of Judaism advises us[41] *"to be of those who are persecuted, not of those who persecute others; to be of those who are put to shame, not of those who shame others"; not to hate another even inwardly (in thy heart[42]);* to believe that all those who are righteous will have a share in the World to Come. Israel claims the distinction of being the *"Chosen People"* not because it regards the Torah as its *exclusive* possession but because it chose to accept that which other nations, who according to legend had received the offer first and had rejected it. Judaism prays for the time when the world will accept the Torah and walk along its paths of peace and righteousness.[43] *"Before Thee, O Lord our God, let them bow and fall; and unto Thy glorious name let them give honour; let them all accept the yoke of Thy Kingdom, and do Thou reign over them speedily, and for ever and ever"* (*Aleinu* prayer, Singer's Prayer Book, p. 77).

III. ETHICS OF CHARITY

The word *Tsedakah* means something more than charity; it means to *do* right and in the best possible way. It is a basic principle of Social Ethics to provide for the welfare of all and to each according to his need. As one

[41]B.K. 93[a]; Shabb. 88[a]; Sanhed. 49[a].
[42]Lev. xix. 17; Abot ii. 15.
[43]Isa. ii. 2-4; Micah iv. 1-5.

of the three pillars on which society rests,[44] kindness can be regarded as a virtue only if it be practised in secret[45] and not regarded merely as almsgiving to be dispensed grudgingly. In the Torah, giving to holy causes is dignified by the word *Terumah*[46] ("*uplifting*"). Since each of us needs the ennoblement which true kindness fosters, it is a virtue from which even he, who himself is dependent on charity, is not exempt.[47] The Rabbis ruled that it is better to give nothing rather than bring a blush to the recipient of alms.[48] The word *Tsedakah* is comprehensive, including any deed leading to the alleviation of the afflicted and resulting in a sweetening of human relationships. True charity bestows as well as receives; "*more than the householder does for the needy, the needy does for the householder*".[49]

The Talmud quotes the parable of the two lambs passing through a stream, one shorn of its wool the other not. The shorn one found it easier to cross.[50] Is not the possession of wealth rather precarious—with *us* to-day, with *another* to-morrow? "*A wheel rotates in this world*",[51] causing some to be on top one day and at the bottom another. The giving of charity is constantly stressed because of this truth. That any Jew should be indifferent to the woe of another is inconceivable.[52]

No duty is more important, and none ushers in salvation more speedily.[53] "*As long as the Temple stood*", declared

---

[44]Abot i. 2.
[45]See B.B. 10[b]; Ps. xli. 1.
[46]Ex. xxv. 2-3.
[47]Gitt. 7[b].
[48]Hag. 5[a].
[49]Lev. R. xxiv. 8.
[50]Gitt. 7[a].
[51]Shabb. 151[b] explaining the words כי בגלל הדבר הזה (Deut. xv. 10).
[52]Lev. xix. 10; Deut. xiv. 29; Isa. lviii. 6ff; Job xxxi. 13.
[53]B.B. 9[a]; Sukk. 49[b]; Ket. 67[b].

Rabbi Eleazer, "*a man would donate his shekel and receive atonement for his soul.*[54] *Now, however, in the absence of a Temple, it all depends on the giving of Tsedakah; if he gives, all is well, if not, hostile forces will come and deprive him of his wealth by force.*"[55] To ignore giving help to any deserving cause is regarded by Rabbi Joshua b. Karcha[56] equivalent to idol-worship; for it brands the man as "*possessed*" by his possessions, a worshipper of the "*Golden Calf*".

The purpose of true charity should be to build up the *morale* of the recipient, taking great precaution not to humiliate or pauperize him, but to heighten his sense of dignity of human personality. Especially should such care be exercised when "*dowering the bride*", an act of kindness (*gemilat hasadim*) which ranks very high. Nothing is dearer in the sight of God, the Rabbis taught, than to help the orphaned girl to set up a home of her own. No Jewish community is considered fulfilling its duty if it has not within its midst a special organization for this purpose. In their interpretation of the verse: "*Happy are they that keep justice, that do righteousness at all times*",[57] the Rabbis applied it to him who looks after the orphans in their home and helps them to marry.[58] Many are the blessings said to accrue as a reward for such kindness, for it spells a consciousness that God is the real owner of our possessions and that we all regard ourselves as members of one large family.

"*He who gives even a* prutah[59] *to the poor*", says a Rabbi, "*is blessed with six blessings; but he who encourages him*

[54]Ex. xxx. 15.
[55]B.B. 9[a]; Abot d'R'Nathan iv; Hosea vi. 6.
[56]Ket. 68[b].
[57]Ps. cvi. 3.
[58]Ket. 50[a].
[59]A small coin, one eighth of an *isar;* Kidd. i. 1; Shevu. vi. 1; B.Metz. iv. 1. Also a thousandth part of the Israeli *pound* to-day.

with kind words (gemilat hasadim), is blessed with eleven blessings." Experience shows that this view is not mere exaggeration. A sympathetic attitude towards those in want will go a long way towards setting them on their feet once more. At the same time, a solemn warning was issued to him who receives alms under false pretences. He who feigns blindness or any other crippling impediment to stir people's mercy will not depart from this life before he is actually reduced to such circumstances.[60] The Divine method of ultimate punishment is *"measure for measure"* (*middah keneged middah*).

In Temple times, the giving of *Tsedakah* became a fine art. Inspiring is the teaching of Rabbi Simlai[61] that the *alpha* and the *omega* of the Torah is *Gemilat hasadim;* for *"God made for Adam and for his wife garments of skins, and clothed them"*[62] soon after He created them. Similarly, the last words of the Pentateuch record that *"And he* (Moses) *was buried in the land of Moab over against Beth-peor"*[63] seemingly by God Himself; for the verse concludes *"and no man knoweth of his sepulchre unto this day"*. The Temple authorities set aside a special chamber[64] with two large coffers, in one of which the righteous could quietly leave their alms, and from the other the poor could unobtrusively take what they needed. So honest were all concerned, we are told, that at no time were the two coffers of this room ever depleted. The coffer into which they deposited their alms was as full as that from which they withdrew assistance. When the one who had fallen on evil days happened formerly to have been a rich man, the assistance afforded to him was of special consideration.

---

[60]Peah vii.

[61]Sot. 14ᵃ.

[62]Gen. iii. 21.

[63]Deut. xxxiv. 6.

[64]Called לשכת חשאים; cf. Shekalim v. 6. There were also specially appointed "overseers of the poor"—גבאי צדקה

Of Hillel it is told that when one who had been the richest member of the community came for help, he gave him generously, providing him with the best horse and the most costly garments that money could buy. Only one thing the poor man lacked of his former glory; that was a footman to ride before him. When Hillel's attempts at procuring such a servant proved unsuccessful, the Rabbi himself undertook to perform this task. Besides such humility and kindness, even the stories of saints and martyrs of other faiths, touching as they are, pale into insignificance. In the field of noble living, others can teach us but little.

"He that is gracious unto the poor, lendeth unto the Lord", sang the Psalmist. Social Ethics echo this refrain by teaching us how to become *"God's bankers"*. When a Roman governor enquired of Rabbi Akiba: "Why does your God, for whom you claim such loving concern for His creatures, not Himself provide for the poor?" the reply was: *"Charity makes wealth a means of salvation. God wishes us to help one another and thus to convert this earthly life into a period of character-moulding."* Our blessings must be regarded as opportunities for serving God and helping man. Why, asks one teacher, do the words *"that they take for Me an offering"*[65] follow so closely on the words: *"And they said: 'All that the Lord hath spoken we will do, and obey' "?*[66] To show Israel that the best way to obey the Torah is to give offerings of all we have, as well as to emphasize that our affirmations must be backed by our readiness to give.

This alacrity to serve has inspired some sublime utterances in our literature, more especially in the literature of the Hasidim. Can one find an utterance more noble than this? *"To love, that is to say, truly to love one's*

[65] Ex. xxv. 2.
[66] Ibid. xxiv. 7.

neighbour, means to know what brings pain to your comrade."[67] *"It may occasionally happen that thine own hand inadvertently strike thee. Wouldst thou take a stick and chastise thy hand for its heedlessness and thus add to thy pain? It is the same with thy neighbour, whose soul is one with thine; who, because of insufficient understanding, does thee harm. Shouldst thou retaliate, it would be thou, as well as he, who wouldst suffer."* (Yerushalmi Ned. ix.)

The Second Temple was reduced to ruins and Israel led into exile because of *"worthless hatred"*?[68] Those who rejoice at the misfortunes of others do not deserve to possess a land of their own.

The ethical incentive of charity was the desire to imitate the example set by God in the Torah. Only that Jew, distinguished for his benevolence, was a worthy descendant of Abraham and was fulfilling the major demands of Judaism. It is recorded, for instance of Rabbi Eleazar that he was exceedingly poor; so much so, that many were the occasions when he had nothing to eat. Yet his poverty proved no excuse for not giving. He always gave away of the little he had to one poorer still, before he commenced his prayers.[69] Moses was said to have been shown by God the treasures in heaven stored up for those who practise *gemillat hasadim*.

It is necessary to state the exact difference between these two terms. *Tsedakah* refers mainly to a money-offering given primarily to the poor, *gemilat hasadim*

---

[67]Attributed to Rabbi Moshe Leib of Sasov, one of the well-known Hasidic houses. For other stories of Hasidism, see the anthology of L. I. Newman, New York.

[68]שנאת חנם. It was Rabbi Kook who expressed the hope that people should rather be accused of אהבת חנם, universal love, than of שנאת חנם. If we learnt to *love* all, we would be *beloved* by all.

[69]B.Bath 10ᵃ. Whereas *tsedakah* is mostly performed by the giving of alms, *gemilat hasadim* comprises help both of a monetary and moral kind.

includes *all* deeds of kindness other than monetary, the
recipients of which may well be the "*poor*" rich. It also
covers acts of respect towards the dead (Sukkah 49[b]).

In a section devoted to the laws of *Tsedakah*,
Maimonides categorizes three of the noblest types of
gemilat hasadim. The *first* is to lend money to the poor
without the taking of any interest; the *second* is to cheer
them with word and deed as well as with the giving of
money; and the *third* is just to evince sympathy with the
misfortune of another without wedding it to acts of a
practical nature. The Jew should give readily and joyfully;
not "*till it hurts to give*"[70] but till one feels the *pleasure* of
having given generously. The very phrase is a contradic-
tion of the Jewish ethics of giving. Why should a *Mitzvah*
hurt?

The Mishnah[71] which glowingly records the joyous
procession of those bringing the first-fruits between
Shavuot and *Sukkot* into the Temple where they recited
the prayer of gratitude,[72] stipulates that if the first-fruits
were tardily brought after the termination of *Sukkot*, no
such recitation was allowed. Why? One should not wait
for the last moment before discharging dues. Man
must give according to his *means*, not according to his
meanness.

The classic Biblical example of such *meanness* in giving
is to be found in the story of Cain and Abel.[73] There we
are told that Cain brought some "*fruit of the ground as an
offering unto the Lord*", but Abel "*brought of the firstlings
of his flock and of the fat thereof*".[74] We are not surprised
that "*The Lord had respect unto Abel and to his offering:*

[70] A popular expression which is alien to the spirit of social
ethics, in which charity is regarded as a joyous privilege.
[71] Bikkurim iii.
[72] Deut. xxvi. 1-11.
[73] Gen. iv. 1-15.
[74] Ibid. vv. 3-4.

but unto Cain and to his offering, He had not respect.[75]
Had mankind learnt the moral of this story from the
beginning, it would have been spared much suffering.
It would seem, however, that though man is gradually
making the earth yield its secret weapons of destruction,
such as the atomic and the hydrogen bomb, he has not yet
learnt the elementary truths of the sanctity of life and the
need for kindliness. Mankind has climbed the mountains
of scientific discoveries but its soul it has left in the valley
below. For it spends most of its energies in acquiring
goods but not the good. When will mankind learn that
there are no pockets in the shrouds in which we are
clothed when our eyes are closed?

If the new State of Israel is to be true to its mission as a
theocracy whose aim is the establishment of *"the kingdom
of heaven"* on earth, it must incorporate in its constitution
some of the agricultural laws that once characterized
Israel on its own land. A mere reference to the most well-
known of these must suffice. The laws governing the
Seventh Year of Release (*Shemitah*) and the Jubilee
(Lev. xxv) should once again become the very fabric of
our agricultural economy. According to the Torah,[76] any
ears of corn that fell from the hand of the reaper when
harvesting, providing they are less than three, must be
left for the poor to collect.[77] This law was known as *Leket*.
It was directly connected with the law governing the
"Forgotten Sheaf" (*Shikkechah*) which demanded that if,
when reaping, a whole sheaf is left unobserved, it must
not afterwards be collected but left for the orphan and
the widow to enjoy.

A similar provision is made for the *"Corners"* of the

[75]Gen. iv. 4-5.
[76]Lev. xix. 9-10.
[77]See the writer's notes on Tractate *Peah* in the Soncino
Talmud.

field (*Peah*). When the harvest is about to end, the fields must not be cut too closely to the path. Let the poor share some of the rich blessings which "*a good earth*" had lavished upon us and let the poor have the benefit of the doubt which may arise in the interpretation of these humane agricultural laws. Charity and kindliness must again be woven into the warp and woof of the political, economic and social structure of the world if it is to survive.

Are these laws based on Israel's possession of a land[78] applicable in the *Diaspora?* The Talmud voted in favour of their retention because of the feelings of charitableness that they arouse in the heart of farmers. This fidelity to Biblical law is not without its own reward. Did not Boaz meet Ruth, his life's partner, on such an occasion when she was gathering what the reapers had left?

All males must appear thrice yearly with offerings of their field and vineyard; that is *all*, save those not enjoying full freedom of mind or body. "*Three times a year shall all thy males appear before the Lord God*" is the Biblical command.[79] The Rabbis deduced that deaf and dumb mutes, minors, those of questionable sex (*tumtum* and *anderoginos*), women and slaves, are exempt because they are not included in the term "*thy males*" (*zechurcha*). Similarly exempted were those afflicted with blindness, because the word "*appear*" (*yeraeh*), used in that connection, implies one who can *see* as well as one that can "*be seen*". Apart from these exceptions, all others were in duty bound to *give* to the needy, if they were themselves to receive from God of His bounty.

To ensure that, as far as possible, only those deserving to benefit from these agricultural laws were benefited, a

---

[78]The Rabbinic phrase is מצוות התלויות בארץ—"*commandments dependent on a land for fulfilment*".

[79]Ex. xxiii. 17; Deut. xvi. 16.

kind of *"means test"*—perhaps the first of its kind—was instituted in ancient Judea. A precise time was fixed for distribution among the poor, in order to sift out those who were not engaged in any other occupation from those who are. Only the genuine poor would be free to come at any specified time. Consideration was always given to the young and the old, as well as to the infirm and to nursing mothers. They were allowed to come at such times best suited to their comfort and convenience.

The fact that it was decided at Usha that no Jew should give more than one fifth for charity[80] is proof that Jewish Social Ethics, though expressed in legalistic pattern, were not comprised of fine phrases and sentimentality and of *minutiae* and *provisos* that ran counter to the fervour of spirituality. The fact that Jews had to be checked from giving more than a fifth shows how eager they were to express their gratitude to God by helping their fellow-man. It is another dispensation which teaches that: *"If thou wilt be perfect, go and sell all thou hast; then shalt thou lay up for thyself treasure in heaven"*.[81] The logic of Judaism precluded us from going to extremes, not only because it was undesirable but also unnatural to impoverish oneself in the act of doing good. It is alien to the spirit of the Torah, given to frail, erring man as a guide towards his perfection and a spur to his ennoblement.

Our faith seeks to create an *active* piety which should take the place of a mechanical religiosity. Hence with all respect to Maimonides and Albu, with their philosophical presentations of Judaism, the rank and file of Jewry have been more interested in such practical ethical books as *Bahyah's "Duties of the Heart"* and *Luzzatto's "Path of*

---

[80]Ket. 50ᵃ המבזבז אל־יבזבז יותר מחמש that "he who distributes
[81](charity) should not give away more than a fifth".
Matt. xix. 21.

the Righteous" than in the *"Guide of the Perplexed"* and *"Fundamentals" (Ikkarim)*. Jews preferred books describing how to be honest in trade and commerce and how to be sincere and truthful in their dealings with men, Jew and non-Jew alike, than to dabble in treatises that endeavour to describe the unknowable and to pronounce on subjects clearly beyond the finite comprehension of man. In all fairness to Maimonides, let it be mentioned that his *"Guide"* was intended primarily for those "perplexed" in such problems. His *"Mishneh Torah"* on the other hand, was a practical compendium of Jewish laws and duties for all.

IV. THE STRANGER IN OUR MIDST

Allied to the kindliness we must show to the weak and the dying, the poor and the orphan, is the sympathetic treatment we must accord to the stranger in our midst. The command *"to love the stranger"* occurs at least thirty-six times in the Torah, for *"were ye not strangers in the land of Egypt?"* So kind has the Jew been to all in need or who have been alone in a strange environment, that it is no exaggeration to say that the word *"stranger"* has almost disappeared from his vocabulary. Each was made welcome to enjoy hospitality; each was asked to *"feel at home"* in our midst. Abraham gladly welcomed the wayfarers, little suspecting that they were angels in disguise.[82]

The rigorous measures introduced against strangers of another faith in the days of Ezra and Nehemiah[83] were born of the desperate conditions of the times. Judaism had to be saved, a drastic step had to be made; with the

[82]Gen. xviii.
[83]Ezra ix. 2, x. 3; Neh. ix. 2, xiii. 3, 23.

result that those homes which were founded on mixed
marriages had to be set up anew, divorced of the non-
Jewish partner. This cannot be regarded as a measure of
exclusiveness and chauvinism with which the Jewish
people are credited by their maligners and detractors.
The early chapters of the Torah and the Books of Ruth
and Jonah, with their accounts of men and women of
other faiths who embraced the Jewish God, are proof that
the racialism of Ezra was the exception rather than the
rule.

The story of the persistent stranger (*ger*) who worried
first Shammai and then Hillel and the reception he
received from each of them in turn, is an illustration of
the different attitudes the Rabbis adopted towards the
would-be proselyte. The Jew has never spoken with one
voice on this problem. All seemed to be agreed that when
the survival of the faith was jeopardized, there must be a
policy of the "*closed shop*" in the religious life of the
community.

In any examination of the Jewish attitude towards the
stranger, two things must be taken into consideration.
The first is that the historic background of any command
must not be lost sight of. Most of the laws governing the
relationship between Jew and non-Jew are the products
either of the bitter experiences during the Maccabean
revolt (165 B.C.E.), or of the sufferings of our heroic
ancestors during their titanic struggles against Titus
(70 C.E.) and Hadrian in the course of the Bar Cochba
Revolt (132-135 C.E.). Even then, it was not the Jew but
the Greek who styled all non-Greeks as *barbaroi*, "*bar-
barians*"—perhaps in mock imitation of the language they
spoke; just as it was the Roman and not the Jew who
termed all strangers as *pagani*, "*boors*".

This brings us to the second point. One has only to
read of the treatment meted out to foreigners by the

Greeks and the Romans—the peoples regarded as the heralds of Western civilization—to realize that even in this aspect of Social Ethics, as indeed in all others, the world has still much to learn from our teachings.

From a study of Fustel de Coulange's book,[84] we learn that the foreigner could not own land either in Athens or in Rome. He was not allowed to marry; if he did, his marriage was not recognized and his children were declared to be illegitimate. For him to make any contract with a citizen was illegal and it was not considered valid in the case of any claim. Roman law, regarded as the sponsor of modern legislation, did not allow a stranger to inherit the property of a citizen, or a citizen to inherit the property of a stranger. The pages of Aristotle, Plato, Demosthenes, Lysias, Pausanias, Aristophanes, Gaius, Ulpian, Paulos, Cicero and the works of the jurists, philosophers, poets and orators of classic antiquity, furnish abundant proof of this differentiation between citizen and stranger. This division existed also in Persia and in India, with its caste-ridden barriers between man and man.

It was in the Greek way of life, not in ours, that a profound distinction was made between citizen and stranger.[85] The Torah warns us to have *one* law for all. It is Demosthenes who bears testimony that a stranger was denied the rights of citizenship and that he had no right to protection by the local deities nor any share in the sacrifices offered to them. Since the stranger had no part in the religion of the Greeks, he had no claims to the benefits of their legislation. If he entered a sacred en-

[84]"The Ancient City", Book III. ch. 12, p. 262.
[85]To avoid any misapprehension, it must be pointed out that by "*ger*", the Torah means the resident alien. It was he who enjoyed full rights. Not so the *nochri*, the stranger of another faith, whose rights were not entirely those of the native Israelite who was linked by ties of the same faith.

closure which the priest had set aside for the assembly, he was punished with death. In brief, the laws of the city did not exist for him. When found guilty of a crime and not enjoying legal protection, one can imagine the trial he had. He was treated as a slave and punished forthwith. These harsh rules were not a result, as in the case of Judaism, of defensive measures against persons disintegrating and corroding the empire of the Greeks, but of a cruel and barbaric strain in the "make-up" of the Greeks and Romans.

By way of contrast, examine the Jewish attitude towards the *ger*. From the Bible, it would appear that two types of such strangers are referred to: one was the *ger toshav*, the member of another nation who came to live in Palestine. The other was the *ger tsedek*, the member of another religion who sought acceptance "*under the wings of the Shechinah*" in his wish to embrace Judaism. The first type was the one who had accepted the seven Noahidean precepts[86] and had forsworn his idols and had become a sincere believer in monotheism. As a reward of his trust, he was entitled to civic and legal equality; he was not to be oppressed; interest was not to be charged him for any loan, nor could his wages be kept overnight.[87] He was to be given every opportunity for his economic welfare. This partial proselyte, who was admitted only when Israel dwelt in its own land, was

---

[86]These seven laws (שבע מצוות דבני נח) were supposed by the Rabbis to have been binding upon mankind, at large, even before the Revelation at Sinai, and are deemed binding still upon non-Jews. Basing their views on Gen. ii. 16, the Rabbis declared that the following seven prohibitions were enjoined upon Adam: 1. Idolatry; 2. adultery; 3. murder; 4. robbery; 5. eating of a limb cut from a living animal; 6. the emasculation of animals; 7. the pairing of animals of different species. See Sanhed. 56[b], and cf. Hul. 92[a], where *thirty* Noahidean law are mentioned.

[87]Lev. xix. 13.

respected as an honest seeker after truth. Apart from certain ritual disabilities, not having accepted Judaism in its entirety, he enjoyed equal rights in Jewish courts of law.

Two kinds of *ger tsedek* existed side by side. One was the true *"proselyte of righteousness"*, who had sought admittance to the faith of Israel because of a genuine desire to adopt Judaism without any compromise, equivocation or ulterior motive. Once accepted, he was regarded as a Jew from every angle, sharing equally all rights and privileges as well as the duties and responsibilities of the one born into the faith. To such a man it was forbidden by our ethical laws to say: *"Yesterday, you worshipped idols"*, or to taunt him in quarrel with the accusation: *"The flesh of the pig is still between your teeth"*.[88]

The second type of *"righteous proselyte"* did not enjoy the *full* confidence of the community which he had recently joined because it was suspected that it was outward circumstances, such as the love of a Jewish partner in life rather than a genuine love for Judaism which prompted him to renounce his former loyalty and ideology. In the reigns of David and Solomon, when Israel flourished in the full strength of its national glory, such proselytes were not admitted. The Rabbis employed many designations for such fair-weather and opportunist Jews. They were referred to as *"proselytes of lions"* (*gerei arayot*),[89] *"proselytes of falsehood"* (*gerei sheker*), and *"proselytes of Mordecai and Esther"*—the latter referring to the popularity enjoyed by Jews in Persia after the downfall of Haman.

Modern days, which have witnessed an increase of

---

[88]Such taunts were condemned by the ethics of our Halachah as אונאת דברים—"oppressing one with words".
[89]Many embraced Judaism when lions attacked the country in Solomon's days.

intermarriages, have coined yet another name for such partial proselytes; this is *gere arayot* (with an *ayin* instead of an *aleph*, as in the first name cited above). This refers to the main and often the *sole* motive for such conversions, namely the love towards the Jewish partner of the other party.[90] In such cases, experience has shown that the tenets of Judaism are very often given up after the marriage. To be forewarned is to be forearmed. A most searching investigation of the motives behind such conversions is conducted by the Beth Din before whom the would-be proselyte pleads his case.[91]

Not with any desire to be unjust but largely as a measure of precaution, the Jewish Courts do not readily receive any would-be proselytes knocking at the door. The proselyte is first asked: *"Do you not know that this nation is downtrodden and afflicted: that it is subjected to much hatred and persecution, and above all, that it is liable to the severest punishments for disobedience to the Torah"*—penalties from which others are immune? Only when persistence is still shown, is he, or she, accepted; but not before they have undergone circumcision and immersion in a *Mikveh* (*Milah Utevillah*) in the case of a male, and the latter only in the case of a female.

Only once, in the entire history of Israel, do we read of a forced mass conversion undertaken against the Idumeans. The very fact of this being an isolated occurrence is further proof that such a move violated the spirit of Jewish social ethics. The fruits of this Idumean conversion proved disastrous. Herod was an Idumean by birth and he added many a sob and tear to the history of our people.

Among the most famous of proselytes, real or legendary,

---

[90]The Hebrew word עריות is the plural of ערוה, meaning "nakedness", or immorality.
[91]Yeb. 47[a].

are included such men as Marcus Aurelius, believed by some to be Antoninus Pius, of whom the Midrash records many a conversation with Rabbi Judah Hannasi, the final *redactor* of the Mishnah. Another is believed to be Aquila, confused by some with Onkelos, the translator of the Bible into Aramaic (*Targum*) and the faithful disciple of Rabbi Akiba.[92] Yet another was King Monobaz of Adiabene, who with his wife Helena, made munificent contributions to the Temple. Even Nebuchadnezzar was not spared. Legend has it that toward the end of his days he embraced Judaism, perhaps in penitence for the destruction of the first Temple. In Talmudic times, we read of Roman ladies of prestige and distinction who were attracted to Judaism by its beliefs and ceremonies. The story of the Khazars who were persuaded by their King Bulan to become Jews, has been immortalized by Rabbi Yehudah Halevi in the "*Cuzari*", which attributes their conversion to the logical arguments advanced for Judaism by the Rabbi.

The fact that Jewish law requires the exercise of great caution before admitting the stranger to our faith, together with the tolerant and respectful attitude manifested towards *devotees* of other monotheistic faiths, militates against the theory that Jews are intolerant of other beliefs. The reluctance before admitting the proselyte was only because he was to share Jewish responsibilities as outlined in the Torah. It never meant a hesitancy to help him when he was in need. Once admitted, the laws of the Torah spread their protecting wings over him.[93]

Ezekiel[94] declares that *gerim* would share the land to-

---

[92]See A. E. Silverstone: "Aquila and Onkelos", Manchester University Press.
[93]Vide Deut. xxiv. 14, 19-22, xiv. 29, xvi. 11, xxvi. 11.
[94]xlvii. 21-23.

gether with the other tribes of Israel when the country came under Jewish rule. A similar reference in Isaiah[95] leads to the conclusion that such strangers were implied that had become converted after the fall of Sennacherib. The most touching passages in the Talmud refer to the consideration that must be shown towards him who has entered the fold, never to utter anything in his presence derogatory to the faith to which he or his ancestors, even up to ten generations ago, had owed allegiance.[96]

Then why is such reluctance displayed in admitting proselytes? The reason is not far to seek. Those who formulated our Codes were shrewd students of human nature and had not forgotten the lessons of history. They remembered only too well what had happened to Israel in the wilderness, when they were led into idolatry and immorality by those whom they had indiscriminately welcomed into the fold, and who joined Israel's ranks only after beholding the miracles attending the Exodus from Egypt and its attendant wonders. The seven aboriginal tribes of Palestine were doomed to extinction because they were considered *stumbling-blocks* to the spiritual development of Israel after the Revelation. Nothing must bar the unfurlment of God's plan in relation to the people chosen to be the trustees of His Will. It was at the door of the Egyptians that the sin of the Golden Calf was laid, as it was the Moabites who were held responsible for Israel's immorality at Peor with their heathen daughters. With these Biblical warnings in mind, a Talmudic Rabbi taught that *"proselytes in Israel are like a festering sore"*.[97]

[95]lvi. 6-7.
[96]The quotation is from Sanhed. 94[a]: גיורא עד־עשרה דרי, לא תבזי ארמאי באפיה
[97]Cf. Kidd. 70[b]; Yeb. 69[b]; Sanhed 94[a]; Nid. 13b. See also the special section *"Hilchot Gerim"* in the *Mishneh Torah* of Maimonides.

The available material on this subject goes to show that Rabbinic strictures were directed exclusively against the partially insincere proselyte (the *ger toshav*). The affection shown towards the *"proselyte of righteousness"* is eloquent from the opinion of one Rabbi that Israel's dispersion among the nations was in order to attract such *gerei tsedek* to the fold.[98] In the Amidah,[99] a special blessing is uttered on their behalf: *"Towards the proselytes of righteousness, and towards us also, may Thy tender mercies be stirred, O Lord our God"*. Some of the most famous sages of the Talmud, like Shemaiah and Abtalion, Rabbi Akiba and Rabbi Meir, Ben *Bag Bag* and Ben *He He* (Abot v. 25-26) and Rabbi Yehudah ben Gerim[100] were reputed to be either proselytes themselves or to have descended from *gerei tsedek*. That they rose to such eminence proves that no barriers were placed in their paths to greatness. Conditions to-day do not warrant any relaxation in our attitude towards intermarriage.[101]

Our records reveal that the *ger tsedek* became an object of affection both to God and to his fellow-Jew.[102] The *ger toshav* could claim similar consideration if he abandoned idolatry,[103] the practice of sorcery, incest and other abominations, if[104] he abstained from eating blood,[105] from working on the Sabbath,[106] from eating leavened food on Pesah,[107] and from violating the Day of Atone-

---

[98]Pes. 87[b].
[99]Singer's Prayer Book, p. 48.
[100]Sabb. 33[b].
[101]Lev. xviii. 2.
[102]Deut. x. 18-19; Lev. xix. 33; Ps. cxlvi. 9. See also Ex. xii. 49; xxii. 20; Lev. xxiv. 22; Num. ix. 14; xv. 16, 29; Deut. xxiv. 17-18; xxvii. 19.
[103]Lev. xx. 21; Ezek. xiv. 7.
[104]Lev. xviii. 26.
[105]Ibid. xvii. 10.
[106]Ex. xx. 10; xxiii. 12.
[107]Ibid. xii. 19.

ment.[108] The Prophets all preach humanitarian feelings towards the stranger and the Bible itself features non-Jews as examples of fidelity,[109] of devotion[110] and of [111]piety. The Pharisees made it clear that their hatred of the heathen was a hatred of what heathenism stood for in the realm of belief and conduct. similar hatred was displayed by them towards the *Am Ha'aretz*, the Jewish boor who was lax in his religious observance.

Intermarriage, or truer to its meaning, *extermarriage* between Jew and Gentile (looked at askance even by enlightened Jews of to-day), is not due to contempt of the Gentile but to the firm conviction that the unity of Judaism and the Jewish people is contingent on the happiness of the home. This happiness is jeopardized by the yoking together of two people with an entirely different background and outlook on life. When one bears in mind the sufferings of the Jew at the hands of a hostile world, such legislation is not to be wondered at. Had the non-Jewish worlds not persecuted the Jew throughout the ages, with the sword in their hands and the words *"God is Love"* on their lips, those laws cited by Jew-baiters as breathing contempt and hatred for all who are not Jews would not have been admitted into our legislation.

Every edition of the Talmud bears a Preface in which it is expressly stated that whenever the words *Akkum* and *Goy* are mentioned in its pages, the reference is only to the pagans of those early days whose word was untrustworthy and whose conduct was immoral.[112] The non-Jew

[108]Lev. xvi. 29.
[109]Eliezer, the *majordomo* of Abraham's household.
[110]Ruth.
[111]Job.
[112]See also the laws codified in *Hoshen Mishpat*, 266; *Yoreh Deah*, 48[18].

is included in the commandments: "*And thou shalt love thy neighbour as thyself*" and in the injunction: "*That thy brother may live with thee*". In his Social Ethics the Jew has a further cause for pride and a stimulus towards kindliness to all his fellow-men.

CHAPTER TEN

ETHICS OF EVERY DAY

I. LOVING OTHERS

EMPHASIZED in these pages is the fact that Jewish ethics are not content merely with *prescribing* love and nothing else. They go further than the *literal* meaning of "*And thou shalt love thy neighbour as thyself*". Not only must our own life be maintained amid all trials as a sacred trust but also the rights, freedom and individuality of others, and especially of those dependent on us for their sustenance and happiness must be guarded. God alone can claim the sole proprietorship of those whom He has created. Accordingly, man is not a slave to any other. "*For they are My servants*"[1] says the Torah; from which the Rabbis concluded: "*but not servants to servants*".[2]

Hillel, it will be remembered, when asked by the would-be proselyte to give him the whole Torah in a nutshell,[3] gave a negative shape to the spirit of the command of Leviticus xix. 18 "*Ve'ahavta le'reacha kam-ochah*". "*What is hateful to thee, do not unto another.*" Kohler is right to point out[4] that this command, in its *positive* form, could not have been literally implemented. It would be *too much* to ask frail and temperamental man to love the stranger and the enemy as himself. It is as much as we can expect of man that he should at least treat

[1] Lev. xxv. 42.
[2] Kidd. 22^b.
[3] The Talmudic idiom is "while standing on one foot"; modern idiom would be "in tabloid form".
[4] See the chapter on "Jewish Ethics" in his "Jewish Theology."

225

others respectfully, not doing unto them those things he would not like them to do unto him. To treat an enemy magnanimously, not to hate him, but to be ever ready for reconciliation, is to ask of man about as much as he is capable of fulfilling.[5]

Social Ethics applied to everyday life means: to put ourselves in the place of another before sitting in judgment on him[6] and to realize that just as *we* cherish our reputation and possessions, so does *he*. The words "*I am the Lord thy God*" follow the first half of the verse "*And thou shalt love thy neighbour*". Why? To impress upon us that He is the Creator of our fellow-man as well as of ourselves. Ethics and religion are one in Judaism. "*God will reward thee only if thou showest love unto all; He will surely punish thee if thou doest injury, or insultest others*" is the advice of one of our sages.[7]

Merely to *preach* love for everybody, in the expectation to be loved in return, is not regarded by Jewish ethics as a principle of action sufficiently potent to mould character or govern society. Man is too much swayed by impulse and emotion and exhibits a partiality that is inimical to strict justice. He must be guided in his actions by the viewpoints of his ancient teachers.[8] Love, without justice, leads to abuse and persecution.[9] The Rabbis read into the two names of God *Adonai* and *Elohim* the attributes of Love and Justice. Only when one is tempered by the other can true kindness be exhibited and real loving deeds be

[5] There is a world of difference between the positive and negative form in which the "Golden Rule" is couched in Judaism and Christianity.

[6] Abot ii. 5.

[7] Vid. Abot d R'Nathan 53, in Schechter's Hebrew edition.

[8] The concluding chapter of Kohler's "Jewish Theology" will be read with profit.

[9] What is the history of mankind's attitude toward the Jew if not a proof of this statement?

performed. It is for man to shape his conduct after the Divine example if he is to lead the life directed in the Torah.[10] "*And see and do according to the pattern thou hast been shown on the mount.*"[11]

At a time when the contemporaries of Israel tolerated slavery, barbarism and blood-vengeance, the Jew was distinguished for his sympathy and benevolence. It was his Lawgiver who described God as righteous, merciful and holy, "*who executeth the judgment of the fatherless and the widow, and who loveth the stranger by giving him food and raiment*".[12] The Rabbinic teachers developed this conception of the Deity and spiritualized the Jewish message, making piety and charity the consecrated aims of life, stressing the importance of motive in human conduct.

This statement does not imply that one will find an elaborate system of social ethics in the Talmud. Such systematic presentations were the products of the Middle Ages when learned Jews came under the influence of Mohammedanism with its love for the philosophy of Aristotle and of Neoplatonism and incorporated in their works the theories and tendencies of the Greek thinkers. In subsequent ages, ethical treatises were written in the form of "*Wills*", popular admonitions varying between the broadly human and the sternly ascetic. Glimpses into this branch of ethical literature have been provided from time to time in these pages.

The thread running through our moral system is that life emanates from a God of Holiness and that all our actions must spring from a desire to be like Him. "*God pleased to make Israel worthy; therefore He gave them a*

[10]Sot. 14ᵃ; see also Schechter's "Some Aspects of Rabbinic Theology".
[11]Ex. xxv. 40.
[12]Deut. x. 18.

copious Torah and many commandments."[13] Kohler[14] sees in Hillel's advice:[15] "*If I am not for myself, who will be for me? And being for my own self, what am I? And if not now, when?*" the best summary of Jewish ethics. The three main spheres of duty are here outlined: duty towards one's self, duty towards the community and duty towards the State. The value of the individual, apart from being a member of a social organization, was stressed as a counterblast to "*otherworldly*" ethics. Man was at first created a lone figure, a Rabbi observes,[16] that he should remember that he forms a world for himself, that he is a self-conscious personality who must unfold in body and soul the Divine power and higher purpose implanted within him. Man must so regulate his actions as to ensure the preservation, improvement and protection not only of himself but of others.

II. BUSINESS AND LABOUR ETHICS

The attitude of Judaism towards labour is manifest from the opening sentence of the Torah where God is described as the *Creator* of heaven and earth. The Torah sings the praises of him who "*goeth forth unto his work and to his labour until the evening*".[17] Most of the sages of the Talmud followed humble crafts in order to be independent "*of the gifts of flesh and blood*" for their sustenance. The Fourth Commandment, which enjoins the Sabbath rest, begins with the prescription of six days in which to labour.

[13]So R. Hananyah b. Akashya; Singer's Prayer Book, p. 186.
[14]*loc. cit.*
[15]Abot i. 14.
[16]Sanhed. 37a.
[17]Ps. civ. 23. See also Ber. 8a; Ned. 49b; Pes. 113a; Sabb. 118a; Kidd. 29a.

Man must work during the week before he can rest on the Sabbath. He must work not only to earn his livelihood but also to contribute his quota towards the maintenance of social order.

In the early chapters of Genesis, God not only blessed the Sabbath; He also declared the work done on the six days of the week to be very good, a lesson in appreciation. Moses was a shepherd before he became the Lawgiver; so were the prophets Amos and Micah. Saul was taken from the plough to become the first King of Israel and David, who succeeded him, was summoned from the field. True to their teaching that "he who engages in work causes the Shechinah to rest upon Israel",[18] the majority of the Talmudic Rabbis were humble workmen who earned a precarious livelihood in order to pay for the barest essentials of life so as to devote most of their time to the study of the Torah.

The poverty of Hillel was proverbial. He was a charcoal-burner who spent more than half of his meagre earnings to be admitted to the academy of the great teachers Shemaiah and Abtalyon. A similar profession was followed by R. Joshua who lived in a house the walls of which were begrimed from his work.[19] R. Meir was a scribe[20]; R. Jose b. Halafta, a tanner;[21] R. Johanan, a shoemaker;[22] R. Judah, a baker[23]; Abba Saul was a kneader of dough[24] as well as a grave-digger.[25] All these translated into reality the advice God gave to Adam: "*In the sweat of*

[18] In Exodus xxv. 8, God assures Israel that if they will con-secrate a sanctuary unto Him, He will dwell in their midst and bless their work.
[19] Ber. 28[a].
[20] Erub. 13[a].
[21] Sabb. 49[b].
[22] Abot iv. 14.
[23] Yer. Hag. Ch. ii. 1.
[24] Pes. 34[a].
[25] Nid. 24[b].

thy face shalt thou eat bread".[26] They sincerely believed that "idleness leads to lewdness; lewdness to mental instability".[27] They emphasized that "great is work, for it honours the workman"[28]; that Torah is good only when it is combined with a trade; for only the practice of both leaves man little time for sin.[29]

Josephus, in his valiant defence of Judaism against Apio, the arch anti-Semite of his day,[30] could write with truth: "*As for us, we do not delight in merchandise; having a fruitful country for our habitation, we take pains in cultivating that only.*" The respect paid by Judaism to those who refuse to eat "*the bread of idleness*" is evident from our Rabbinic sources. All extol the dignity of labour and the influence for good it exerts. Usurers who live on the efforts of others are condemned in no uncertain terms and are accounted as shedders of blood.[31] The ancient sages of Israel taught that man cannot be brought under the yoke of work too soon[32] and that a parent who does not teach his son a trade teaches him to steal.[33]

Man is advised to make a habit of four things and to weave them into his daily routine. These are: Study, Charity, Piety, and Work.[34] When Adam was told "*Thorns also and thistles shall it bring forth to thee; and thou shalt eat the herb of the field*" (Gen. iii. 18) he began to weep, says a Rabbi. To be likened to a beast of the field was a condemnation against which every manly instinct within him revolted. Only when he was told: "*in the sweat*

[26]Gen. iii. 19.
[27]Ket. v. 5.
[28]Ned. 49b.
[29]Abot ii. 2.
[30]"*Contra Apionem*", i. 12.
[31]See B. Metz. 61b; 71a; Sanhed. iii. 3.
[32]Mid. Echah R. iii on Lam. iii. 27.
[33]Kid. 29a; cf. Ber. 65a.
[34]Ber. 32.

of thy face shalt thou eat bread"[35] did his self-respect return.

Man should never say, another teacher observes, that to work is not in keeping with the office he holds, or with the family from which he stems. Idleness causes death and the loss of the World to Come.[36] God has ordained that each individual should find agreeable his own work, however burdensome it may be, even preferring it to any other.[37] To pursue an honest trade is to rank higher than an idle nobleman. "*Any kind of work is more honourable than being indebted to others; for this reason, if needs be, flay a carcass in the street and say not I am a great man.*"[38]

Since labour was raised to the rank of a religious command, there was a danger lest the grasping and irresponsible employer take advantage of the one he employs. Hence come responsibilities one owes towards another. In its earliest stages, the Torah manifests concern for him compelled to serve others. Take the humanity of our slave-laws as an example.[39] After six years, the Hebrew slave must be released and his wants liberally supplied from the flock, threshing-floor and the wine-press of his employer. The honour of the bonds woman was even more meticulously safeguarded. If she were espoused her food, raiment and marriage rights were not to be diminished.[40] Should the master injure his non-Jewish slave, the latter was to be immediately emancipated; if the injury proved fatal, the master must be punished. Long before slavery had ceased in Israel (as it did almost at the beginning of the current era), the

[35]Gen. iii. 19.
[36]See Midrash Rabba and the Pirke d'R. Eliezer.
[37]Ber. 43[b].
[38]B. Bath. 110[a].
[39]Ex. xxi. 2-11.
[40]Ibid. xxi. 7-11.

humanitarian spirit that inspired the relationship between master and slave had grown into tender regard.

The employer was held responsible for the failure to provide for the safety of those he employed.[41] The labourer could not be compelled to do work that might injure his health,[42] or to work overtime against his will,[43] even for extra pay. If he were not paid within twelve hours of the time when his work was done, he could summon his employer before the religious court.[44] To delay payment due at "*the setting of the sun*" is to be deserving of severe punishment.[45] The labourer must be guarded against fraud and exploitation and his hours of work must conform to local usage.[46] The Sabbath was ordained as a day of rest also for him who works for another—a motive which classes this commandment as one of the greatest acts of social legislation of all times. To oppress the poor labourer is to forfeit the share in the Hereafter[47] and to put him to shame is to be guilty of homicide.

Consideration and justice were to be shown not only by the employer.[48] The labourer, too, was reminded that his time and energy, in return for his wages, must be given willingly and unstintingly. To botch work and not to give of his best is as deceitful as a shopkeeper who gives false weights. When one realizes the importance attached by Judaism to regular prayer, one will be interested to learn that in a case where the recital of all the statutory prayers means the robbing of some of the time

[41]B. K. 33[a].
[42]B. Metz. 77[a].
[43]Ibid. 83[a].
[44]Ibid. 3[a].
[45]Ibid. 111[a].
[46]Ibid. 83[a].
[47]Ibid. 112[a].
[48]Amos iii. 9; Hos. xii. 8; Prov. xxviii. 6-11; II Samuel xii. 1-14.

scheduled for his employer, these must be curtailed. The Rabbis condensed for the workman engaged on his task the *nineteen* blessings of the Amidah[49] to seven and they also appreciably shortened the Grace After Meals.[50] The workman who is performing a task for his master on a scaffolding or on the top of a tree, is permitted to say his prayers while still there; to descend would take up time which was not his.[51] An employee who disregards the instructions of his employer cheats as much as the employer who withholds from the labourer his hire. The contract between the parties must be scrupulously obeyed.[52]

The Torah holds the scales equally balanced between rich and poor, employer and employed; but it is clear that the heart of the Lawgiver was with the oppressed labourer. Did he not himself leave a royal palace in order to go out and relieve his people from their burdens?[53] No less than seventy times does the word *'ani* (*poor man*) occur in the Bible (with *evyon* "*needy man*") a close second with *sixty-one*)—an indication that the needs of the poor were uppermost in the mind of the Lawgiver. No Socialist ever denounced more trenchantly than did our prophets the evils of their times, thundering against the grinding of the poor and the violence and immorality committed by the rich.[54] In education, the children of the poor were to be given first consideration, for from them would scholarship emerge.[55] Even the Messiah, according to one Rabbi,[56] will be found among the ragged poor. When

[49]See Singer's Prayer Book, p. 55.
[50]Ibid. p. 286; Ber. 45[b].
[51]Ber. ii. 4.
[52]B. Metz. 78[a].
[53]Ex. ii. 11.
[54]See especially Amos ii. 6-16 *et passim;* Is. iii. 14-15; Jer. xxii. 13ff; Job xxiv. 2-11.
[55]Ned. 81[a].
[56]Ex. R. xxii.

God was asked by Israel: *"Who are Thy people?"* the answer they received was *"The poor"*.

III. JUDAISM AND SOCIALISM

Is it surprising that the sympathies of Jews have in all ages veered towards Socialism in its broadest sense, that is towards Socialism with a difference? But whereas Karl Marx, a Jew by birth only, regarded Capitalism as the deadly enemy, in the way of the revolution which would *"break the chains of the proletariat"*, *"unite the workers of the world"*[57] and result in the State ownership of all property, Judaism sought to achieve the same millennium by *peaceful* means. The revolution had to come from *within*, from a change of heart and from a new spirit; not from *without*, from bloodshed and passions let loose. The modifications of *"Das Kapital"*, the authorized *"Bible"* of the *Marxians*—introduced by the Fabian Society, in which a distinction was made between personal and collective property may have been due to the moderating influence of Jewish teachings; for among its first leaders were Jews. Logic is on the side of those moderate Socialists who, while eager to see all means of production, distribution and exchange controlled by the State, agree that possessions, personal and intimate, could be privately owned. Many collective settlements in Israel have arrived at this conclusion after much experimentation with other ideologies.

This is the policy pursued, more or less, in the State of Israel to-day; a policy which, if undisturbed by war and faction from within and without, bids fair to become the model of enlightened statecraft. The new Jewish State can teach the world that Socialism has a spiritual back-

[57]The slogans of Marxian Socialism.

ground behind its economic and political doctrines. Man has a right to private wealth which he holds as a trust from God to be used for the benefit of all. Our Codes contain laws for the transfer of property, for the relationship between capital and labour, landlord and tenant. The Sabbatical and Jubilee laws did *not* mean the abolition of private ownership. Their main intention was to give the debtor a fresh chance to reverse his shattered fortunes and the soil a breathing-space to gain new strength after its enforced idleness. The world, it seems, will always be composed of rich and poor. No man is exactly like another; some will spend, while others will save. The Torah asks those who have to help those who have not; not to use their money for selfish or oppressive purposes.

Rebellion against the laws of the State or constituted authority is considered obnoxious to ethical conduct. The laws of the civil Courts must be obeyed (*dina d'malchuta dina*). They can be brushed aside only if loyalty to them means a violation of the essential commandments given by the Source of all authority—God, "*the Holy One of Israel*". When will those who cannot reconcile their Judaism with their socialist leanings and who admire every way of life except their own bear in mind that the Greek gods are pictured as residing on Mount Olympus indulging in endless revelry and pleasure and that the Brahma and the Buddha are described as living in philosophic repose, undisturbed in their contemplation of *Nirvana?* Whereas the Jewish God is revealed as the Maker of heaven and earth, identifying Himself with Israel as their Protector and Saviour and daily renewing His work of creation. One can be a Jew and yet be active in support of any movement the sincere aim of which is the ennoblement of mankind and the amelioration of want and suffering.

This reconciliation between Judaism and Socialism is important in life to-day, and especially in our national homeland Israel. Both have so much in common that it is a pity a gulf has been erected in partisan minds between them. Their common denominator is the study of man in relation to society. It can be claimed for Socialism that which is certainly true of Judaism— namely, that the basic concepts of their ideology is the consciousness that *all* men stand in the same social relationship with one another and that equality of opportunity must be provided for all. Both are emphatic that riches and social station are mere accidents of birth and do not constitute claims to dignity or power.

The credentials to respect and affection among men should be decency of life and the contributions made by manual labour or mental talent towards the emergence of a better world. These should be the criteria by which character and rank in society should be judged. If Socialism agrees with Judaism thus far, then Judaism certainly agrees with Socialism that slums must be cleared; that the spectres of unemployment and misery must be banished and that the equal sharing of the opportunities of life must be firmly organized in our national life. The discrimination between rich and poor, the *haves* and *have-nots*, is due to human weakness.

In Jewish Social Ethics, God is revealed not as a respecter of persons but as the Father of *all* His created beings. This, in fact, is the most prized contribution of Judaism towards the advancement of civilization and towards the unfolding of the Divine plan on earth. All men are equal; all are entitled to a fair share of the good things in this life. Who, more than the Jew with his unbroken record of loyalty to the Torah, is so qualified to be the torchbearer of the ideal design for living?

IV. ETHICS IN FAMILY LIFE

The basis of Jewish social life being the family, Judaism has exercised a ceaseless vigil over its purity and stability. The relation between the sexes is based upon the ideal of *tohorat ha'mishpachah*, that is, upon chastity and purity which border on holiness. The Jew does not regard woman as his inferior but as his co-partner. The sole reason why she is exempt from certain precepts, the fulfilment of which is circumscribed by the occasion, is the fact that male and female have been cast into different physiques, making it biologically necessary for a division of labour between man and woman. It was *never* intended that the sphere of the home, delegated to the wisdom and tenderness of the wife and mother, should be considered as *secondary* to the study of the Torah or to the pursuit of a livelihood, occupations set aside for the programme of men. The Bible knows no such distinction, for *"male and female created He them"*.[58] When those who arranged the order (*Siddur*) of our daily prayers prescribed the blessing[59] thanking God *"who hast not made me a woman"*, all they meant was, as can be seen from the context of the blessings, that the Jew is grateful to His Master for so conditioning him that he is not deprived, as a woman is by reason of her domestic responsibilities, from fulfilling such duties as *Tsitsit*, *Tephillin*, *Sukkah* and similar duties which must be performed within a limited, stipulated time.[60]

Apart from this category of commandments, known in

[58]Gen. i. 27. See an excellent study by Margaret Mead, "Male and Female", published by Gollancz, 1950.
[59]Singer's Prayer Book, p. 6.
[60]Kidd. i. 7; Men. 43[b]. See also the writer's "Jewish Customs" (1949) *passim*.

the Talmud as "*mitzvot aseh she'hazeman grama*", no differentiation in our ethical codes exists between male and female. On the contrary; because the Fifth Commandment tells the child to honour father and mother, the Lawgiver felt that he must remove the mistaken idea that the father is mentioned first because he is the more important partner in marriage by putting the mother *first* when he repeats the command elsewhere in the Torah.[61] Redress could not be more noble, nor equality of the sexes more colourfully stressed.

Moreover, when the Rabbis explained the verse "*Now these are the ordinances which thou shalt set before them*",[62] their comment was: "Scripture places men and women on an equality with regard to all the laws of the Torah".[63] If woman is not encouraged to higher study, no qualms of conscience need assail her; her merit consists in the help she gives her men-folk to become learned in "*the Word of God*".[64] Moreover, God endowed woman with more intuition and tact than man.[65] Biblical support for this statement was found in the word *Vayiven*,[66] used when woman was created from the rib of man. God used special intelligence (*binah*) before coming to the decision that the best material from which to shape woman was the rib, the symbol of modesty, for it is that part of the body which was always covered.[67]

The answer given by the daughter of Rabban Gamaliel when her father was challenged by a Roman to defend the action of God in taking a rib from the slumbering

[61]Lev. xix. 3. "*Ye shall fear every man his* mother *and his father*".
[62]Ex. xxi. 1.
[63]B. K. 15ᵃ.
[64]Ber. 17ᵃ.
[65]Nid. 45ᵇ.
[66]ויבן which is made a denominative from בינה "intelligence"; Gen. ii. 22.
[67]Gen. R. xviii. 2.

Adam displays the Rabbinic chivalry towards woman. "Was that not a dishonest action, savouring of stealth? Adam should have been asked permission first", argued the Roman. When the Rabbi was for a moment nonplussed as to the best answer to give to this accusation, his daughter volunteered the reply: "Since God immediately replaced the rib of flesh and bone by presenting Adam with a partner for life (whose value cannot be prized by ordinary standards of wealth) such permission before the exchange was made was unnecessary".[68]

When God advised Adam that "*it is not good for man to be alone*",[69] this meant that man would never achieve perfection alone, unaided by a good wife. To live in so-called "*single blessedness*" is an error, resulting in loneliness and frustration. "*Without a wife, man lives without joy, blessing, peace or anything that can really be called good*."[70] He is not the complete man, and in the Life to Come he will have to answer, on Judgment Day, the question why he remained unwedded throughout his earthly pilgrimage.[71] Further, by not marrying, man is prone to be held in suspicion, thus transgressing the command "*then ye shall be clear before the Lord and before Israel*".[72] A Rabbi cautions us that "in order to appear blameless before men and God, one must remove any cause for suspicion".[73]

A wife *completes* a man's outlook on life; she is also the architect and builder of the home. She *is* the home.[74] "Never", said R. Jose,[75] "have I called my wife by any

[68]Sanhed. 39[a].
[69]Gen. ii. 18.
[70]Yeb. 62[b].
[71]Shabbat 31[a].
[72]Num. xxxii. 22.
[73]Yoma 38[a].
[74]Yoma i. 1.
[75]Shabb. 118[b].

other name than that of *my home*." In gratitude for all this, her feelings are to be the prime study of her husband. To cause tears to flow from her eyes is to sin in the eyes of God.[76] As these tears come lightly, man can never be too careful in his married relationship. The Rabbis realized the difficulty of always pleasing woman. "Women are a law unto themselves."[77] "They are fickle-minded."[78] "They are less generous to wayfarers than their husbands are."[79] "But they are more active than man"[80] and more merciful.[81] They are more expert in the art of speech, since *"she talks while she spins"*.[82] She is more desirous of marrying than man is.[83] With such discrepancies in her character, the task of ensuring the happiness of married life is difficult; but Judaism insists that it is worth the effort. There is no greater earthly bliss than domestic happiness. Man is blessed in his home if he makes happy those who live with him, and blessings come to a home because of a good wife.

The Rabbis believed that "no one is above temptation to sexual desire".[84] They accordingly advised early marriage, emphasizing it by declaring it to be the *first* command of the Torah.[85] Marriage was essential to the holiness and happiness of the Jew. Woman was of purpose created from the body of man to impress upon him that she is his equal in dignity and is the main source of his earthly blessings. Both together have been made *"partners in the work of creation"* in order to preserve the human

[76] B. Metz. 59[a].
[77] Shabb. 62[a].
[78] Ibid. 63[b].
[79] B. Metz. 87[a].
[80] Yerush. Ket. vi.
[81] Meg. 14[b].
[82] Ibid.
[83] Yeb. 113[a], 118[b]. ‏(טב למית בטך דו מלמיתה ארמלתה)‎.
[84] Ket. 13[b] ‏(אין אפיטרופוס לעריות)‎.
[85] Gen. ii. 18-24; Abot v. 24; Kidd. 29[b].

race. Many are the blessings promised to the virtuous couple.[86] To violate the marriage law is to merit punishment,[87] besides nullifying that which heaven has decreed.[88] Equally wrong is it to marry for lust or for money; he who does so, will have children who will bring shame upon his head.[89] The Torah, as a warning, records the case of the rebellious son immediately after the laws to be obeyed when a heathen woman is taken captive after a victorious battle (Deut. xxi. 10-21) to show that the "fruits" of a lustful union taste bitter in the mouth.

Polygamy, though not expressly forbidden in the Torah, is mentioned as the cause which turns the hearts of kings away from the true worship of God. It is to be eschewed as a potential danger to the peaceful married life.[90] Maimonides, in the special section dealing with forbidden sexual relationships,[91] deduces from the command to the High Priest "*And he shall take a wife in her virginity*" (Lev. xxi. 13), that even he was allowed to marry only *one* wife at a time. The prophets do not seem to have been polygamous, though the Kings do appear in that rôle. Among the people, monogamy appears to have been the rule, polygamy the exception. One Talmudic Rabbi rules that: "*he who adds another wife to the one already at his side must divorce the newcomer and grant her*

[86]Proverbs xii. 14; xviii. 22; xix. 14; xxxi (*passim*).

[87]Ibid. ii. 16-19; v. 8-22; vi. 24-35; vii. 5-27, *et passim*.

[88]Gen. R. lxviii. 4, which tells the story of the Roman lady who thought that she could also arrange marriages when the Rabbi told her that only God can make happy and successful unions, but who discovered that "*marriages are made in heaven*".

[89]Kidd. 70[b].

[90]Gen. ii. 24, where the words "*and he shall cleave unto his wife*", explicitly show that man is to possess only *one* wife at a time.

[91]Issure Biah, xvii. 13.

a marriage settlement (*Ketubah*)".[92] It was only the
Oriental Jews who did not accept the *Takkanot* of
Rabenu Gershom, "the Light of the Golah" (1000 C.E.)
and adhered to Mohammedan law and married four
wives, living with them at one time.[93]

Nothing must be done to endanger the holy alliance
(*Kiddushin*) of man and wife. The Rabbis devote five
tractates of the Talmud to this theme. *Kiddushin* and
Ketubot deal mainly with marriage settlements; *Yebamot*
with Levirate and prohibited marriages; *Sotah* with the
woman suspected of adultery and *Gittin* with divorce, not
to mention the references to these themes scattered over
the other tractates. The Rabbis found it necessary to deal
with these themes exhaustively in view of the vagueness
of the Biblical laws. These Talmudic views have been
systematically collected in two works that are still the
authoritative sources of every Rabbi. These are the
Mishneh Torah of Maimonides and the *Eben Ha'ezer* of
Joseph Karo.[94] These authorities warn that intermarriage is likely to mar family purity and sow dissension
and produce disreputable children.[95] Though one Rabbinic view states that *"Gentiles in the Diaspora cannot
really be termed idolaters"*, yet marriage with them is
disallowed.[96]

---

[92]Yeb. 65ᵃ. It is interesting that the numerical value of the
word והוא in Lev. xxi. 13 (*supra*) is 18, the age which the
Rabbis prescribed as the most suited for the male to marry.

[93]See L. Finkelstein, "Jewish Self-Government in the Middle
Ages", New York, 1924. *Takkanot* were Decrees made by
Rabbinic Courts during the Middle Ages for the self-govern-
ment of their communities in civil and religious matters.

[94]No fewer than one hundred and seventy-eight sections dealing
with marriage and divorce appear in Karo's work.

[95]Deut. vii. 3-4; Ezra ix. 1-2, x. 10-11; Neh. x. 31, xiii. 23-25;
Ab. Zara 31ᵇ; *Eben Ha'ezer* xvi. 1; Maimonides *Issure Biah*
xii. 1.

[96]Hull. 13ᵇ.

Underlying all these restrictions is the ethical contention that just as virtue and righteousness flow from the worship of God, so do vice and oppression issue from the ungodly marriage, especially with daughters of the heathen. This will explain the seemingly harsh measures taken, especially by Ezra, against idolatry and immorality, both of which are to be eliminated.[97] A "*holy people*" must remove all obstacles to the purity of family life and regard them as abominations.[98] Marriage is something more than a civil contract; it is an institution based on morality and implying the most sacred duties. It was wrong for one to betroth a wife before he had seen her,[99] or to marry a partner much younger or much older than himself.[100] In either case, the main object of marriage, procreation, would be jeopardized on account of age and impotency.

The wife must be fully conscious of the implications of her marriage vow which, as the name *Kiddushin* implied, meant that she had been consecrated for her husband alone. It was R. Abba Areka of Sura (Rav) who emphatically protested against the practice of infant marriages, declaring it to be morally wrong for a father to contract a marriage on behalf of his daughter before she had attained the age of consent.[101] This Rabbi also protested against the husband who acquired a wife not by one of the two usual methods of money and document (*Kesef* and *Sh'tar*), but by *Biah* (consummation) alone.[102] Though it was essential for man to marry, he was advised not to hurry into marriage unduly. Let him first build a house

[97]Ex. xx. 3; Lev. xix. 4; Deut. iv. 15-25.
[98]Deut. vii. 3.
[99]Kidd. 41ª.
[100]Yeb. 101ᵇ.
[101]Kidd. 41ª.
[102]Ibid. 12ª.

and plant a vineyard; marriage could then be considered.[103]
Sage advice, indeed, which to ignore is to court marital
disaster. When economic stability is precarious, love
between the partners may be absent; and when love goes,
the reactions upon the character of the children will be
undesirable and harmful.

V. DIVORCE IN JUDAISM

The high ideal of married life inculcated by Judaism,
added to the experience that an irksome marriage could
be ended if absolute necessity arose, raised the lofty
standard of Jewish marriage to a very high level. Though
the *ethical* principles of Judaism are against dissolution,
life reveals circumstances, the influences of which sometimes so undermined the basis of marriage as to make any
modus vivendi almost impossible. In such cases, it was
contended that divorce was the external dissolution of a
relation which had already inwardly been destroyed.
From the Codes, it would appear that our divorce laws
did not press heavily to the disadvantage of woman.
Despite the facility with which a union could be dissolved
(as would appear from a *hurried* glance at the sources),
the evidence does not suggest that this facility was abused.
In the figurative words of one teacher, the altar weeps
when a man divorces his first wife (Gittin 90).

The Jew, despite the utterances of his detractors,
could not divorce his wife upon any slight pretext or
whim. He had to find some serious flaw in her.[104] What
this *uncleanness* was is the theme of much Talmudic
debate. He could not banish her from his home just by

[103]Sotah 44[a], quoting, in support of this view, Deut. xx. 5-7.
[104]Deut. xxiv. 1-2.

mere word of mouth and in an unceremonious, peremptory manner, but after a long and dreary formality which ended in the placing into her possession of a *Get*. This process was made deliberately odious and laborious for two reasons: one, to prevent an undue haste to divorce occasioned by an outburst of anger; two, to afford an opportunity to either party, even at the twelfth hour or during the actual writing of the Bill of Divorcement, to become reconciled. In the case of a *Cohen*, reputed by ancient Jewish tradition to be more temperamental than others, the delivery of the *Get* was made a more complicated affair, taking longer in the writing and the delivery thereof (*Get Mekushar*). As he is liable to be quick to anger, longer time was given him to calm down. In addition, though an ordinary Israelite may remarry his former wife if she remained unmarried since the divorce, a Cohen cannot do so. Hence let him take longer over his contemplated divorce.

The Talmud cites two instances in which the husband was denied the right of divorcing his wife. The first was the case described in the Bible,[105] when the accusation of pre-marital immorality brought by him against his wife proved untrue; the second was when he himself had seduced his wife before marriage. In that case, it was an act of justice that he should not be allowed to shame her by summarily dismissing her. The detailed and complicated process of legal separation could be performed only by experts, a stipulation that ensured exactness, minimized mistakes and misunderstandings and settled with reasonable certainty the legal status and mutual obligations of the two parties. One unfamiliar with its various aspects was counselled not to take part in such matters, being sternly warned that "*he who divorces his wife is hated before the Lord*". He must not by his incom-

[105]Deut. xxii. 13-19.

petence aid and abet the act of breaking up domestic happiness and disrupting home life.

We turn again to the ideal family life with its happy home and the sound of joyous children within. To be happy, children of one family must not be treated differently from one another. The story of what happened to Joseph serves as a warning. Because his father made for him *"a coat of many colours"*,[106] was he sold into Egypt and Israel made to serve bondage to the cruel Pharaohs.[107] A father should not terrorize his child; and lest the child be taught to deceive, the parent is urged to keep *all* the promises he makes at home.[108] What is said by the parents in the presence of children should be carefully weighed and guarded, for children repeat in the street what they have heard in the home.[109]

VI. THE IDEAL FAMILY LIFE

The ideal Jewish home is created by the conviction that a blessing unfolds itself within the life of husband and wife and their children through the family. This is both of a natural and of a spiritual order. Home life is on a partnership basis; there is the love and the care of the parents for their children and there is the obedience and the respect of the children towards their parents. In their father and mother, the children have before their eyes that union between man and wife which is *Kiddushin* (holy). It is from the care and love for him that the child first learns the meaning of God as "Our Father who art in Heaven (*avinu she'bashamayim*).

[106]Gen. xxxvii. 3.
[107]Shabb. 10b.
[108]Gitt. 6b.
[109]Ibid. 56b.

One of the many answers that could be given to the question "What is Judaism?"[110] is this: It is a religion in which the family is in possession of God's blessing and in which the parents hand down this blessing to their children. It is in the happiness of the family life that the Jew experiences his nearness to God.

The question might also be asked *"What is marriage?"* The answer could equally be given very simply. It is *not* merely a *social* relationship but an attempt to create joy and peace in the world, to build a sanctuary out of a worldly institution. Husband and wife are enabled through marriage to share in the creative work of God, *"renewing the creation every day continually"*.[111] Both can sustain life and make it holy; empowered by their life together to bring out the best that is in them.

"Thou art consecrated unto me by this ring according to the Law of Moses and Israel"[112] is the translation of the nine Hebrew words by which the bride becomes a wife. They form a gateway through which the couple proceed towards their future life of joy and holiness, at the same time impressing upon them that they are now dedicated to each other for life.

Jewish family life will always be the main reason for the survival of our people; for it is the ideal home that forges characters able to withstand extinction. No gain in national territory could ever offset the tragedy that would ensue were those ideals of Judaism—marriage, the Sabbath and *Kashrut*—to suffer a decline in the State of Israel. Thucydides, the historian of the Peloponesian Wars, records that Greece fell not because of the clash of arms but because home life was being destroyed.

[110]See Appendix II at the end of this book.
[111]Singer's Prayer Book, p. 37.
[112]See ibid. pp. 298-299 for the words of the entire marriage ceremony.

Rome had a similar tale to tell. On account of the danger existing to the sanctity of marriage not only in the *Golah* but also in Israel, it is the task of spiritual leaders constantly to be on their guard to defend and explain the ethical import of a Jewish union.

The enemy of a happy marriage is the childless one. This may not always be due to the selfish indulgence of parents. When Abraham cried: "*O Lord God, what wilt Thou give me, seeing I go hence childless?*"[113] he echoed the yearning of every Jewish parent. Similarly, when Rachel pleaded with Jacob: "*Give me children, or else I die*",[114] hers was the *cri de coeur* of every mother pining for the "*fruit of her womb*". *Father* and *mother* are the most tender words in the language; because of this, they describe God's relationship to us. "*As a father hath mercy on his children, so will I have mercy on you*", says God. "*As one whom his mother comforteth, so will I comfort you*"[115] are the words used in a house of mourning. It is the bearing of children that makes the home like a Temple of God and the table its altar.[116] A family is the natural fulfilment of marriage. However devoted to each other husband and wife may be, there is a place in their natures which only children can fill. Children cement the structure of family life more solidly together.

Marriage is holy, for it gives to men and women the opportunity of taking part in the miracle of creation and provides for the children resulting from such a happy union the best environment for their sound and healthy

[113]Gen. xv. 2.
[114]Ibid. xxx. 1.
[115]Is. lxvi. 13.
[116]Much useful advice on how to be happy in married life will be found in "The Threshold of Marriage", 1949, a practical guide for all who intend to be married, issued by the Church of England Moral Welfare Council. Also in "Men, Women, and God", by Dr. Herbert Gray.

development—a united and happy home and the love and care of devoted parents. It is also blessed, because it offers to the majority of men and women the greatest chance of achieving personal happiness and the joy of companionship with a beloved and chosen partner. Judaism sees in marriage a mitigation of the essential loneliness of life and the opportunity of shared interests which gives content and significance to things around us.

True, some of these things may be found to a certain degree in other relationships, but in marriage there is the *greatest* promise of daily companionship, of lifelong partnership, of sharing joys and sorrows, of the building up of a living philosophy of existence. The family is proof positive that man is not intended to live for the good of himself alone but is to care for the welfare of those in his charge, giving of his best to the claims and duties of a common life.[117]

Nowhere are the ethical ideals of married love more tenderly expressed than in Judaism. In our religion, it means ideals and spiritual experiences shared; it signifies the struggle to work out together the will of God in everyday life and the effort to make the home a place of friendliness, refreshment and peace. In the happy home, God becomes more real to all who dwell there and to those who visit it. This aim is suggested by the other word for marriage, *Nissuin*, which means an *uplifting* of the soul and an ennoblement of human desires.

There is a verse in the Bible which contains both a warning and a definition of the true marriage of souls. *"And Isaac brought her into his mother Sarah's tent, and took Rebekah, and she became his wife; and he loved her.*

[117]The reader will find useful the pamphlet entitled "The Marriage Relationship", 1950, the excellent report of a Commission appointed by the direction of London Yearly Meeting of the Society of Friends in 1949.

And Isaac was comforted for his mother."[118] The words
"*and he loved her*" come after the words "*and she became
his wife*". Logic would have reversed the order. What
lesson does the verse convey? To teach that love *after*
marriage is the *sequel* and the effect of a perfect partnership
in which joys, anxieties and responsibilities are shared
jointly and unstintingly. Cynics say that marriage is
wonderful *at the start* but soon romance fades away and
then all is not "*happily ever after*". A dull monotonous
round in "*double harness*" takes the place of what seemed,
"*once upon a time*", such a thrilling state of existence.
Some marriages are like that; but they need not be.
"When husband and wife", says the writer of "The
Threshold of Marriage',[119] "are purposed to work for
happiness, to learn by mistakes in their understanding of
one another, then marriage becomes more interesting and
more joyful each year. Here is an illustration. You light
your sitting-room fire. At first, the wood and paper flare
up, and the flames flicker and dance. Yet it is only when
the fire settles down to a steady glow that it really does its
job and provides the comfort and the satisfaction you
look for. So it is with marriage. The later years of mature
love and deeper experience may have lost some of the
sparkle of '*first love*'; but what they have gained is
precious beyond compare."

It is in the relationship of the partners *after* marriage
that our ethical teachings are seen at their best. The
husband is to honour his wife more than himself and to
supply her with all the comforts of life she needs; of
course, in measure of his means. If he does so, he will be
a happy man; for blessings come to a home on account of
a good and virtuous woman. Here are some of these
blessings: she rears his children; she it is who makes it

[118]Gen. xxiv. 67.
[119]p. 9.

possible for him to pursue his studies undisturbed by attending to his physical wants; she alone can fill the house with happiness and holiness. More than one religious historian of our people has borne witness that the wonderful and mysterious preservation of the Jews is due to the Jewish woman. This is her glory not alone in the history of her own people but in the history of the world.

Is it a wonder that the Rabbis were of the opinion that for a husband to witness the death of his wife is to see the destruction of the Temple with his own eyes? If to this day, nearly two thousand years after the event,[120] the Jewish year is still dotted with so many poignant memories of the event—memories which have been embalmed in our fast days and in our abstention from joys otherwise legitimate—it does not need much imagination to picture the depths of mourning into which our ancestors at the time were plunged. The feelings occasioned by the death of a good wife are significant of the Jewish view of marriage. Had marriage been regarded as a semi-religious contract, as a permitted living together of man and woman with privileges heavily loaded on the side of the man, such tender statements would not have been possible when marriage formed the theme of those penetrating discussions in the Babylonian Academies of learning.

It is like stepping from a breezy mountain-top swept by gusts of invigorating air into an over-heated room of an invalid when one compares the relationship of man and wife among Jews with that among ancient peoples. In the pages of Greek and Roman writers, woman is designated for work of a menial nature and is regarded as an instrument for propagation. Weighted down from birth by injustice, she appears as a low creature from whom obedience to her lord and master was required as a spinner

[120]In the year 70 C.E., when Titus destroyed the second Temple.

of wool and a preserver of grain. Civilization, in the form of art and literature, owes much to the great nations of Greece and Rome; but have they added much towards the ideal home life? Let their own sources give the answer.

According to Homer, the ideal wife was "*one who weaves the loom and prepares the couch*". Plutarch, writing on "*Love*", states that "*true love is impossible between man and woman*". Xenophon narrates that when Socrates, so fond of asking the youths in the Athenian market-places the most embarrassing questions, enquired of an average citizen what his attitude towards his wife was, the reply he received was: "*First of all, I insist that my wife should, as much as possible, spin the wool and leave off drinking and eating excessively. Secondly, I rarely remain at home.*" Such outrageous views apparently earned the approbation of Socrates, than whom none was wiser in ancient Greece.[121] The current impression seems to have been that since woman was instrumental in bringing death to the world by causing Adam's disobedience to the first command of God, she was to be an object of contempt all the days of her life.

The Romans capped this unfair treatment of the "*fair*" sex by their harsh teachings. It was possibly from them that early Christianity learnt to consider both woman and matrimony as "*necessary evils*". Celibacy of man and virginity of woman were displayed as the acmes of virtue. Despite the dissolute life of many of the priests, Pope Gregory VII made the celibacy of the priesthood the law of the Church. This law is binding to this day, though it constitutes a violation of all legitimate instincts and serves as a challenge to human reason. It was this stern

---

[121]In fairness to Socrates, it should be remembered that he married a shrew, with the result that his views on women were rather biased by his experience with Xanthippa, his wife.

decree that was mainly responsible for the Dissolution of the Monasteries in England in the early part of the sixteenth century.[122]

In a treatise entitled "*Ornaments of Woman*",[123] one of the saints of the early Church, Tertullian, writes bitterly: "*O woman! thou shouldst always wear mourning and rags, in order to show thy penitence and thy weeping and atoning for thy great crime of having corrupted humanity soon after the Creation. For thou art the one who first tasted of the forbidden fruit and who first transgressed the law of God. It was thou who hast seduced man whom the devil himself did not dare to approach.*" The Jew found it therefore hard to heed the claim of Christianity that it was the first to teach that "*God is love*". He preferred, though threatened by the inquisition and the torture-chamber to embrace the new creed, to remain a member of "*a stiff-necked people*" ever ready to *die* for Judaism than to *live* for Christianity.

From the Gospels, especially from the Epistles to the ancient Greek and Roman communities sent by Paul, the real architect of Christianity, it is evident that it was Judaism that first liberated woman and converted marriage into an inviolable sacrament. [In Hebrew, the words for man and woman—*ish* and *ishah*—contain the same two letters (*aleph* and *shin*), sharing equally between them the two letters (*yod, he*) which form one of the names of God.[124] Could the equality of the sexes have been more

---

[122]From this date, England ceased to be a Catholic country; but it was much later that the Church began to consider marriage as a *Sacrament*.

[123]The reader will find striking material on this subject in "The Jewish Woman", a book written by Nahida Remy, a non-Jewess, who cannot, therefore, be dismissed as biased.

[124]This will be more closely seen from the Hebrew איש (man) and אשה (woman); the word for God is יה. Incidentally, R. Meir points out, if you leave out the two letters spelling the name of God, the word left, in both cases, is אש (*fire*), indicative of the consuming nature of such a godless relationship.

forcibly and picturesquely described?] The words *Kid-dushin* and *Nissuin*, described above, should be sufficient guarantee for the protection of woman in Judaism and should convince all but the bigot that marriage is a loving alliance of godliness and happiness. In such an ideal union, the wife is *not* the slave of the husband but his *better* self with whom her husband should always confer and whose good advice he should ever be ready to follow. "*Whatever Sarah shall tell thee to do, listen to her*", was the behest God gave to Abraham when he felt disinclined to act on her advice of banishing Hagar from his home.[125] The Jew does not "*fall*" in love; he *rises*. Our religion never wearies in reminding its adherents that "*to be fruitful and to multiply*" is the first command in the Torah. "*A man's home is his wife*" (Yoma i. 1). If he treats her as an inferior being, he will be responsible for the destruction of his home-life and of his general welfare.

What we have tried to say on this subject is so delight-fully condensed in the last of the *Seven Blessings* (*Sheva Berachot*) recited at every wedding ceremony that it may well serve as a postscript to this chapter. "*Blessed art thou, O Lord our God, King of the universe, who hast created joy and gladness, bridegroom and bride, mirth and exultation, pleasure and delight, love, brotherhood, peace and fellowship. Soon may there be heard in the cities of Judah and in the streets of Jerusalem, the voice of joy and gladness, the voice of the bridegroom and the voice of the bride, the jubilant voice of bridegrooms from their canopies, and of youths from their feasts of song. Blessed art thou, O Lord, who makest the bridegroom to rejoice with the bride.*"[126]

[125]Gen. xxi. 12.
[126]Singer's Prayer Book, p. 299.

CHAPTER ELEVEN

ETHICAL INSTRUMENTS IN CHARACTER BUILDING

IN the shaping of character we are asked to make the attributes of God our pattern. An ingenious mnemonic for this advice has been found in the three Hebrew letters spelling the word *Melech* (מלך) "a king"; and when used of God, as the *"melech malechei hamelachim"*, *"the King of Kings"*. The *mem* (shortened from *min*, meaning *"from"*) reminds us *from whom* all authority emanates; the *lamed* (meaning *"to"*) exhorts us to be aware *to whom* all should turn, and the *chaph* (a comparative prefix meaning *"like"*) urges us all to try to be *like* Him. The reward of the implementation of this threefold reminder is that He will repay us *"measure for measure"* (*middah keneged middah*), or in the colourful imagery of the Psalmist, *"The Lord is thy shade upon thy right hand"*.[1] Just as the shadow faithfully reproduces what we do, so will He reward us for the good and punish us for the evil. Let us now consider some of the ethical tools which seek to shape our character.

I. HUMILITY

First among these aids to the godly life is humility. The greatness of God is best seen in His modesty, says R. Johanan.[2] Humility avoids the extremes of self-effacement on the one hand, and of self-glorification on the other. Jeremiah does not consider it sinful to rejoice in achievement so long as one recognizes that all blessings

[1] Ps. cxxi. 5.
[2] Cf. Meg. 31ᵃ. See Singer's Prayer Book, pp. 214-215.

flow from His gifts. The prophet only denounces the boastfulness which results from the mere acquisition of wealth, strength or wisdom.[3] Haggai[4] echoes this declaration in his statement that God is not impressed with material riches without a corresponding wealth of the spirit; to which the Psalmist[5] adds *strength* and the Book of Proverbs[6] *wisdom*.

Among men material things are considered things that matter most; but He loves "*a broken and a contrite heart*".[7] His chief d mands of man are "*Justice, Mercy and Humility*".[8] Abraham spoke of himself as "*but dust and ashes*";[9] and the glory of Moses was his humility.[10] The fact that this quality is singled out in the character of one who was the paragon of all virtues is the measure of its importance. Isaiah ranks this virtue above the building of religious shrines,[11] a belief expressed in other parts of the Bible.[12] Besides Abraham and Moses, Gideon,[13] Saul and David are also displayed as models of meekness.

Jewish suffering implemented what the sages taught regarding the humble life; for in defiance of persecution, the finer Jewish minds set themselves out to inculcate patience and gentleness. They took the symbolism of the hard-boiled egg on the *Seder* table to heart; the longer it was boiled, the harder it became. So were their natures refined in the crucibles of suffering and religious intolerance. The revenge they took of their persecutors was to be of the persecuted rather than of those who persecute; to be of

[3] Jer. ix. 22-23.
[4] ii. 9.
[5] cxlvii. 11.
[6] xxi. 30.
[7] Ps. li. 19.
[8] Micah vi. 8.
[9] Gen. xviii. 27.
[10] Num. xii. 3.
[11] lxvi. 1-2.
[12] Deut. viii. 10-18; Isa. x. 13-15; Ps. cxxvii. 1.
[13] Who refused a crown; Judges viii. 23.

those who are put to shame rather than of those who shame others. The ideal Jew will be humble, as beseems a servant of God and a member of a people who bear the Divine name in their very appellation (*Israel*—prince of God). He will not retaliate when wronged nor be angry with those who slander him. To those who curse him, his soul will be dumb.[14] Silent, he will endure for His sake.

The Talmud is full of praise for this virtue. Humility is the deterrent to self-conceit; it teaches man not to rely on his own merits and achievements. Humility should avoid the extreme of self-effacement favoured by Buddhism on the one hand or the disregard of life preached by early Christianity on the other. It takes pride of place among the ten degrees of moral perfection enumerated in the Talmud.[15] The proud man is compared to an idolater;[16] the *Shechinah* will dwell only among the humble in spirit,[17] whether he be prophet or scholar.[18] When Hillel died, he was mourned not so much for his great learning but for his piety and humility.[19] God will elevate those who are humble; but He will humiliate those who seek aggrandisement. From him who pursues greatness, greatness will flee; but he who flees *from* greatness, him will greatness follow.[20]

Hillel taught: "*Remove thyself from thy place some rows behind and wait until they call thee to come in front.*"[21] It is better to be asked to take a more prominent position than to be asked to shift to a less exalted one. Man was

---

[14] See the thoughts expressed in the Amidah prayer; Singer's Prayer Book, p. 54.
[15] Arakhin 16[b]; Ab. Zara 20[b].
[16] Sot. 4[b].
[17] Ned. 38[a].
[18] Erub. 13[b]; 54[a].
[19] Sot. 48[b].
[20] Erubin 13[b].
[21] Lev. R. 1 quotes this in the name of R. Akiba, who in turn, cites R. Shimon b. Azzai as its author.

created last at the creation of the world, so that in the event of overweening pride assailing him, he should gently be reminded that the worm and the gnat had preceded him at Creation.[22] The Creation was all finished before man arrived on the scene. Another Rabbi taught: "*Happy is the generation in which the great listen to the small; for how much more then will the small listen to the great?*"[23] Pride leads to destruction, and the man or nation that boasts superiority soon begins to attack others.

Lack of humility begets hatred; hatred begets strife; strife leads to destruction. The more one criticizes oneself, the greater one is. The ideal man is pictured as one walking through life humbly, doing his duty come what may, without thought of self-glorification. The extent to which the proud was held in abomination by the Rabbis can be gauged from their teaching that "*a scholar who is proud is like a carcass lying in the street; those who pass it by, turn away in disgust*".[24]

The reason, according to the Mishnah,[25] why the High Priest was not allowed to officiate in his garments of gold on Yom Kippur was a reminder that God was not to be worshipped in the panoply and *regalia* of majesty but in simplicity of humility, attired in plain linen garments.[26] Because of their haughtiness, the generation of the Flood merited destruction.[27] If a scholar will scorn humility, warned R. Judah (in the name of Rav[28]), his learning will

[22]Sanhed. 38ª. More favourable to man is the view that he was created last so that he should find ready for him all the things needed (*Tanhuma*).

[23]See R. Hash. 25ᵇ; Taan. 15ª, 18ª; Meg. 11ª, 13ᵇ-14ᵇ, 18ᵇ; Sanhed. 88ᵇ; Ber. 10ᵇ.

[24]Abot d'R. Nathan ii.

[25]Yoma vii. 4.

[26]Lev. xvi. 4; Zeb. 88ᵇ; Hull. 5ᵇ.

[27]Sanhed. 108ª.

[28]Pes. 66ᵇ: כל־המתיהר, אם חכם הוא חכמתו מסתלקת

depart from him; if he be a prophet, he will cease to prophesy. Addressing the thorn-bush from which Moses first heard the Voice of God in the wilderness when tending the sheep of Jethro, a Talmudic Rabbi thus apostrophizes: "O thorn-bush! Not because thou art the highest of all trees did God choose thee as the scene of His revelation unto suffering mankind. On the contrary, thou wert chosen because thou art the lowliest among them."[29] Humility is especially fitting to Israel;[30] to walk about life haughtily is to insult the *Shechinah*.[31]

The daily affirmation of a *Jabneh* sage is worth repeating. *"I am God's creature, so is my fellow-man; my sphere of usefulness is in the city, his is in the country. I have no more right to be overbearing on account of my work than he has on account of his."*[32] The Messiah will come only when haughtiness has ceased to plague Israel.[33] R. Jonathan b. Amram, during a famine, it was told, insisted on receiving no more bread than anyone else.[34] Because of the self-denial of Moses, who after the Golden Calf pleaded with God to erase him from the Torah rather than to destroy Israel, God rewarded him by calling the Torah after him.[35] *"Remember ye the Law of Moses My Servant"* (Malachi iii. 22).

Pride was the downfall of five men otherwise highly endowed by Divine grace. These were: Samson, intoxicated by his physical powers; Saul, proud of his grand

[29]Sabb. 67[a].
[30]Haggigah 9[b]; Ned. 20[a].
[31]Ber. 43[b].
[32]Ibid. 17[a].
[33]Sanhed. 98[a]; Arakhin 16[a].
[34]B. Bath. 8[b].
[35]Shabb. 89[a]. It is interesting that the absence of the name of Moses from the Sidra *Tetsaveh*—the only instance in the Torah from the recording of his birth till his death—as well as the omission of his name from the Passover *Haggadah*, are attributed to the Divine granting of his request to *"blot out"* his name.

physique, being head and shoulders above the people;[36] Absalom, vain on account of his beautiful, curled locks; Asa, boastful because he was fleet of foot and Zedekiah, unforgetful that he was blessed with beautiful eyes.[37] David, on the other hand, was characterized by his humility. When recalling retrospectively the events of his life,[38] he is claimed to have said: "*My heart was not haughty when I was anointed king by Samuel the prophet, nor when I conquered Goliath.*" The decisions of Hillel,[39] rather than those of Shammai, were accepted because of his humility. "*If you minimize your merits*", observed a sage, "*people will minimize your faults.*"[40]

God despises the slightest flaw in the animal sacrifices brought to Him but he cherishes the broken heart and contrite spirit.[41] Commenting on the words of Isaiah (lv. 1) "*Ho, every one that thirsteth, come ye for water*", a Rabbi says: "*Just as water in its course seeks the low land and not the high ground, so will the Torah find an abode not with the haughty but with the humble.*"[42] To possess even an infinitesimal fraction of pride is an abomination in the eyes of God.[43] Not the proud cedar was chosen for the purification of the leper but the humble hyssop. God ignored the exalted mountains, choosing instead Sinai for the giving of the Torah.[44]

The spirit of God refuses to rest on the haughty;[45] the humble are to be ranked higher than the arrogant.[46]

[36]1 Sam. ix. 2.
[37]Sotah 10[a].
[38]Hull. 89[a].
[39]Erubin 13[a].
[40]R. Hash. 17[a].
[41]Lev. R. vii. 1.
[42]Taan. 7[a].
[43]Sotah 5[a].
[44]Ibid. 5[a]: הניח כל־הרים וגבעות והשרה שכינתו על־הר סיני
[45]Shabb. 92[a]; Ned. 38[a].
[46]Ab. Zara 20[b]: ענוה גדולה מכולן

"Wilt thou be a participant in the blessings stored up for the righteous in the World to Come", asks another Rabbi; *"then be thou humble and constantly enrich the store of knowledge without the least sign of self-conceit."*[47]

It must be emphasized that Jewish Ethics do not intend that humility be carried to cowardice, or practised at the expense of manhood. It is a manly and heroic virtue. The disciple of the wise should have sufficient pride to stand in defence of the Law he represents.[48] For this reason, is the *Talmid Hacham* allowed to possess a small fraction (one sixty-fourth) of pride. He must have sufficient pride in his principles to stand up for them, if necessary.

II. JUSTICE AND CHARITY

Humility will occasion a sense of justice in all things. It will teach a man to be scrupulously honest in all he does and not to take any unfair advantage of the ignorance or trust of another. It will instil in him the determination to loathe any usurious transaction and abhor exploitation in business and all other kinds of fraudulent dealing. Few vices come more under the lash than the abuse of the confidence placed in us by a trusting fellow-man.[49] To be impartial is only the *passive* side of justice and is not enough. Justice has an *active* side also; this is to right wrong and to vindicate the cause of the oppressed. Isaiah is fond of describing the justice of God side by side with His holiness.[50]

[47]Sanhed. 88[b].
[48]Sotah 5[a].
[49]See Lev. xix. 15; xxv. 14; Deut. xvi. 19; xxv. 16; Isa. xxxii. 7; Jer. xxii. 15; Zech. vii. 9-10; Hab. ii. 6-11; Prov. xxi. 21; xiv. 34; xxviii. 8; Job xxxi. 7; Ps. xv; *Talmud:* Sanhed. 25[a]; Kidd. 56[b]; Hull. 94[a].
[50]xxvi. 9.

18

The just man is "*He that walketh righteously and speaketh uprightly; he that despiseth the gain of oppressions, that shaketh his hands from holding of bribes, that stoppeth his ears from hearing of blood (guilt) and shutteth his eyes from looking upon evil. He shall dwell on high; his place of defence shall be the munitions of the rocks; his bread shall be given, his waters shall be sure.*"[51]

Not only in action but in disposition[52] must one be just; not only honest in intention but also in deed. One must be upright in speech and mien; perfect in rectitude; neither taking advantage of ignorance nor abusing confidence.[53] A sense of justice will deter a man from betting and gambling, from acquiring wealth by unfair means,[54] and will remove from him the temptation to acquire food illegally or to raise the market-price of goods.[55] The promise of the just man will be his bond; his word will be as reliable as his weights and measures.[56]

A medieval ethical teacher[57] explains the command "*Justice, justice shalt thou pursue*" (Deut. xvi. 20) thus: "*Justice you must follow, irrespective of whether it be to your profit or loss, whether in word or in action, whether to Jew or non-Jew.*" Justice is comprehensive in its sweep, covering consideration for the honour and welfare of our fellow-man. We must not harm his peace of mind by the tongue of the back-biter (Ps. xv. 3), by the ear that listens to calumny (Pes. 118[a]), or by the suspicion cast upon the

---

[51]Ibid. xxxiii. 15-16.

[52]B. Metz. 58[b].

[53]B. Bath. 88-90[b]; Makk. 24[a]. The reader will find some apt quotations on all the virtues treated in this chapter in Bialik's *Dibre Haggadah;* A. Cohen's "Everyman's Talmud"; Newman's "Hassidic Anthology" and Browne's "Wisdom of Israel".

[54]Sanhed. 24[b].

[55]B. Bath. 90[b].

[56]Lev. xix. 36; B.M. 49[a].

[57]R. Bachyah b. Asher (13th cent.) in his כד הקמח s.v. גזלה

innocent.[58] It is so easy yet so wrong to save one's own honour at the expense of another's reputation. The Rabbis warned that God avenges those whose honour has been violated by their fellow-men. *"He who publicly puts his fellow-man to shame forfeits his share in the World to Come."*[59]

Justice is more than a mere abstention from hurting our fellow-men. It is a *positive* conception, including charity and philanthropy. The word for charity (*tsedakah*) actually means *Justice*, for the poor have a claim upon the rich. To prevent the poor from being helped is to class oneself a robber, said one Rabbi.[60] In support, he quoted the Scriptural verse *"Remove not the ancient landmark; and enter not into the fields of the fatherless; for their Redeemer is strong; He will plead their cause with thee"* (Prov. xxiii. 10-11).

Charity is not only a gift of touched sympathy; it is also a *duty*. It behoves the fortunate to rescue the unfortunate from their plight; for what they possess was given to them for this purpose. *"The poor are God's people"*, says the Tanhuma; *"does it not say 'If thou lend money to any of My people, even to the poor with thee?'* (Ex. xxi. 24). *Do not forget that 'There is a wheel which rotates in this world', and that the turn of the wheel which made you rich one day may make you poor another."*

This cry for social justice is heard throughout the prophetic writings. It was the demand of Isaiah,[61] and the lack of it was condemned by Amos.[62] The Book of Proverbs[63] imposes curses upon him who withholds the corn from the people in need. Judaism laid the foundations

---

[58]Yoma 19^b; Shabb. 97^a.
[59]B. Kama 79^b; B. Metz. 58^b.
[60]Peah v. 6.
[61]v. 8.
[62]viii. 4.
[63]xi. 26.

of a higher justice not satisfied with the mitigation of misery by pittances but insisted on a readjustment of the social conditions that create poverty. If the rest of the world has become more philanthropically-minded, it is due in great measure to the "*Poor Laws*" of the Torah, to its institutions of *Shemitah*[64] and *Yovel*,[65] and to its provisions for the release of debts and the restoration of fields and houses to those forced to sell what had once been their patrimony.

These humane regulations aimed at preventing the tyranny of wealth from becoming a permanent source of oppression. From them arose all efforts in modern times to alleviate the lot of the poor and check the causes of corruption in the social organism. Jewish Social Ethics seek not only to *alleviate* but to *cure;* not only to serve as a *panacea* for many ills but as a prophylactic; not only to add to the happiness of mankind but to arm the good instincts inherent in society and in man that they may overcome the evil rampant in the world. Justice demands a consciousness of individual responsibility and an interdependence of one man on another. In Jewish ethics, virtue is not a sedative, but a stimulus; not a dope, but a dynamic.

The passage dealing with a dead man who is found outside a city[66] must be instanced again here, though passing reference has already been made to it. The elders of the city, responsible for the administration of its affairs, were bidden to slaughter a heifer and to wash their hands in public and exclaim *"Our hands have not shed this blood"*. The Rabbis ask:[67] "How could the elders be suspected of murder?" The reply is *"If they failed to*

[64]Deut. xv. 1-6.
[65]Lev. xxv. 8-19.
[66]Deut. xxi. 1-8.
[67]Sot. ix. 7.

*provide the poor in their charge with the necessary food,
with the result that the needy man had to have recourse to
highway robbery for his means of existence, losing his life
while so engaged, it was the responsibility and the blame of
the elders that a life had been taken. Similarly, if they left
him without the necessary protection and he fell a victim by
the roadside from starvation, it was again the responsibility
of the elders before God."*

In this graphic way Judaism impresses upon its
adherents that each one according to his station is
responsible for the social conditions which create crime
and poverty. A strict sense of justice sets the highest value
upon all things that make man increase his power of
doing good and of removing the causes of evil. From
whatever angle we examine our ethical teachings, we see
that our faith recommends and encourages a robust
morality. It looks upon life as a continual battle for right
against injustice, for truth against falsehood,[68] for survival
against extinction.

III. TRUTH AND FALSEHOOD

Truth is the seal of God, the beginning and the end of
all things.[69] It is therefore a profanation of the name of
God to avoid the truth with the intent to deceive. Perjury

[68]Deut. i. 17.

[69]The Rabbis draw attention to the fact that the three letters
א מ ת (truth) are the *first, middle* and the *last* of the Hebrew
alphabet. They are each broad-based, whereas the word for
falsehood (ש ק ר) consists of three letters close to each other,
as if to hint that one lie breeds another. Furthermore, they
are composed of letters which, in the old Hebrew form of
writing (still seen in the Sepher Torah), tail off to a point.
Hence the Talmudic expression that שקר אין לו רגלים—
"*falsehood has not a leg to stand upon*", but חותמו של הקב״ה אמת
(Shabb. 55[b]).

is vigorously denounced in the Decalogue (Ex. xx. 7) and in other parts of the Torah.[70] False witnesses, in certain cases, were punished with that penalty which their victim would have received had their plot not miscarried.[71] Lying is an abomination which receives the lash of fury in all our teachings;[72] it is a direct offence against God "*who lieth not*".[73] On this account liars, mockers, hypocrites and slanderers cannot appear before the Heavenly Throne.[74] To speak the truth is a duty which admits of no limitation; only where domestic peace is threatened by the *whole* truth can "*the white lie*" be uttered.[75] It is the duty of the Israelite to deceive no man, to speak the truth in his heart and to suffer no false word to be uttered in his presence.

Here are some further Rabbinic observations on this theme.[76] The punishment of the liar is that even when he is speaking the truth he is not believed.[77] Just as science without ethics is dangerous to the welfare of society, so is a man who affirms one thing and does another. To break a spoken promise is to be guilty of idolatry; for both are manifestations of faithlessness.[78] Duplicity, resulting in concealing the truth and in creating a false impression, even when the excuse be that it was for a

[70]Ex. xxiii. 7; Lev. xix. 11.

[71]Deut. xix. 15-21. These false witnesses are called עדים זוממין that is, witnesses who had plotted against an innocent man.

[72]Ps. xv. 2; xxiv. 4; ci. 7; Zech. viii. 16-17; Zeph. iii. 13.

[73]1 Sam. xv. 29; Ps. lxxxix. 34.

[74]Sot. 42a.

[75]Yeb. 65b. On account of *shelom bayit*, of not destroying that domestic peace and happiness that is so highly prized in our way of life, can a slight modification of the rigidity for truth be allowed.

[76]See Newman's "Hassidic Anthology", pp. 486ff., and his "Talmudic Anthology", pp. 517ff.

[77]Sanhed. 89b. Readers will recall Æsop's fable of "Wolf, Wolf".

[78]Sanhed. 92a.

good purpose,[79] is to transgress the Biblical command *"Keep thee far from a false matter."*[80] To pretend to harbour for another an affectionate feeling not actually there, in order to curry favour, is to sin against truth. To be lavish in the singing of a bride's praises when she does not deserve them was considered by the School of Shammai as a transgression against the canons of strict truth. The School of Hillel, purely out of consideration for the peculiar circumstances, took a more lenient view.[81]

As a precaution against telling an untruth, the advice is to train the tongue in cases of doubt to utter the words *"I do not know"*.[82] Especially on our guard must we be when speaking to children. *"Never tell a child: 'I shall give you so and so' unless you actually will give it to him; lest he learn from you to tell untruths."*[83] Truth is the hall mark of character. *"Sin has many tools, but a lie is a handle to fit them all"*, a warning to be heedless of which is criminal folly.

The liar seeks to deceive from some selfish motive. It is wrong to offer hospitality to one who, we know, is certain not to accept it. Similarly it is deceitful to enquire about the price of goods when one has not the slightest intention of buying them.[84] To lie even in jest is forbidden. Only when telling the complete truth involves a risk to life is one permitted to utter a falsehood.[85] The reason being (as in the case of a threat to domestic peace), lest truth become a *fetish*, the worship of which leads to the breaking-up of love or life, peace and hope.

The Jew is taught to pray each morning: *"At all times,*

---

[79]Shevuot 31ᵃ.

[80]Ex. xxiii. 7.

[81]Ket. 17ᵃ.

[82]Ber. 4ᵃ.

[83]Sukk. 46ᵇ.

[84]This is called גנבת דעת *"stealing one's mind"*.

[85]Ned. ii. 4; *Yoreh Deah*, 232¹⁴.

*let a man fear God in private as in public, acknowledge the
truth and speak the truth in his heart.*"[86] Many Talmudic
Rabbis are held up as models of those who never allowed
a lie to escape their lips; such a one being R. Safra, whom
nothing tempted to deflect from his path of virtue.[87]
Rav advised R. Kahana to engage in the most menial
trade rather than utter falsehoods.[88] The overthrow of
Sodom and Gomorrah, the Flood, the Tower of Babel and
other calamities mentioned in the Bible should serve as
a warning to those who do not keep word that destruction
will be their nemesis.[89]

IV. ETHICS OF PRAYER

Prayer is the measure of one's faith and its outward
manifestation. Since man was stamped in His likeness, he
must show that he is ever conscious of this great compliment. A life of prayer, reflecting his dependence on the
Heavenly Father, will be a perpetual reminder of this
relationship. Not to pray is to stamp oneself ungrateful
and possessed of little faith, an attitude of mind scorned
by our sages[90] because it displays a dependence on self
that is alien to Jewish philosophy. When the Rabbis
debated which was the Biblical passage on which the six
hundred and thirteen Mitzvot rested, they awarded the
palm of their decision to Habakkuk (ii. 4): "*But the*

[86]Singer's Prayer Book, p. 7; Tana d'be Eliahu xxi.
[87]Makk. 24ª. This Rabbi refused to take advantage of the
higher price offered to him for an article when he had finished
his prayers.
[88]Pes. 113ª.
[89]B.M. 44ª.
[90]Sot. 48ᵇ cites this statement as an example of doubt in God's
power of providing our wants. "*He who has bread in his pantry,
but is nervous lest he has no food for the morrow, is one who has
little faith.*"

righteous shall live by his faith".[91] Prayer means a declaration of man's helplessness and God's omnipotence; of man's ignorance and God's omniscience; of man's limited scope and God's omnipresence.

It is called "*the service of the heart*",[92] to be accompanied, both when praying communally in the synagogue or in the intimacy of one's home "*with eyes downward and heart turned toward heaven*".[93] Tenderness toward all should suffuse every fibre[94] and the joy of fulfilling this great act of faith should banish gloom or despair.[95] The *Shechinah* does not rest on one who makes a burden of communion with God[96] but on one swayed by the *joy* of fulfilling a religious precept with all his heart and soul.

God loves nothing more than the sight of His pious ones at prayer,[97] swayed more by feelings of genuine love for Him than by the pangs of a guilty conscience.[98] Such prayer has charm and grace[99] and reflects gratitude to Him especially when performed at the break of day; pleasing Him in the same way as the offering of first-fruits (*Bikkurim*) did in Temple times. To dedicate our first words to Him on awakening, or the last words after having resigned ourselves to rest is to manifest a faith worthy of that possessed by our ancestors. They began their journey in the wilderness, "*in a land that was not sown*",[100] as

[91]Makk. 24[a].

[92]Taan. 2[a].

[93]Yeb. 105[b]: המתפלל צריך שיתן עיניו למטה ולבו למעלה

[94]Sotah. 5[a].

[95]Ber. 31[a]: אין עומדין להתפלל מתוך עצבות

[96]See Ber. 24[b] for some Rabbinic observations on the attitudes man should adopt in prayer; also the writer's "Jewish Customs" in the chapters dealing with Prayer.

[97]Ber. 3[a]: אשרי המלך שמקלסין אותו כך

[98]Sot. 31[a]; Ber. 33[b].

[99]See R. Hama b. Papa's statement in Sukk. 49[b].

[100]Read Jeremiah's (ii. 1-3) tender references to this act of sublime faith.

soon as the midnight hour of freedom had sounded in Egypt on that historic night of Exodus, armed for their unknown destination only with faith as their weapon.

To convert the Jewish life into one long Divine service, three statutory prayers and many blessings have been prescribed for man to be said daily. When man communes with his Maker regularly and devoutly nothing can intervene between them.[101] Let man pray for mercy "*even when the sword is about to sever his head*" is the advice of another Rabbi.[102] Any man who abstains from adding his own prayers to those of another in misfortune brands himself a sinner.[103] One need not be hesitant in his approach to his Creator when his heart is broken. On the contrary, "*The Lord is nigh unto all them that call upon Him . . . . in truth*" (Ps. cxlv. 18).

The Midrash,[104] commenting on the words of Isaiah (lv. 8) "*For my thoughts are not your thoughts*", reflects: "*Whereas men spurn vessels that are cracked as possessing no more value, God takes especial delight in healing hearts that are broken and spirits that are torn with anguish; for 'the sacrifices of God are a broken spirit, a broken and a contrite heart, O God, Thou wilt not despise'*" (Ps. li. 19). The act of publicly appealing to God for help in trouble inspires the congregation to join in prayer and is thereby efficacious in itself from on High.[105] Not the *length* of prayer is the deciding issue but the devotion of heart and the concentration of mind (*Kavanah*).[106] Moses used *five* Hebrew words only when he asked God to remove the

[101]Sot. 38[b] for the figurative expression used by R. Joshua b. Levi.
[102]Ber. 10[a].
[103]Ibid. 12[b].
[104]Mid. Haggadol, xxxviii.
[105]Hull. 78[a].
[106]Ber. 5[b] ‏(אחד המרבה ואחד הממעיט ובלבד שיכון לבו לשמים)‏

stroke of leprosy which He had brought upon his sister Miriam as a punishment for slandering him.[107]

Prayer is not to be made into "*a fixed mechanical task, but an appeal for mercy and grace before the All-present*".[108] The correct attitude to be adopted is to have the hands and feet together at the side, as if to symbolize that without the help of Heaven man is helpless and tied. Such an attitude was to serve as an aid to achieve the purpose intended by the worshipper. The right mood will be introduced when we approach Him not in a spirit of levity and irreverence[109] but with the consciousness that prayer ushers us into His presence.[110] David, whose Psalms form the *matrix* of the prayers of a believing world, taught us the mood in which to pray when he sang: "*I have set the Lord always before me; surely, He is at my right hand, I shall not be moved*".[111]

The giving of charity is recommended by R. Eleazar[112] as helpful towards the right frame of mind for worship. It was David who exclaimed "*As for me, I shall behold Thy face in righteousness*" (*betzedek*).[113] Apart from these aids towards the prayerful attitude, the word *Tephillah* (literally "*judgment*") teaches us to approach God in a spirit of trusting resignation; only He knows what is good for us.

There are four kinds of prayer in our liturgy: Thanksgiving, Intercession, Praise and Confession. The Dedication Prayer of King Solomon[114] contains all four and was

---

[107]Num. xii. 13: אל נא רפא נא לה
[108]Abot ii. 18.
[109]Ber. 30[b].
[110]Sanhed. 22[a].
[111]Ps. xvi. 8.
[112]B. Bath, 10[a].
[113]Ps. xvii. 15, where the play is on the word בצדק. Charity must precede "*beholding Thy face in prayer*".
[114]I Kings viii. 12-53.

addressed to God on behalf of *all* who would ever come to the Temple to pray. For this reason, the Temple of Solomon was described by Isaiah (lvi. 7) as "*a House of prayer for all peoples*".

Prayer began to occupy its dominating position in Jewish life after the destruction of the Temple in the year 70 C.E. when R. Johanan b. Zakkai taught the people that the place formerly occupied by sacrifice was now taken by prayer. Yet so strong was the nostalgic yearning for the Temple and its sacrifices that the face of the Jew was always directed towards the East in prayer and his liturgy is studded with innumerable references to the priestly and sacrificial system. The synagogue, with its Women's Gallery (*Ezrat Nashim*) and its *Bimah* in the centre, was modelled on the Temple. The reason why no instrumental music is allowed at its services is a sign of mourning for the glory that once was that of Israel. Three services were instituted daily[115] to correspond with the belief that it was our first three patriarchs who instituted the morning, afternoon and evening services, respectively (תפלות אבות תקנום). Into these three services, the most important tenets of our faith were woven. The language was to be Hebrew, so as to provide a further strong link with a past which it was hoped to reproduce in a more glorious future.

Public prayer was considered more efficacious than that of individual worship because Jews must be united in their dispersal among the nations. *Tephillah Betzibbur* was more likely to foster this unity than prayer in the privacy of one's home. A common language of prayer, with little reference to the need of the individual, would help to link the bands of scattered Jewry. Subsequent Jewish history has proved how correct in their suppositions the formulators of our liturgy were.

[115]See Ps. lv. 17.

Fears that prayer means interfering with God's Providence are unfounded. Though the Rabbis taught that "*everything is foreseen*" and that "*no man bruises even a finger here below without it having been ordained in heaven*",[116] yet prayer can change the Divine Will if so it is deemed just by Him. R. Eleazar used to pray: "*Do Thy will in heaven above and give rest of spirit to those that fear Thee on earth, and do that which is just in thine eyes*".[117]

To pray *post eventum* for the reversal of something which has already happened is considered futile (*Tephillat Shav*); for it expresses a lack of faith in the judgment of God. The Rabbis tell the story of the young man who was overheard praying for the love of a young woman seemingly indifferent to his attentions. They reminded him: "*If she be destined in heaven to be your wife nothing on earth will make her part from you; if, however, she has been reserved for another, you deny Providence in praying for her*". In other words, "crying over spilt milk" is regarded as throwing tears away and an act of folly.

To express praise and thanks to God will help to mould that humble and grateful character desired by our ethical system. Our prayers are couched in the form of thanks and not merely as supplications for favours to come. Prayer moulds character. Apart from expressing the jewels of human thought, it is a manifestation of the harmony which should exist between that which is *human* and that which is *divine* in man. It is the "*half-way house*" where man *ascends* and God *descends*. It is the altar on which man lays his most intimate yearnings and from which the words to heaven go. For this reason, Judaism

---

[116]Hull. 7[b]: וְאִי אָדָם נוֹקֵף אֶצְבַּע מִלְמַטָּה, אֶלָּא א״כ מַכְרִיזִין עָלָיו מִלְמַעְלָה

[117]Ber. 16[b]. The "*Lord's Prayer*" has been proved by G. Friedlander in his "Jewish Sources of the Sermon of the Mount" to be reminiscent of the prayers current among the Jews at the time of the rise of the new creed.

demands that man should always pray. "*If thou canst not go to the House of Prayer, pray on thy couch. If thou art unable to frame words, then let thy heart meditate in silence.*" The English poet who sang:

> "He prayeth best who loveth best,
> All things both great and small.
> For the great God who loveth us,
> He made and loveth all,"[118]

summed up this Jewish approach to prayer beautifully.

Mention has been made that the Jew does not pray for himself alone. A typical example of this is told of the young woman, exceedingly beautiful in appearance, who prayed each night before retiring that her striking beauty be not a pitfall to young men and a source of unholy thoughts in their hearts. This is prayer *in excelsis*, expressing the ethics of prayer more forcibly than many a large volume dedicated to the subject.

The Jew is exhorted to pray for his foes, as well as for his friends, so that he win them over by his humanity rather than by his enmity. The advice given in the Book of Proverbs[119] is: "*If thine enemy be hungry, give him bread to eat; and if he be thirsty, give him water to drink; for thou wilt heap coals of fire upon his head, and the Lord will reward thee*". Had Shylock been a real Jew and not the figment of a very imaginative brain, his revenge on those who had wronged him would have taken the form of clemency and not of that travesty of justice—"*the pound of flesh*" without a drop of blood being shed in so doing. This is a caricature of Jewish life which, to this day, has been falsely represented as characteristically Jewish. If Shakespeare had mixed with Jews (which he could not have done in Elizabethan England), or if he

[118]Coleridge in the "Ancient Mariner".
[119]xxv. 21.

had had but an elementary knowledge of Judaism, he would have known that the Jew is forbidden to be elated even when his enemy is dejected. Moreover, to cut a limb from a living organism was forbidden even in pre-Torah days.

The angels at the Red Sea were silenced by God with the rebuke: "*What! Those whom I have created are drowning in the sea, and you dare to sing?*" (Meg. 10[b]). Moses prayed on Pharaoh's behalf for God to remove the plagues sent in punishment for the stubbornness of their despot. The Talmud denies Jewish ancestry to those who are not kind unto all. The Jew prays for *all* the children of God on earth. It is not the sinner that he wishes to see destroyed from earth but sin, as Beruriah, the scholarly wife of R. Meir pointed out.

The words of the *Amidah* for the Solemn Festivals adequately summarize our attitude towards those who hate us. We quote the paragraph in full.[120] "*Then shall the just also see and be glad; and the upright shall exult and the pious triumphantly rejoice. Then iniquity shall close her mouth, and all wickedness shall be wholly consumed like smoke, and the dominion of arrogance will pass away from the earth.*" Nowhere in this paragraph does it mention the disappearance of the *wicked;* for the removal of *arrogance* and *cruelty* do we pray. As long as the Temple stood, sacrifices were offered daily to atone for the sins of nations. Prayer ennobles character by teaching us to rely on the judgment of God of what is good for us. Yes, "*More things are wrought by prayer than this world dreams of.*" Judaism endorses this truth uttered by Lord Tennyson,

[120]Singer's Prayer Book, p. 239[a].

V. BRINGING OUT THE BEST IN US

As a spur towards mental perfection, man was created with two instincts—the good and the evil; but it will ever be to his glory if he allow his better nature to triumph.[121] As this duel will constantly be waged within him, man must be on his guard so that the evil instincts obtain not the mastery. "*For so artful is the Evil Inclination that to-day it will entice thee to do this and that, but on the morrow it will succeed in making thee worship idols.*"[122] "*Evil is very treacherous*", says another Rabbi, "*it may taste sweet at the outset, but how bitter is it at the end!*" It crowns this treachery by leading man into temptation on earth and is the first to testify against him in the World to Come.[123]

What should a man do to be able to defy the machinations of Satan? R. Johanan, quoting R. Banaah, answers: "*Israel is, indeed, fortunate. When they engage in Torah and good deeds, their evil instinct lies powerless in their hands; they are then the masters, not the slaves of their passions.*"[124] The Torah is the remedy which God created before He brought plagues into the world as a deterrent to wrong-doing.[125] Mastery over evil will add to our years; for it will exorcise anger from our system, a vice as dangerous as a malignant disease.[126] When R. Adda b. Ahabah was asked to what special merit he attributed his longevity, his reply was: "*I never allowed anger to possess me when I was at home with my family*".[127] A further sign of good breeding was the restraint exercised by a man in

[121]Ber. 61ª. לעולם ירגיז אדם יצר טוב על־יצר הרע
[122]Shabb. 105ᵇ; Nid. 13ᵇ.
[123]Sukk. 52ᵇ; B. Bath. 17ª: הוא שטן, הוא יצר הרע, הוא מלאך המות
[124]Ab. Zara 5ᵇ.
[125]B. Bath. 16ª. בראתי לי מכה, ובראתי לי תורה תבלין
[126]Ned. 22ª; Pes. 66ᵇ.
[127]Ta'anit 20ᵇ.

the face of the provocation of another. In ancient Judea, it was a firm belief that if one of the contestants maintained a dignified silence in answer to vituperation, his was the finer nature and the more distinguished origin.[128]

Man is seen at his noblest when he is at peace with himself and with others. The story is told in the Talmud[129] of the two men whom Elijah pointed out as worthy of the World to Come because they always strove to reconcile friends who had quarrelled. According to one medieval ethical writer, the ideal Jew is one who is shamefaced, modest, humble, gentle, courteous, peaceful and forgiving. He must not envy nor disparage any man but speak well of all; he must shun honours and not jest at serious things; he must not talk overmuch. He must be able to keep a secret, to possess a frugal mind and a grateful heart, to harbour no malicious joy, to consort only with true and faithful men and strive to form other men after his own pattern. Such a man can claim that he is the master of his fate and the captain of his soul.

Once he has subdued his baser instincts, man will not take vengeance or bear a grudge against another; he will realize that revenge lowers character, spelling a descent to those things one should hold in abhorrence. True blessing and strength lie in a readiness to forgive all who have sinned against him. Nothing compensates for that friendship which comes to man as a reward for turning strife into forbearance. His better nature will teach him that it is desirable to work *for* peace; to work *against* it, is to be detested.[130]

[128]Kidd. 70[b].
[129]Ta'an. 22[a].
[130]The Book of Proverbs is so full of this teaching that the reader is advised to study the *whole* book in this connection. It will well repay the time spent on this exercise. Cf. also Ex. xxiii. 4; Deut. xxxi. 35; Ps. xxxiv. 15; cxxxiii. 1; Job xxxi. 28-29; Eccl. vii. 8-9; ix. 17; B.K. 93[a]; B.M. 32[b]; Meg. 28[a].

The Rabbis insisted on this subjugation of the evil within us which *"crouches at the door"* and is ready to pounce upon us, like a beast in the jungle. To hate another is to possess one of the three vices that *"put a man out of the world"* (Abot ii. 16). The other two are, according to R. Joshua, *"the evil eye, and the evil inclination"*. The question and answer of a teacher in Abot d'R. Nathan is worthy of note: *"Who is mighty? He who turns the enemy into a friend."*

The man of virtue was one who, hearing shame cast upon him, never retaliated; who, being persecuted, never persecuted others; who accepted the outrageous treatment he received in a resigned and chastened spirit. Of him the Scriptures write that *"those who love Him, will be as strong and as glorious as the sun at the height of its strength"*. Which bird is more hunted than the gentle dove? Yet it is the only one of its kind that is acceptable as a sacrifice on the altar[131].

God loves three types of people: those who do not fall into easy paroxysms of rage; those who are not at any time the worse for drink and those who do not persist in exacting their revenge for wrong done to them. Three classes He hates: those who are insincere, saying one thing and meaning another; those who are able to act as a witness (and so help another in his trial), but who refuse to do so and him who, being the *only* witness of another's corruption persists in testifying against the sinner, knowing full well that it is only his evidence that can bring punishment on the culprit.[132]

Censure by a friend is more valuable than insincere flattery by a stranger. When R. Tarfon doubted if

[131]R. Abahu in B.K. 93a.
[132]Pes. 113b. Only *two* witnesses can condemn a man, but suspicion can be aroused by one witness.

anybody in his generation could take correction with grace, he was challenged by R. Eleazar b. Azariah with the question whether there be anybody of his generation who knew how to rebuke.[133] That is an art in itself. R. Hizkiah places the art of chastisement and the gift of reconciliation above all others; for whereas all other precepts in the Torah are to be performed only as occasion arises—such as chancing on a nest with the mother bird and the fledgling, or helping the ass of our enemy as it struggles under its heavy burden—the effort to establish peace among men must be a constant quest. Does it not say "*Seek peace and pursue it*" (Ps. xxxiv. 15); meaning seek it from thy place and pursue it even to another town?[134]

Only by being a lover of peace and possessed of a power to forgive will one earn the esteem of his fellows. Defamation of character, slander, scorn, ridicule and tale-bearing are deadly sins—the stock-in-trade of the flatterer, the hypocrite and the liar. "*He who carries evil reports from one to the other, though they be true, destroys the welfare of man*" is the view of one Palestinian sage.[135]

To be ethically-minded is to be pure in the eyes of God;[136] avoiding the slightest breath of suspicion[137] and being always pleasant[138] and respectful of another's views. In the words of *Derekh Eretz Zuta*—he must not be "*awake among those who sleep, or asleep among those who are awake; not weeping when others laugh, or vice versa; not sitting*

---

[133]Lev. R. ix.
[134]Lev. R. ix.
[135]Tal. Yerushalmi Peah i. Some other references are: Lev. xix. 16; Ex. xxiii. 1; Arakhin 16ᵃ; B. Metz. 58ᵇ; Ab. Zara 18ᵃ; Pes. 118ᵃ.
[136]Num. xxxii. 22.
[137]Hull. 44ᵇ: אמרו חכמים הרחק מן־הכעור ומן־הדומה לו
[138]Ket. 17ᵃ.

*when others stand, or vice versa; not learning aloud, when
others are reading quietly, or the reverse*". In general, he
will not be awkward or angular in the company of others.
He will be considerate of others. When the three angels
visited Abraham in his tent they ate and drank with
him, though it was not their custom so to do.[139] When
Moses ascended on high he did not eat for forty days and
nights, for such was the custom in heaven.[140]

Jewish ethics teach us to speak gently with all, be they of
our own faith, or of another;[141] assure us that a good
name is the best crown a man can wear[142] and fortify us
with the knowledge that our *own* actions will either
promote our station in life or degrade us in the eyes of
our fellow-men.[143] They teach us to shun that which is
sensual and profane by being *Kedoshim* (holy) in the
literal sense of the word—that is, *a part of* a noble mankind
but *apart from* a world addicted to base appetites and
passions.[144] Our safest guide in this holy quest will be
our codes with their standards of ethical purpose in
life's issues, with their minute precepts concerning every
action in order to spiritualize existence, with their
insistence on holiness in such human relationships as
marriage and business, and with their stress upon chastity.
R. Meir taught:[145] "*Keep thy mouth from sin and thy body
from wrong, and God will be with thee.*"

Peace and holiness will prolong life; anger and hatred
will undermine man's stability, leading him in extreme
cases to commit crime and murder. The character
moulded by social ethics will pray regularly and be on

---

[139]Gen. xviii. 8.

[140]Ex. xxxiv. 28.

[141]B. Metz. 87ª: לא כאלישע שדחפו לגחזי בשתי ידיו

[142]Abot iv. 17.

[143]Eduyot v. 6-7; Yoma 38ª: ומעשיך יקרבוך ומעשיך ירחקוך

[144]See *Sifra Lev R. Kedoshim* i.

[145]Ber. 17ª; Yoma 9ᵇ.

guard against those who distort truth for their own ends. The Talmud[146] records the advice which King Jannæus gave to his Queen Alexandra just before he died: "*Fear neither the Pharisees nor their opponents, but fear the hypocrites who pretend to be Pharisees and whose deeds are those of Zimri, but who claim the reward of Phinehas.*"[147]

R. Johanan quotes in the name of R. Simeon b. Johai:[148] "*Why has it been ordained that all our prayers should be recited from a low place (de profundis[149]) and in silence?*"[150] The answer is: not to put to shame those who have been guilty of transgression. The Torah differentiates between him who erred in ignorance and is required to bring a sin-offering (*hatath*), and him who sins deliberately and must seek atonement by means of a burnt-offering (*olah*) though both are called sinners. Such consideration is born of "*a love which covereth all transgressions*" (Proverbs x. 12) and which is capable of producing a nobility of character that will hide the infirmities of another and not gloat over them. The ideal man, says the Psalmist,[151] is one who "*hath hath no slander upon his tongue*", lest he causeth thereby a shedding of blood.[152]

Nor is the *actual* doing or speaking of evil needed to constitute a wrong. Often a look or a smile is enough. A sudden silence is, at times, more eloquent than speech; as if one should say "*I could a tale unfold, if I so wished*". Such insinuation is called by the Rabbis "*the fine dust of*

---

[146]Sot. 22b.
[147]A reference to Num. xxv. 14-15.
[148]Sotah 32b.
[149]Ps. cxxx. 1.
[150]A reference to the prayer of Hannah; 1 Sam. i. 13. cf. Ber. 31a.
[151]xv. 3. Called the "Gentleman's Psalm".
[152]Lev. xix. 16. לא תעמד על־דם רעך—the ethical meaning of this verse.

evil speaking" (*abak leshon hara*). God hates him who says one thing with his mouth, while he thinks another in his heart.[153] The Talmud attaches much importance to honesty in all things, especially in commerce and industry. Jerusalem was destroyed when honest men ceased to be therein.[154]

To help the shopkeeper to maintain scrupulous honesty, he is advised *"to wipe his measures twice a week,*[155] *his weights once a week, and his scales after each weighing"*.[156] When explaining Leviticus xix. 35 *"Ye shall do no unrighteousness in judgment, in meteyard, in weight, or in measure"*, it was taught:[157] *"in meteyard"* refers to the measurement of land. One may not measure equally for one in summer and for another in winter, for in summer the measuring-line is dry and contracted. The words *"in weight"* mean that he may not keep his weights in salt, so as to make his weights heavier; and *"in measure"* means that he may not make his liquid produce a foam. Does not the Torah expressly say *"A perfect and just weight shalt thou have; a perfect and just measure shalt thou have: that thy days may be long upon the land which the Lord thy God giveth thee"*?[158]

Our ethical literature abounds in stories describing the meticulous honesty of great men who shunned every form of deception, especially when the victim was a non-Jew.[159] The most famous being that of R. Shimeon b. Shetah who returned the gem found in the saddle of an ass he had bought from an Arab. This honesty caused the owner of the gem to praise the God of the Jew.

[153]Pes. 113[b].
[154]Shabb. 119[b].
[155]Bezah 29[a].
[156]B. Bath. v. 10.
[157]B. Metz. 61[b].
[158]Deut. xxv. 13-16.
[159]Hull. 94[a]; B. Bath 90[b]; Deut. R. iii. 3.

One of the most inspiring stories found in the Talmud[160] concerns Abba Umana whose profession was *"blood-cupping"* (*hakkazat dam*), an operation he conducted with the utmost modesty and generosity, refusing to take fees from the poor or the scholar. When Abaye heard the many praises sung of this humble man, he decided to test their validity for himself. What did he do? He sent him two of his disciples as patients without revealing who had sent them. Abba Umana received them most courteously, operated upon them, gave them food and drink and further insisted that they spend the night under his roof. Acting on the instructions of their teacher Abaye, they stripped their beds of the most costly rugs with which their host himself had covered them and offered them for sale in the market-place the next morning. To their surprise, none other than their former owner approached them as a would-be buyer. They were anxious to know whether he would expose them as thieves or, in order not to shame them in public, would silently buy the rugs.

Imagine their surprise when, though he recognized the rugs as his, he did not dispute the high sum demanded but gave the price asked for them. When the disciples refused to take such mean advantage of this saint's thoughtfulness, Abba Umana was adamant that they accept the sum offered. He explained that when he found the rugs missing, he did not at all suspect the two of being thieves but thought that they had taken the rugs in order to redeem with their great value those who had been taken captive and were being held up for ransom.[161] Besides, he continued, he could not possibly take back the money he

[160]Taan. 21[b].
[161]To redeem captives (*pidyon shevuyim*) was considered an act of saving souls (*Pikkuach nephesh*), before which all other commandments pale.

had offered them for the rugs as he had already dedicated their value to the Temple for holy purposes. When the disciples returned and told him the story, Abaye realized that here was a man of the finest calibre, the paragon of a life modelled on Jewish teachings.

CHAPTER TWELVE

PHYSICAL AND SPIRITUAL WELFARE

I. CARE OF THE BODY

IN maximizing spiritual welfare, Jewish ethical teachings do not seek to minimize bodily health. On the contrary, to neglect an enfeebled body is sinful. Take the rest ordained on the Shabbat. It has been commanded not to serve as an imposition and an additional restriction to the liberty of man, but as an opportunity for physical rest and the *re-creation* of the soul after six days of work. The object of Judaism is to guide us in the enjoyment of the gifts with which God has endowed us. To reject such legitimate gifts is to be guilty of an ingratitude for which man will have to give account on Judgment Day.[1] The Jew must not hate his body; he is in duty bound to preserve his health, not to jeopardize his life.[2] Foods that are injurious to health are to be avoided even more than those ritually forbidden.[3] This may well be another reason for our Dietary Laws.

The body must be kept pure and fresh, as the temple of the soul.[4] Our garments must be spotlessly clean.[5] He who castigates and tortures his flesh with fasting is a sinner.[6] Judaism places itself in complete variance with

[1] Yer. Kidd. iv. 66ᵈ.
[2] Ber. 32ᵇ, explaining Deut. iv. 9: רק השמר לך ושמר נפשך מאד
[3] Hull. 10ᵃ with its teaching that חמירא סכנתא מאיסורא; B. Kama 91ᵇ; Shabb. 82ᵃ.
[4] See the story told in Lev. R. xxxiv. 3 of Hillel who regarded the purification of his body as a sacred act.
[5] Shabb. 113ᵇ; Ned. 81ᵃ.
[6] Taan. 22ᵇ; Ned. 10ᵃ.

Hindu asceticism which encourages the flagellation and emaciation of the body as the seat of sin. The voice of Hillel is the voice of Jewish ethics. When he explained the meticulous care he paid to his physical welfare, he quoted this simile: "*See what care is bestowed upon the statues of the Emperor to keep them clean and bright. Ought we not, likewise, to keep His image, our body, containing the divine soul He breathed into us at birth, also pure, free from every blemish? Does not Scripture tell us that 'The merciful man doeth good to his own soul: but he that is cruel, troubleth his own flesh'* " (Prov. xi. 17).[7]

The Rabbis *practised* as well as *preached* cleanliness. They were emphatic that we are first to adorn ourselves before adorning others.[8] Only if we first ennoble ourselves can we contribute to the betterment of the world. If we are ourselves industrious, others will be inspired to act likewise. If we ourselves display parasitic tendencies, then harm is done to others as well as to ourselves.[9] Spiritual welfare is stressed because of the belief that a vicious soul will corrupt the body. Similarly, a diseased body cannot be the effective instrument through which a pure soul can function. Both body and soul are responsible for man's welfare.[10] Physical cleanliness leads to spiritual purity.[11] One should wash his hands, face and feet every day out of respect for his Maker.[12] No scholar should reside in a city in which there are no baths or other public conveniences,[13] described elsewhere[14] as the chief delights of man.[15]

---

[7] Lev. R. xxxiv. 3.
[8] See Sanhed. 18[a] for the familiar quotation:
קשוט עצמך, ואח״כ קשוט אחרים
[9] Ket. v. 5.
[10]Sanhed. 91[b].
[11]Ab. Zara 20[b].
[12]Shabb. 50[b].
[13]Sanhed. 17[b].
[14]Gitt. 68[a].
[15]Eccl. ii. 8.

Without physical purity, the mind will be unable to concentrate on the devotion necessary to prayer at the dawn of each day.[16] God takes pride in those who are of splendid physique[17]; hence those chosen to sit on the Sanhedrin had to possess twofold perfection—physical as well as moral.[18] Of Rabbi Hanina it was said,[19] that even when he was eighty years of age he was able to stand on one foot when tying up his shoe; and this because his mother cared for him well when he was young by frequently giving him warm baths and anointing his body with fine oil. No man should reside in a place where a doctor was not available; for he would be endangering life to no purpose.[20] It is the duty of the doctor to heal;[21] ours to be healed. To eat with unwashed hands is fraught with many dangers[22] and the vessel from which we eat and drink must be rinsed before and after it has been used.[23] Especially important is it to wash the hands when arising from sleep in the morning.[24] Moderation in food, as in all other physical pleasures, is the counsel of perfection.[25] Prevention is better than cure.[26]

This moderation is the outcome of self-conquest and self-control. Explaining the words of the Psalmist[27] *"There shall be no strange god in thee"*, the Rabbis said: *"No anger and passion, nor any evil desire or overbearing*

---

[16]Ber. 15[a].
[17]Bekh. 45[b].
[18]Sanhed. 17[a]: אין מעמידין בסנהדרין אלא בעלי קומה ובעלי חכמה
[19]Hull. 24[a].
[20]Sanhed. 17[b]. Though the passage speaks of a תלמיד חכם, yet it also refers to all. Each Jew should be a scholar of Torah.
[21]Ber. 60[a].
[22]Sotah 4[b].
[23]Tamid 27[b].
[24]Shabb. 108[b].
[25]Gitt. 70[a].
[26]Ned. 81[a].
[27]lxxxi. 10.

pride shall retain their mastery over thee. In braving temptation and overcoming sin, man asserts his godly origin." The ideal man is the one who, in self-mastery, can sacrifice himself in a great cause.[28] Such sacrifice means an assertion of divine life in the midst of death.[29] To desert life from selfish motives, to be what the Talmud styles a *me'abbed atzmo Leda'at* and commit suicide in the face of ordeal, is, according to Jewish standards, despicable. A man, though greatly to be pitied, forfeits his claim in the Hereafter if he sell his birthright of life to escape pain or disgrace. Has not the Torah warned us "*And surely your blood of your lives will I require; and at the hand of man, even at the hand of every man's brother, will I require the life of man*"? (Gen. ix. 5).

To take life deliberately is unpardonable and to endanger the life of another is heinous. Both acts mean the extinguishing of the lamp which God has kindled within us—the soul.[30] The accent put on hospitality and charity is to impress each man that he is held to be responsible for the welfare of the community.[31] Hospitality became an art. The guest must be welcomed to our home and, when he departs, one should not close the door behind the visitor before he has crossed the threshold. The host must in fact accompany him part of the way. How far?—was the question asked in the Babylonian schools. The Rabbis replied: "It all depends. If it be a teacher who was visited by his disciple, the former has to see him off till the outskirts of the city, and if it be a scholar who is visited by another scholar, he has to escort his visitor until he has walked two thousand cubits outside the boundaries of the city.[32] If it be a pupil seeing off his teacher no

[28]Abot iv. 1.
[29]B.K. 91[b].
[30]Shabbat 30[a].
[31]Sotah 38[b].
[32]Known in the Talmud as תחום שבת

limit is prescribed." It is an indication of the love for learning in Israel that the veneration for the teacher bordered almost on that in which God was held.

Judaism is insistent on physical welfare. Austerity on the one hand and hedonism on the other are matters for censure, both being injurious to bodily health.[33] No virtue is attached to poverty; on the contrary, "*where there is no food, there can be no Torah*".[34] Since a Jewish life is inconceivable without learning, the significance of this statement is apparent. Man is recommended to acquire three assets in order to enjoy life. These are: a good home, comfortable furniture and a virtuous wife.[35] Asceticism was discouraged because man sins when he spurns lawful pleasures created by God for human enjoyment. Merely to "*sit and fast*"[36] for the sake of bodily emaciation is to sin. Those mentioned in the Talmud as having practised asceticism are not exhibited as examples to follow, but as men whose lives were graphic denunciations of the luxury and materialism rampant in their day.

The sage who practised fasting during the day the year round, partaking of food only on those days when fasting was not allowed, could have had no other purpose in mind.[37] Of Rabbi Hanina b. Dosa—one of the saintliest figures in the Talmudic gallery—it is told that he was satisfied with one measure of carob-beans for his food from one Sabbath to another; though the whole world, on God's own evidence, was fed on account of the virtues

[33] Sot. 46[b].
[34] Abot iii. 21.
[35] Ber. 57[b]. A good mnemonic for these three prerequisites is אשה, standing for home—דירה, furniture—כלים, wife—אשה
cf. Ps. xc. 3: תשב אנוש עד־דכא ותאמר שובו בני אדם
[36] Taan. 11[a].
[37] Pes. 68[b].

of this godly man.[38] Judaism bids man to regard bodily
and mental welfare as two priceless possessions and to
shun excesses of all kinds. Man should make wise use of
the faculties with which God has endowed him and of
the joys provided for his happiness. He should understand
that the laws of the Torah place a check upon appetites
which lead to immoderate indulgence. To go beyond the
limits prescribed is to err to our own detriment.

The preservation of life is one of the main aims of our
legislation. Man can achieve this by heeding the wise
counsels offered by men who were past-masters at the art
of living. Here are a few of their observations. "The
world grows dark for him who has to depend on the
table of others; such a life is really not worth while."[39]
Could independence wish for a better advocate? "A man
takes greater delight in *one* measure of his own than in
nine belonging to his fellow-man."[40] Who does not recall
the advice placed into the mouth of the dove when, with
an olive-leaf in her beak, she returned from the flood
without to the safety of Noah's Ark?[41] "*Let my food be
bitter as an olive, O God, but dependent on Thee, than
sweet as honey, but dependent on the gifts of flesh and
blood.*"[42] "He who eats of his own bread is like the child
reared at his mother's breast."[43] "He who eats of the
bread of another fears to look at him.[44] "The mind is not
contented unless man eats of the fruit of his own
labour."[45]

[38]Ber. 17[b].
[39]Betz. 32[b].
[40]B. Metz. 38[a].
[41]Gen. viii. 11.
[42]A prayer so acceptable, that it has been incorporated, with
some slight changes, into the Grace After Meals; see Singer's
Prayer Book, p. 281.
[43]Abot d'R. Nathan xxxvii.
[44]Orlah i. 3.
[45]Shekalim iii. Cf. Hull. 7 of R. Pinhas b. Yair.

The Jew is to be grateful for the contributions made by others towards his welfare. How much labour, asks one Rabbi,[46] must Adam have expended before he could eat bread? The whole process from the sowing of corn to the baking is enumerated; now we find our loaf awaiting us at the breakfast table. What would the wealthy, or indeed any one, do without the menial tasks performed by the navvies and scavengers? The posing of such questions was considered barriers to class distinction.

Co-operation does not spell dependence on others; it means working together for the good of all. Each of us has been created for a specific purpose and an allotted task; it is folly, therefore, for the scholar to boast over his humble fellow-man whose work carries him into the field or workshop.[47] The Rip Van Winkle of the Talmud,[48] (*Honi Ha'meagel*) story taught that friendliness and companionship prevent existence from becoming a living death. Another Rabbi,[49] when explaining the verse of Ecclesiastes (iv. 9) that "*two are better than one*" issued this warning to his pupils: "*If you will lift the load, I will lift it too; but if you will not lift it, I will not do so either.*" In other words, "God helps those who help themselves".

Food being essential for physical health, many are the laws concerning meals. One is advised not to rush a meal, for to spend time at the table is to add length to our years.[50] A proverb current in ancient Judea was: "*He who eats luxuriously, will hide from his creditors in the attic; he who eats frugally, will not be afraid to sleep even in the high-*

---

[46]Ber. 58[a].
[47]Ibid. 17[a].
[48]Taan. 23[a]. The conclusion people arrived at from Honi's experience was: מיתותא או חברותא
[49]B.K. 92[b].
[50]Ber. 54[b]. It provides opportunity also for the poor to participate in the meal (*Roslin ad locum*).

road."[51] Woman is urged not to drink intoxicants at the table; though a sip or two may be beneficial, the more she indulges, the more immoral her actions may tend to become.[52] In refined circles in Jerusalem, none would sit down to a meal unless he first enquired who his fellow-guests were.[53] The meal was to be accompanied by words of Torah to save it from becoming a pagan ritual.[54] In the academy, the usual order of seating was a measure of scholarship; but at a meal, age would take precedence over learning, for at the table, the aged need more attention.

So condemnatory were our teachers of those who eat in the street,[55] that they were compared to a dog who is always hungry and even disqualified them to act as witnesses in a court of law. It is desirable to go suitably dressed and especially when sitting down to a meal,[56] a lesson derived by the School of Rabbi Yishmael from their explanation of "*And he shall take off his garments and put on others.*"[57] Appearances are very important, and man was advised to spend more on dress than on food. Such advice was considered unnecessary for woman; nature has seen to that. "Woman's armour which she carries about with her, is her beauty", of mind, as well as of body, if we are to be chivalrous.

Judaism is a religion of reality, teaching us to live and love and to enjoy what is ours *legitimately*. The sages do not curb their disdain of the man who, beholding a child drowning in the river, excuses himself from jumping in

---

[51]Pes. 114[a].

[52]The quotation in Ket. 65[a] is far more descriptive.

[53]Sanhed. 23[a].

[54]Abot iii. 4.

[55]Kidd. 40[b].

[56]Shabb. 114[a]. Spoken of the High Priest, who was not to appear in the Holy of Holies in the vestments in which he prepared the sacrifices.

[57]Lev. vi. 4.

on the plea that he was praying with the phylacteries on his head at the time.[58] Equally blameworthy is he who, seeing a woman drowning, refuses to save her because that would entail looking at her closely. Such a man is condemned as a *hasid shoteh*, an idiot who happens to be pious.

A man should not be so self-sacrificing as to throw his own life away to save another. The question once arose in the Schools as to the right course of conduct to be adopted if two travellers in the desert have only a little water between them with which to slake their thirst. Only if one drank the water would he be able to reach the nearest village; not if both shared the precious drops. What should they do? Let one drink himself and the other die? Or should they both sip and die? Rabbi Simeon b. Patura taught that it were better in such an emergency for *both* to die; for "Is the blood of one more red than that of his brother?" Rabbi Akiba said: "No! Let one only drink; for his *own* life comes *first*."[59] An ethical system which does not allow Shabbat and Yom Kippur, Kashrut or Leaven on Pesah, or any other precept to stand in the way of life, deserves to be in the forefront of creeds to which a believing humanity pin their trust.

II. SPIRITUAL WELL-BEING

To aid our spiritual advancement, we are asked to be kind to all created things, be they men or animals. From

[58]Sot. 21[b].
[59]B. Metz. 62[a]. Since the Torah says: "*So that thy brother may live with thee*", the meaning is that he is to live, not to die, before the other in such a contingency. He who drinks is the possessor of the water. The law is according to R. Akiba.

the Fourth Commandment it is clear that one of the objects of the Sabbath was to provide rest for the beast of burden.[60] Only he who has mercy on all created things is entitled to the mercy of God. Leaders in ancient Israel were chosen from those who exhibited tenderness towards the flock they tended; the argument being that such consideration was an earnest of the sympathy they would evince towards those whom they would have to lead. The appointment of Moses was due to such tenderness,[61] as was the call to prophecy of Amos and Micah and to Kingship of Saul and David; all were shepherds.

To be unkind to animals is to court suffering. Rabbi Judah Hannasi suffered great agony because he was inconsiderate to a calf that sought his protection as it was being led to the slaughter.[62] Not to alleviate their pain, is to break a command of the Torah.[63] From the Shema,[64] it is clear that one should not sit down to his own meal before giving food to the domestic animals under his protection.

This consideration towards animals is important not only because it is another precision tool in the carving of character but also because it expresses gratitude for their service. Had the Torah, which teaches us these virtues, not been given to us, says a teacher,[65] we would have learnt modesty from the cat; from the ant, industry and honesty; good manners from the cock and chastity from

[60]Ex. xx. 10.

[61]See the story about Moses and the straying lamb told in Ex. R. ii. 2.

[62]B. Metz. 85ª.

[63]Shabb. 128ª: צער בעלי חיים דאורייתא

[64]Deut. xi. 15. "*And I will give grass in thy fields for thy cattle, and thou shalt eat and be satisfied.*" Note the order of the words: first grass for the cattle then "*thou shalt eat*"; Ber. 40ª; Gitt. 62ª.

[65]Erub. 100ᵇ.

the dove. The slaughter of animals for food is to be as painless as possible.[66]

One of the methods to promote moral perfection is to display the folly and the futility of sin. The man who is prone easily to fall into one temptation after another is compared with the donkey that refuses to be led, only conceding when a child walks in front dangling a carrot. The man who refuses to be guided by the Torah and is tempted by sensuous pleasures, mostly of a questionable nature, and at their best only sufficient to gratify a few passions, manifests similar stupidity. If it be folly to sin, it is wise to take an active share in the weal and woe of communal life. Hillel taught[67] "*Separate not thyself from the congregation*". Another Talmudic sage urged that a scholar is in duty bound to make no communal need alien to him.[68]

Co-operation with others must not lapse into lordship over them; for that way lie worry and a shortened life. Why did Joseph die before his brothers though, next to Benjamin, he was the youngest of his family? asked a Rabbi. Because he took authority and prestige for himself, was the answer. Lordship and supremacy over others shortens one's days.[69] Collaboration with others is a virtue, but independence of spirit must never be sacrificed. Our moralists, to emphasize this, reflect that it is because the oil does not mix with other liquids, being ever intent

[66]See the writer's article on "Shehitah" in Vallentine's Jewish Encyclopædia, 1938. One reason why the blood of birds and wild beasts is covered after the *Shehitah*, is because one had no right to kill them for food if nothing was done to feed them whilst they were alive. In the case of domesticated animals, the blood was not covered after the *Shehitah*.

[67]Abot ii. 5.

[68]Moed Katon 6ª: נתמנה אדם על־הצבור ,כל־מילי דציבורא, עליה רמיא

[69]Ber. 58ª.

on successfully retaining its independence, that it was chosen for the anointment of priests and kings. Tolerance of others does not mean the suppression of one's own views and ideals.

III. FORGIVENESS

The hall-mark of character is to forget and forgive wrongs. Judaism teaches to view wrongs done to us as a punishment for sins; for the Divine law runs on the "measure for measure" principle. We should be the first to forgive those who sin against us; "*he who hath a forgiving spirit, is himself forgiven*";[70] accordingly, "*be you the first to be reconciled with those whom you have offended*".[71] One seals the *Amidah* prayer thrice daily with the imploration: "*O my God! guard my tongue from evil and my lips from speaking guile: and to such as curse me, let my soul be dumb; yea, let my soul be unto all as dust.*"[72]

Signs of spiritual well-being are: the pursuit of peace;[73] gentleness and conciliation in all dealings; forgoing, should necessity occasion, our own rights to avoid strife and dissension and an undespairing bid to bind others closer together in amity and concord. Judaism has no patience with a morality that is merely conventional, or with a righteousness that betrays its superficiality by being content to take its tone from the shifting conceptions of the world. The true Jew does not shun evil because he is afraid of the opinion people will hold of him, but because it is wrong to perpetrate misdeeds and cause hurt. He shrinks from it, even when it would involve him in no loss of reputation; that is, even when evil-doing is

[70]Yoma 23ª.
[71]Yoma 87ª.
[72]Singer's Prayer Book, p. 54.
[73]Vid. Ps. xxxiv. 14.

condoned by public opinion and general practice. He does not follow the majority for evil, but the minority who do good.

Forgiveness is urged, not only because it is human to err (for life provides many occasions for friction with those who move in our circle), but because grievances have a tendency to grow and become strong. To ensure complete reconciliation, two prerequisites are considered essential. The wrongdoer should express sorrow, and the one wronged should be ready to forgive. "*Never*", was the proud boast of a Rabbi,[74] "*did the curse of my fellow-man ascend my bed*"; he always succeeded in pacifying, before he retired to rest, any one whom he had offended during the day. Should one wrongly suspect another, he must at once seek to conciliate him; nay more, he must bless him.[75]

A man should be as soft as a reed when it comes to reconciliation, not hard as a cedar.[76] "*To forgive him who caused me distress*", was the prayer to God of many of our noblest characters. The Abot d'R. Nathan[77] has excellent advice on this subject: "*If you have done your fellow a little wrong, let it be in your eyes great; if you have done him much good, let it be in your eyes a little. If he has done you a little good, let it be in your eyes great; if he has done you a great wrong, let it be in your eyes little.*" The man who declines to forgive, transgresses an express command of the Torah.[78] He will receive the rod of chastisement,[79] because he has incurred Divine displeasure

---

[74] Meg. 28[a].

[75] Ber. 31[b], where Eli wrongly suspects Hannah of being drunk; on learning of her true condition, he dismisses her from his presence with a blessing on his lips.

[76] Taan. 20[b].

[77] xli; in the edition of Schechter.

[78] Lev. xix. 18.

[79] Yoma 23[a].

by preserving enmity and being glad when misfortune befalls another. If to forgive is God's *métier*, as Heine said on his death-bed,[80] how much more should it be the predominating characteristic of frail and impulsive man?

IV. REPENTANCE

Allied to this virtue of Forgiveness is the virtue of Repentance. God who has planted within man a *Yetzer Hara*, an Evil Inclination by which he is tempted to sin has, in justice, provided an antidote—*Teshuvah*—a *return* to the godly road. The Evil Inclination is both a barrier and a stepping-stone to perfection. Without this sense of divine forgiveness, an attribute of God which preceded Creation,[81] mankind would be overwhelmed by a sense of frustration which it would be unable to endure.

The Rabbis cap one another in their estimations of the efficacy of *Tshuvah*,[82] even claiming that sinners who have repented before death take precedence in Heaven over those who have never tasted sin.[83] The gates of Prayer are sometimes closed; those of Repentance are ever open. As the sea is always accessible, so is the Hand of the Holy One always ready to receive penitents.[84] "*Have I any pleasure at all that the wicked should die*"? pleads Ezekiel (xviii. 23) in the name of God. "*Is it not rather that he should return from his ways and live?*"[85]

Jewish ethics do not seek to *defend* human suffering.

[80]"*Dieu me pardonnera; c'est son metier*". "God will forgive me; this is His business".

[81]See Pes. 54ᵃ.

[82]Yoma 86ᵃ.

[83]Ber. 34ᵇ; Abot iv. 22.

[84]Deut. R. ii. 12.

[85]See the whole of this remarkable chapter, the ideas of which have been incorporated in our Yom Kippur Amidah for Neilah.

They try to *explain* it as a gateway to repentance, paving the way to nobility of character and a philosophical outlook. Suffering, especially when it results in death, is a sure sign that God has forgiven the sinner,[86] a thought that colours the confession on a death-bed.[87] During Temple times, a sacrifice accompanied the confession (*vidui*) of guilt; since its destruction, prayer occupied the place of the animal-offering. A stipulation was made that prayerful repentance *alone* will not suffice, unless it is accompanied by a complete change of conduct. *"Only he who is filled with shame at a wrong committed, not perpetrating it again in similar circumstances, will have his sins forgiven."*[88] The best advocates (*saneigorim*) before the Heavenly Throne are Repentance and Good Deeds.[89] These, combined with Charity, form a *trinity* of virtues before which no evil decree can stand.[90]

Is it sometimes too late to ask God's forgiveness, the breaking heart may ask? Never, replies Judaism with a myriad voices. *"Even if one has been wicked all his life, but repents at the end, he will be forgiven."*[91] When Rabbi Eleazar made the cryptic remark[92] that *"one should repent one day before his death"*, he meant two things. One: man should not leave his repentance to the last minute, lest he may be unable to collect his thoughts before the end. Two: since life is crowded with uncertainties—the only certainty being its end at a time unknown—it behoves him to regard each day as the one before his last and to repent.

---

[86] Sanhed. vi. 2.
[87] Singer's Prayer Book, p. 317.
[88] Ber. 12[b]; Yoma viii. 9.
[89] Shabb. 32[a]; Abot iv. 13.
[90] Gen. R. xliv. 12. Cf. the phrase in our liturgy for the *Yamim Noraim:* ותשובה ותפלה וצדקה מעבירין את רע הגזרה
[91] Kidd. 40[b].
[92] Shabb. 153[a].

The proneness of man to sin is occasioned by the nature
of his composition—being half angel, half animal. In
three things, wisdom, upright walk and a knowledge of
Hebrew—he resembles an angel. In three other things—
eating and drinking, reproduction and the functioning of
his body, he is comparable to an animal.[93] True, "*there
is not a righteous man upon earth, that doeth good, and
sinneth not*";[94] nevertheless, to sin is to revolt against the
express wish of God, as revealed in the Torah. The evil
in man should be checked before it gets the mastery.
Once a sin is repeated often, it comes gradually to be
regarded as permissible.[95] Temptation of all kinds,
obscenity of language, selfishness, dishonesty, are so
many pitfalls that fling us headlong into sin. To avoid
them is the counsel of Jewish ethics. "*It is not the mouse
that is the thief, but the hole.*"[96]

Idleness being a conspirator of vice,[97] the Jew is asked
to keep his mind occupied with wholesome thoughts and
his hands engaged in toil. "*An excellent thing is the study
of Torah combined with some worldly occupation,*" taught
Rabban Gamaliel, the son of Rabbi Judah Hannasi;[98]
"*for the labour demanded by them both makes sin to be
forgotten. All study of the Torah without work must in the
end be futile and become the cause of sin.*" Torah and
Derekh Eretz are the best defences against the Evil
Inclination, a force described by the Rabbis as the
fermenting ingredient[99] that stirs up the baser elements
in man's nature and results in sin. It must be overruled by
the finer instinct (*Yetzer tov*) which should always battle

---

[93]Hag. 16[a].
[94]Eccl. vii. 20.
[95]Yoma 86[a]: כיון שדש בה נעשה כהותרה
[96]Gitt. 45[a]: לאו עכברא גנב ,אלא חורא גנב
[97]Sot. 3[a]: אין אדם חוטא ,אלא א״כ רוח שטות נכנסה בו
[98]Abot ii. 2.
[99]Sin is the שעור שבעיסה—"the leaven in the dough".

against its evil companion, the *Yetser Ra* Man has the freedom to choose the noble.[100]

V. STUDY AS ANTIDOTE TO SIN

The Rabbis would have been the first to deny that *they* were the originators of the Jewish design for living. All they would claim would be that they were excavators in the inexhaustible mine of the Torah, bringing to light the treasures hidden beneath the surface. It was their incessant study of the Bible that fired their minds with those deathless utterances recorded in the Midrash and Talmud. Characteristic of the Jewish passion for learning are the songs and lullabies with which former Jewish mothers in Israel used to sing their babies in the cradles to sleep, in which the hope was expressed that the child (if it were a boy) would choose the study of the Torah as his main occupation in life. ("Torah iz die beste *Sehorah; Mein Kind vet lernen Torah.*")

Such devoted study of the Bible made the Rabbis teach that "*Each man should always consider himself poised equally between guilt and innocence. If he does a good deed, happy is he; he has weighed down the scale of merit; if, on the other hand, he commits a sin, he has made the scale of guilt heavier in the balance.*" Did not Ecclesiastes (ix. 18) warn that "*one sinner destroyeth much good*"?[101] Let man try to do good and he will be helped from heaven;[102] for in the way a man chooses to walk, will he be guided.[103] Despite the teachings of Providence and of Predetermina-

[100]Ber. 33[b].
[101]Kidd. 40[a]: יראה אדם עצמו כאילו חצי חייב וחצי זכאי
[102]Shabb. 104[a].
[103]Makk. 10[b].

tion, the will of man is unfettered; his is the choice to do good, or to misuse his opportunities. If he falls low, so that the nature of his life be moulded by his desires, the responsibility is his, and his alone. Man will not be able to escape punishment *in public* for a sin committed *in secret*, was the *caveat* of Rabbi Meir;[104] he will soon painfully discover that sin simply does not pay.[105] On the other hand, should man wish to do a good deed but be prevented through no fault of his own, it will be accounted unto him as if he had performed it.[106] God alone knows the secret intentions of our heart.

The Creator expended much ingenuity when He formed man, taking care to see that none be exactly like another in looks, opinion, or in the *timbre* of his voice,[107] but He left the moulding of our moral welfare to ourselves. The Midrash records that:[108] *"Everything created by God needs perfection. Mustard and lupins need sweetening; wheat needs grinding at the mill for flour; so does man need the Torah-process of perfection."* This wisdom to live *"the good life"* will not always be found in youth, *"for counsel is not among infants"*.[109] With advancing years will come experience. "If old people advise you to destroy and youth counsels to the contrary, follow the advice of the elders; for the destruction they suggest may be the means of a fresh start in your life; whereas the building programme of youth may result, in the long run, in ruination."[110] Accordingly, let not youth be impetuous,

---

[104]Sot. 3[a].

[105]Shebiit ix: אין החוטא נשכר

[106]Kidd. 40[a]. Though Abraham was finally prevented from sacrificing Isaac, yet he was told *"because thou hast done this thing, and hast not withheld thy son, thine only son"* (Gen. xxii. 16).

[107]Rabbi Meir's statement in Sanhed. 38[a].

[108]Gen. R. xi.

[109]Shabb. 89[b]: ולא בדרדקי עצה

[110]Meg. 31[b]; 40[a]: סתירת זקנים בנין ,ובנין נערים סתירה

acting as the cynic in Oscar Wilde's play, "*who knows the price of everything, but the value of nothing*". "*The bad things a man does in his youth will bring the blush of shame to his cheeks when he is old.*"[111] Above all, let youth avoid immorality; for nothing ages man more,[112] dulling his finer instincts and carrying greater punishment than for any other crime. "*For seven causes do plagues occur: slander, bloodshed, swearing in vain, immorality, pride, robbery and envy*", declares a Talmudic sage.[113]

Let not man be dismayed when he sees the righteous suffer and the wicked prosper. The place for Reward and Punishment will be in the World to Come;[114] secondly, no man is so perfect that he does not deserve punishment for an evil he has once done. Equally, no man is so hopelessly corrupt as not to have done some good for which he deserves compensation. How are we to judge—we whose outlook is often blurred, whose mentality is at times jaundiced—as to who is righteous and who is wicked? Nittai, the Arbelite,[115] advises us not to abandon the belief in Retribution as long as we live. The thoughts of God are not as our thoughts; He does not judge man with the eyes of human beings. Man should do good "*for goodness' sake*", following the advice of Antigonos, of Socho,[116] that is, doing good, not for the thought of reward, but because we are impregnated with the "*fear of heaven*".

Spiritual welfare is a by-product of love and of consideration for all. It is born of a minimizing of the good done *for* another and a maximizing of the good done *by*

[111]Shabb. 152[a].
[112]Ibid.
[113]Arakhin 16[a].
[114]The Talmudic teaching being—היום לעשותם ומחר לקבל שכרם (Erub. 22[a]).
[115]Abot i. 7.
[116]Ibid. i. 3.

another.[117] It will express itself in altruistic friendship, ever ready to be the first to greet others[118] and regarding the honour of another as equivalent to one's own.[119] Rabbi Johanan b. Zakkai was always the first to greet a person, be he a non-Jew;[120] to be polite to others is equivalent to being polite to the *Shechinah*.[121]

If one has nothing to offer a poor man save courtesy and a smiling face, it is good enough; life has shown these things to be worth more than treasure.[122] Nothing is more injurious to moral well-being than to hate another inwardly,[123] and to take vengeance is a boomerang; for both suffer. If we are to love another as ourselves, the logical inference is that to hurt another, for wrong done to us, is like cutting off our right hand because it has injured our left.[124]

This love need not be spineless. A love which never has a word of rebuke for another is not real love but sycophancy.[125] Friendship is like looking into a mirror; the glass returns the look we bring to it, be it a smile or a frown. As we sow, we reap, and as we love so shall we be loved. The company in which we mix is indicative of our moral character, for "every raven goes to its own kind" (Lev. xi. 15). The Midrash to Proverbs xiii. 20 ("*He that walketh with wise men shall be wise; but the companion of fools shall smart for it*") gives this simile. "It can be compared to one who enters a tannery; though he purchase nothing, his clothes will carry about with

[117]*Derekh Eretz Zuta;* Abot d'R. Nathan, *passim.*
[118]Abot iv. 20.
[119]Ibid. 15.
[120]Ber. 17a.
[121]Erubin.
[122]Abot d'R. Nathan.
[123]Lev. xix. 17; Arakhin 16a.
[124]A striking thought of the Yerushalmi Ned. ix.
[125]Gen. R. liv. 3: כל אהבה שאין עמה תוכחה אינה אהבה

him the whole day the rank smell of that place." The Talmud has this striking thought: "Consort with a fat man, and you become fat".[126] To choose good friends is to go on the right road to ideal living;[127] but to consort with evil-doers is fatal. The warning against bad companionship should be heeded since the good is often punished with the bad.[128]

Though "*man can take nothing away with him and his glory not descend after him*" (Psalm xlix. 18), we are not on this account to lead abstemious lives of self-negation. In the name of Rav, it was taught that man will have to give an account in the World to Come for all the things spurned which were his here below to enjoy.[129] One who abstains from lawful pleasures immoderately,[130] violates the command of *bal tashchit*,[131] of destroying something useful and is a sinner. Man should strive after holiness, but not through *extreme* means. Physical well-being will not be stimulated for lasting good by rigorous treatment of the frail body.

When the Rabbis discussed aids to longevity, asceticism was never mentioned. Rabbi Nehunya was once asked to what he attributed his ripe old age, and he replied: "*Because I have always zealously guarded the honour of another. I have never received gifts or insisted on my rights even if they were just; and I have always been*

---

[126] קרב לגבי דהינא ואידהן. To touch a man smeared with oil is to become greasy. The moral application needs no stressing.

[127] B. Kama 92[b].

[128] The Aramaic phrase is בהדי הוצא, לקיא כרבא—"In removing the fence, some plants are also destroyed"; B. Kam. 92[a].

[129] Yer. Kidd. iv.

[130] Num. vi. 11; Ned. 10[a] (in the case of the Nazir who at the expiration of his thirty days' vow to abstain from wine and the cutting of his hair, had to bring a sin-offering.

[131] The reference is to Deut. xx. 19-20. In the case of the Nazir, he is destroying his health (בל תשחית דגוף). Cf. Shabb. 129 for a discussion on this point, where it is ruled that to destroy the body (גוף) is more serious than to waste money (בל תשחית דממונא)

generous with my money." Rabbi Zera, when the same question was put to him, replied that he never allowed anger to overcome him when at home with his family; that he never took pride of place before somebody greater than he, that he was never elated when another was dejected, nor dejected when another was elated, and that he never was disrespectfully intimate with another so as to call him by his nickname. To have done so would have been, in his estimation, frivolous and offensive.[132]

Gratitude for what others have done was indicative of the health of the soul. The Rabbis expressed this in a proverb: "*Into the well from which you have drunk, throw no stones*".[133] Does not Scripture tell us not to despise the Egyptian "*because thou wast a stranger in his land*"?[134] It is imperative that we ourselves do not suffer from the defects of which we complain in another.[135] We must take care to speak about a thing only when we know it for *certain;* at no time must we repeat anything about another, especially if it be derogatory to him and of which the truth is doubtful.[136]

VI. TRAINING THE YOUNG

The purpose of all democratic social legislation is to increase the power of the ideal to the end that it may become the dominant force in life. The Jewish design for living regards faith as a medium for the enjoyment of fellowship with God, as well as an aid in the development of what is purest and highest in human nature—moral

[132]Meg. 27[b]-28[a].
[133]B.K. 92[b]: בירא דשתית מיניה, לא תשדי ביה קלא
[134]Deut. xxiii. 8.
[135]B. Metz. 107[b]; B. B. 60[b]: ר' נתן אמר: מום שבך, אל־תאמר לחברך
—Is it not ridiculous when the pot calls the kettle black?
[136]Yeb. 65[b].

welfare. Parents and teachers have a tremendous responsibility to teach this view of life to the younger
generation. A people not sure of its posterity is in danger
of losing its glorious ancestry. The ideal to be aimed at
is to make our youth worthy members of society and to
forge them into secure links in the chain of continuity.
Our religious and cultural heritage, bequeathed to us
unsullied by preceding generations, must be transmitted,
in turn, unimpaired to the generations that will follow.

The survival of our people depends on such a diffusion
of knowledge.[137] It was only when Israel speaks un-
haltingly with *"the voice of Jacob"* according to Torah
principles, that it will survive the machinations of *"the
hands of Esau"* and the persecutions of a hostile world
bent on its destruction. The child must be taught that
religious knowledge is all-powerful and all-embracing,
that *"if thou lackest knowledge, thou lackest everything;
but if thou possessest knowledge, thou wilt not feel the lack
of anything"*.[138] So earnestly did one sage take this
parental duty that he is reported not to have eaten his
breakfast before he had taken his child to school.[139]
Another was of the opinion that Jerusalem was destroyed
because parents neglected to send their children to
school.[140] These schools were established for children
from the age of six or seven years upwards by Rabbi
Joshua b. Gamla, whose memory on this account is
recalled in the Talmud with a blessing.[141]

---

[137]See Shabb. 119[b].
[138]Lev. R. i. 6: ‫דעה קנית, מה חסרת? דעה חסרת, מה קנית?‬. Another
interpretation of these words may be this: "When you have
knowledge, then you know what you lack".
[139]Kidd. 30[a]; B. Metz. 85[a].
[140]Shabb. 119[b].
[141]B. Bath 21[a]. For the most interesting method used in the
Babylonian *"Kindergartens"*, see Shabb. 104[a], where we are
told how the alphabet was taught. Cf. also "The Jewish
School", by Dr. N. Morris.

Little differentiation was originally made between the education offered to a boy or a girl, except that women were discouraged from what was known as *"higher learning"*. It was feared that adolescent co-education might lead to promiscuity and laxity, as indeed did happen in the schools of Greece and Rome. Anxiety went further; so absorbed would women become in study, that they might tend to neglect the fulfilment of the first precept of the Torah—marriage. Not an imaginary fear in view of the encouragement of women by Catholicism to become nuns.

A Mishnaic teacher[142] has some uncomplimentary views regarding those *"female Pharisees"* who practise excessive piety at the expense of wifely and motherly duties. The syllabus for boys and girls was otherwise essentially the same; the aim being to endow them with the characteristic features of the Jewish life—piety and chastity, modesty and decency in all things. They were taught that the religion of others must be respected and that though Judaism does not claim to be the *only* repository of the noble life, it does consider itself the most perfect expression of the godly existence on earth.

Only idolatry, with its concomitants of cruelty and immorality, was condemned. Those who are sincere in their beliefs and whose conduct is noble, will be equal heirs in the Life Hereafter.[143] The *Yalkut*[144] puts into the mouth of God these words: *"Heaven and earth I call as witnesses that every one, be he Jew or Gentile, male or female, slave or free, partaketh of the Divine Spirit, provided his deeds do not run counter to his creed."* In his *Mishneh Torah*, Maimonides gives the opinion—an opinion whose breadth of vision singles it out as outstanding even now—

[142]Sot. iii. 4.
[143]Sanhed. 94ª; B.K. 38ª.
[144]On Judges ch. xlii.

that both Christianity and Mohammedanism help towards the perfection of mankind. When the Messiah comes, all will return from their errors and say to one another: "*Come ye, and let us go up to the mountain of the Lord, to the house of the God of Jacob; and he will teach us of His ways, and we will walk in His paths.*"[145]

In those ancient Babylonian schools, the young were taught that life must be led communally-minded and that no man can be a law unto himself. There must be a *temporal* authority to legislate in all civil matters, to rebel against which is to be guilty of an offence deserving death.[146] The civil laws of a State, provided these do not militate against the basic teachings of the Torah, must be respected.[147] To be loyal citizens has been considered a duty since Jeremiah (xxix. 7) first taught: "*And seek the peace of the city whither I have caused you to be carried away captive, and pray unto the Lord for it; for in the peace thereof shall ye have peace.*" The prayer for the Royal Family[148] still forms a salient feature of our public services on Sabbaths and Festivals. Especially was the child taught that he must not separate himself from any communal effort, for the welfare of *all* should be the concern of each.

Characteristic teachings of our ethical codes are: that "*all Israel are responsible one for another*"; that only "*he who mourns for Zion with the community, will one day witness its rebuilding*". The pupil was taught not to chase glory and crave lordship over others; for these ambitions bury those eager for such things.[149] Joseph died before his elder brothers because the title "*Viceroy of Egypt*" was his.[150] "*Be rather a tail to lions than a head to foxes*", was

[145]Isa. ii. 3.
[146]Sanhed. 49ª.
[147]B.K. 113ª: דינא דמלכותא דינא
[148]Singer's Prayer Book, p. 153.
[149]Yoma 86ᵇ.
[150]Ber. 55ª.

the advice given to his disciples by Rabbi Mattithyah, the son of Cheresh.[151]

Reluctance to assume authority was never intended as an excuse to shirk the responsibilities of office, but as a deterrent against an eagerness motivated by selfish ambition. On the contrary, wherever work had to be done for the community it could not be shelved but had to be performed selflessly, without self-assertiveness. It was imperative to take up a cause if it were neglected by others;[152] for "*in a place where there are no men, strive to be a man*".[153] Such principles, woven into everyday life, lead to brotherhood and international peace—the lodestars of Jewish ethics—and causes for which Jews, in common with others of goodwill and noble repute, must work for without end.

The child was to be taught respect for his parents. The fifth Commandment occupies in the Decalogue a position mid-way between the duties man owes to his Maker and those he owes to his fellow-man and is significant of its paramount importance. It follows immediately the injunction to observe the *Shabbat* perhaps to stress that on this day there is no valid excuse for parents not to interest themselves in the lives and education of their children on the plea that they are too busily preoccupied in their several tasks. For on the Sabbath, man does not go forth "*unto his work and to his labour until the evening*".[154] Affinity of interests between parent and child on educational subjects and communal efforts, on ideals and daily topics, will inspire filial obedience, love and respect. Based on such foundations, filial love will outlive the passing of the parent. This filial respect, which can

[151]Abot iv. 20.
[152]Ber. 63ª.
[153]Abot ii. 6.
[154]Ps. civ. 23.

only be disregarded when the child would break a law of the Torah in the fulfilment of his parents' behest, should remind the parent that he was responsible for the religious training of the child.

The *only* teachers of children mentioned in the Bible are parents. "*And thou shalt teach them diligently to thy children*" (Shema); "*Thou shalt tell it to thy son*";[155] and "*Hearken, my son, to the instruction of thy father; and abandon not the teaching of thy mother*".[156] The professional teacher was a product of economic stress when parents no longer had the time to look after this duty themselves. At the best, he was only a substitute for the parent. Only when the parent has succeeded in equipping the child with a sound Jewish education leading to nobility of action, is the parental task discharged. This education must commence as soon as the child can speak "*in order to introduce him to a performance of Mitzvot*". The first three years were to be devoted to building up the body of the child; after that, the needs of his mind must also be catered for.

Jewish ethics is seen at its height in the perfect relationship between parent and child. Whereas among the early contemporaries of Israel, the father had *absolute* right to dispose of his child, Jewish law recognized the inalienable prerogative of children as persons. Only in the case of minors not able to look after themselves, was the father given unquestioned authority; but even then was it qualified and restricted. The right to inflict punishment on children was less an expression of arbitrary authority than a means of instruction; for "*he who spares the rod, spoils the child*". Parents were warned to lead good lives themselves, physically and spiritually, for "*the iniquity of the fathers is visited upon the children, upon the third and*

[155]Ex. xiii. 8.
[156]Prov. i. 8.

upon the fourth generation of them that hate me".[157] The best guarantee that their children would remain loyal to their ancestral tradition was to teach them by personal example.

No difference was made between the respect due to the father and the mother; both must be *equal* sharers of the affection and regard of the child. The last charge Rabbi Judah Hannasi made on his death-bed to his sons was: "*Be careful of the honour due to your mother. Let the lamp be in its place and the table set as usual.*"[158] The tenderness shown by Rabbi Tarfon to his mother is touching.[159] The Talmud bestows high praise on a heathen youth of Ashkelon for the respect he paid to his father, refusing to sell a Red Heifer for a fabulous sum because he did not wish to disturb his parent when asleep. When he later attained exalted office, he remained respectful towards his parents, often under the most trying circumstances.

A special section in our Codes is reserved for the laws governing this parental and filial relationship.[160] The first Book of the Torah puts the emphasis on home life; its fifty chapters providing intimate glimpses into the family life of our Patriarchs. As a result of this emphasis on home environment, cases of unfilial conduct, disturbed home life and juvenile delinquency are comparatively rare among Jewish communities.

The Jew is constantly reminded that "*God dwells in a pure and loving home; and that marriages are arranged in heaven forty days before a child is born*".[161] Our religious ceremonial was so designed as to constitute a bulwark of

---

[157]Second Commandment of the Decalogue; Ex. xx. 5.

[158]Ket. 103[b].

[159]Kidd. 31[b]. He would rise to his feet at her approach, and remain standing in her presence.

[160]See the הלכות כבוד אב ואם in the Yoreh Deah.

[161]Shabb. 22[a].

the Jewish spirit, cemented by the love and respect between parent and child. No excellency in any other direction can compensate for the lack of this ideal relationship. The Jew best honours God by honouring his parents; and a good way of showing reverence for the teachings of the Synagogue is to honour the sanctity of the home.

The parent who is wise will follow the example of Rabbi Nehorai who taught that the most profitable thing to teach a child is the Torah; because whereas other professions will not be of much help to him when he becomes old and weak, the Torah alone will be his support and his hope right down to old age.[162] *"Unless Thy Law had been my delight, I should have perished in my affliction. I will never forget Thy precepts; for with them Thou hast quickened me"* (Ps. cxix. 92-93).

Next to the respect due to parent and home, the child was taught to respect his teacher, the school-house and the Synagogue; they being responsible for the fostering of his Jewish consciousness. The Rabbis vied with each other in stressing the importance of attending regularly the House of Prayer and the House of Learning. *"No one has ever come before me into the Beth Hamidrash; neither has any one left before me"*, was the proud claim of one scholar. Not to be outdone, another sage assured his disciples that *"he who goes from the synagogue to the school to study Torah will merit one day to be received in the Presence of God"*. He will go *"from strength to strength"*. Tradition demands that a Jew live in proximity to a synagogue, so that regular attendance may help to colour his life. To live in a place without a house of prayer is forbidden. As an incentive, long life was promised to him who comes early and stays late in its holy precincts.[163]

[162]Kidd. 31[b].
[163]Ber. 8[a].

Who will gainsay that the teaching of such a syllabus by parents in the home and by teachers in the school—teachings complemented by the example and integrity of those who taught them—left an indelible impression? In the ears of the teachers of Israel there rang the assurance of Isaiah that only when "*all thy children shall be learned of the Lord, shall the peace of thy children be great*".[164]

[164]liv. 13.

CHAPTER THIRTEEN

A RETROSPECTIVE SURVEY

THE thesis we have tried to develop in this book is that Jewish ethics are indissolubly linked with a fervent belief in God—the essence of whose virtues we are asked to possess ourselves. It is significant that the six chapters of *Abot* (Sayings of the Fathers), should begin with the words: "*Moses received the Torah*[1] *on Sinai, and handed it down to Joshua: Joshua to the elders: the elders to the prophets: and the prophets handed it down to the men of the Great Synagogue.*"[2] Why? To impress upon the Jew that his system of moral and ethical regulations bears the same impress of Divine authority as the Torah received on Mount Sinai. Though Judaism is essentially a religion which stresses "*good deeds*", the Torah is insistent that the motives propelling action should be equally noble. No fewer than *six* of the Ten Commandments deal with social ethics.

When we spoke of the ethical background of the *Halachah*,[3] an endeavour was made to show that it flows

---

[1] Left untranslated in this book. It is variously used for the Pentateuch, the whole of the Bible, the Talmud, as well as for the entire body of religious truth, study and practice.

[2] Singer's Prayer Book, p. 184; Hertz's Prayer Book, p. 614. The *Great Synagogue*, or "*the Great Assembly*" was instituted by Ezra and consisted of Prophets, Scribes, Sages and Teachers. They continued the spiritual regeneration of Israel begun by their great founder, laid the foundations of the Liturgy, edited several Books of the Bible and "restored the crown of the Torah to its pristine splendour".

[3] Chap. iv. *supra*.

from the same stream as the Torah; that behind the Rabbinic *façade* of interminable legal *minutiæ* was the urge to teach that the full Jewish life will not be led unless ethical theorizing is exchanged for concrete practice. When our ancestors were thrilled into a ready acceptance of the Torah, their instantaneous reaction was "*We shall do and we shall understand*".[4] This truer translation is apt to be misunderstood. What they intended to imply was this: "We promise to make our religion one of belief and action". To translate that promise into deed, the Sidra of *Yithro*,[5] containing the Decalogue, is immediately followed by *Mishpatim*,[6] with its summary of some of the most essential laws of the Mosaic legislation.

The "*Duties of the Heart*" are essential; but these must not lead to a paralysis of the limbs of the body, to each of which has been allotted some act of service. "*All my bones shall declare: 'O Lord, who is like unto Thee?'*"[7] Oxygen is administered only to the patient too ill and weak to breathe normally. Similarly, a mere protestation of ethical-mindedness can be no excuse for nonconformity to traditional practice. It is an admission of an anæmia of the intellect when one seeks to brush aside custom and observance before vague theological idealism.

I. PRACTICAL ETHICS

In this blending of *creed* and *deed* is the genius of Judaism seen at its best. To take one example. What other Statute-Book, ancient or modern, has tabled such a law as "*Thou shalt not covet*",[8] implying that one can wrong

[4] Ex. xxiv. 7: נעשה ונשמע
[5] Ibid. xviii–xx.
[6] Ibid. xxi–xxiv.
[7] Singer's Prayer Book, p. 126 (*Nishmat*).
[8] Ibid. xx. 17; Deut. v. 18.

a neighbour in the heart no less than by bodily injury? The many laws[9] *"not to hate our brother in our heart"; not to curse the deaf"; "not to place stumbling-blocks before the blind";* not to take a mean advantage of the ignorance of another, end with the stern reminder *"I am the Lord, thy God".* The deaf and the blind may be unaware of our malicious intention, but He who knoweth all, will in due course exact severe punishment for such double-dealing.

A medieval teacher summed up this stress on sincerity of intention and action succinctly when he explained the verse: *"And the Angel of the Lord appeared unto him (Moses) in a flame of fire out of the midst of a bush".*[10] The two Hebrew words for *"in a flame of fire"* are *Belabbat aish,* implying that God wishes us to perform all our duties as His witnesses sincerely and eagerly, with a heart (*lev*) aflame for righteousness. To illustrate this thought, take the conspicuous part allotted to charitable acts. It has been explained that the reason why the middle one of the three Matzot at the *Seder* table is broken in two (*Yahatz*), is to indicate that our aim as Jews should be to halve another's sorrows by practical sympathy and by sharing with him the blessings that a good fortune has brought our way.

Further, the half *Shekel* which each Israelite was asked to contribute towards the mobile Tabernacle in the wilderness and later towards the upkeep of the Temple, was an earnest of communal responsibility and a reflection of *"the coin of fire"* God showed Moses on the Mount. All our actions were to be inspired by a warm heart and a loving consideration for the recipients of our goodwill. One of the reasons advanced for the fact that no blessing is recited when performing an act of kindness, though it is a *Mitzvah* so to do, is the consideration that the joy in

---

[9] Especially in Lev. xix.
[10] Ex. iii. 2: וירא מלאך י׳ אליו בלבת־אש מתוך הסנה

the performance of the *Mitzvah* may simultaneously cause some pain or shame to the beneficiary. It is an irrevocable principle of Jewish ethics that wherever a good deed involves some discomfort to the object of our kindness, no blessing was to be recited.[11]

We have dealt with the ethical implications of charity and justice in the preceding pages. The additional thoughts advanced here are intended solely to lend emphasis to what has already been said. One of the reasons, explain our moralists, why Scripture insists that "*Justice, justice, shalt thou follow*" (Deut. xvi. 20), is to stress that justice must be dispensed with absolute impartiality. The Jew is not to employ *unjust* means in order to secure the fruits of justice. In this conception, that the end does *not* justify the means, our Torah differs from the laws of the ancient Greeks and Romans, as it does from those of many nations of the world to-day.

It was the peoples of antiquity who emphasized the *difference* between human beings; Judaism emphasized *equality* of opportunity for all created in the likeness of God. To be unjust to another is to violate the respect due for his personality—a respect we owe to God whose likeness we all bear. This respect must be made manifest especially to the weak and the oppressed, for it involves the positive act of charity. Since the poor and the needy are the victims of social injustice, it is our duty to rehabilitate them and to endeavour to eliminate the

---

[11]Other examples are that no שהחינו blessing is recited by the Mohel at his first circumcision of a child; at the *Shehitah* of an animal; when donning shoes made of leather; or when counting the *Omer*. The memories of a Temple destroyed are too bitter to be sweetened by this blessing. See the author's "Jewish Customs". In the "Responsa" of the *Rashba* (No. 18), the reason for no blessing on the giving of alms is lest the poor will not accept the gift, and we will thus make a blessing in vain.

causes that lead to the denial of their rights. This redress of wrongs is an act of justice binding on nations as well as on individuals. International justice is meaningless if it does not protect the citizens of any nation to live their lives in their own way.

Judaism holds the line evenly between excess and defect. Our religion is not exclusively an affair of the spirit but also a participation in the social life around us. Judaism has brought *conduct* down from heavenly spheres to dwell among the children of men. Judaism deliberately does not thrust forward its teachings on the "*Life to Come*" so as not to dwarf the significance of our duties towards our neighbour and the community. This harmony of serving God and man, of matter and spirit, can be accomplished by hard, practical work in the highways and byways of life.

II. ETHICS OF JEWISH EDUCATION

The Jewish mode of life has been transmitted to us across the ages by a system of education unparalleled by any other people; by an education which was not *taught* as we saw in the previous chapter, by professional teachers, but was *caught* from paternal example. Jewish pedagogues do not subscribe to the derivation of education from the Latin *educere*, which means "*to lead out*", on the grounds that you cannot develop the personality, be it of a child or adult, just by drawing *out* from that which is *within*. This objection is logical. There may be little to extract, and what may be within may not deserve the extraction. They prefer to derive the word from *educare*, which means "*to feed*", a connotation more in agreement with the Hebrew term for education, *hinnuch*, derived from *hech*, a word meaning *palate*. Jewish education in the ways of life is not a process of extracting what is there already, but an endless process of imparting, enriching, feeding and adding to that which has been put in.

The ideal method of education is not one or the other; it is both. Putting in and drawing out; putting in our minds and hearts the laws of the Torah, and drawing out by means of thought and action the fully-formed character. To advocate one or the other method is to fall into the trap laid for those to whom party politics are more sacred than the cause. The existence of such freak schools of thought that argue that it is wrong to impose upon the child at an early impressionable age the religion, discipline and moral guidance of adults, which it may find irksome when manhood comes, is alien to Jewish ideas.

Their contention is that the child must be allowed to discover for itself, as it grows up, all the hidden treasures of life. The logical corollary of such a view is that the child should be allowed to do what it likes, provided it does not interfere with others. Such teaching has led to what was popularly called "*the new morality*" of a generation ago; the caustic comment upon which was that "*it was neither new, nor was it morality*". (Readers will remember Lord Bryce's criticism of the so-called Holy Roman Empire: "It was neither *Holy*, nor *Roman*, nor an *Empire*".)

Jewish education refuses to subscribe to these freakish experimentations with their ideal of the uninhibited child, free from every hampering complex and encouraged to indulge in all the emotions with which nature has endowed him. How can it agree with such notions since the basis of our social ethics is the fact that man was *not* created perfect, that his task in life is to make his evil inclination subservient to his better self and thus to achieve balance of mind and beatitude of spirit? If the child be not impregnated with religious values and fired with ancestral ideals, he will be tormented by animal instincts and primitive emotions.

Judaism cannot concur with the opinion expressed by Plato in his *Phaedo* that *"education is a training in public and social virtue"*, because such an aim is dangerous and inadequate. The history of dictatorships of our own day, be they Nazi, Fascist, or Communist, is ample warning that a training divorced from religious influence leads to the disintegration of society and to the periodic convulsion of civilization. Man becomes a puppet, an *automaton*, dragooned by a narrow patriotism which puts national loyalties above every sanctity.

The claim persistently made in these pages is that the Jewish viewpoint of life has at no period been more essential than it is to-day. Now that the world is threatened by new mass methods of extermination undreamt of before, must mankind (to save itself) see that ethical conduct be not outdistanced by the rapid advances in science. A hundred years ago, scientists cheered their contemporaries by describing the beneficial possibilities of their discoveries; now they throw us into gloom by speaking of their potential dangers. The fable of *"The Sorcerer's Apprentice"* that Goethe spun from his fertile brain has become a reality.

Many symptoms appear from a diagnosis of the ailments from which society is suffering to-day. While it is true to say that the world, in general, seems to have cast off religion as a guide through *"the lands of the living"*, it is equally true to assert that organized religion is not making any significant contribution to the problems besetting mankind. There may be justice in the widespread belief that a system of ethics is possible *without* a belief in Revelation, for practical experience teaches that religion usually trails behind the social consciousness. Religion does not lead advanced thought; it follows it. Were the religions of the world to bestir themselves more, moral values would not have been, at every turn, outstripped by technology and industrial discovery. Instead, they would serve as guides showing how to use to the advantage of mankind those new forces unharnessed from nature. Man would learn, instead, to be more humble, more ready to accept the conceptions of justice and peace that are taught by divine authority.

Life to-day issues a challenge to men of goodwill of all nations to unite and present the world with an ethical programme of conduct. In this task Judaism must play a conspicuous part. It was a Jewish teacher who, nearly two thousand years ago, made God exclaim to Israel:[12] "*If you come to My house, then shall I go to yours*". Life will be worth while and safe only if our daily actions are motivated by holiness and if the heavenly pattern of life be reflected on earth. The aim of Jewish ethics is not to distinguish the Jew from those around him so much by racial, social or political features but to mark him out by his spiritual characteristics.

Even in money matters—considered by our detractors as our Achilles' heel—the Jew is distinguished by generosity, especially when the cause touches his heart. The history of philanthropy and of all the essential social services—as of all humanitarian movements for the alleviation of injustice—contains many glorious pages written by Jews. Holiness is possible in the midst of life without tearing asunder body and spirit, material and spiritual, as two unconnected parts. Both strands are vital to the welfare of society; both forces must be enlisted into the service of God and man. Man may achieve anything, provided he is holy and humble in thought and purpose, doing everything in moderation and out of consideration for others. To be too "*otherworldly*" is to

[12]Sukk. 53ᵃ; Ex. xxv. 8.

be as foolishly sinful as it is to be addicted to earthly pleasures. The Torah was not given to angels, but was meant to be a Book of Life to ordinary, erring mortals. To be weary of this life, so as to inherit the *Life to Come*, is to forfeit eternity. Man was created to prove himself worthy in this hard school of life of the bliss awaiting the righteous in heaven.

III. WHAT JUDAISM SHOULD TEACH TO-DAY

So scientific has our world become that even the milk of human kindness has been *condensed*. Nations are becoming as heartless to universal suffering as the inventions that inflict their misery. Now, more than ever, must Jewish ethics be again promulgated from the New Judea if humanity is to be restored to a balanced mode of existence. Solicitude for the rights of the weak, the poor and the lowly; kindness towards all, be they men or animals, are the *desiderata* to-day. "Tenderness to animals", says Lecky, "is one of the most beautiful features of the Old Testament writers."[13] The lives of the leading characters of the Bible bear ample evidence of their reaction towards sympathy and consideration for all. Rebekah's qualification to become the wife of Isaac was her kindness to Eliezer and his camels;[14] Jacob was chosen as the father of the founders of the Twelve Tribes of Israel by reason of his tenderness for his flock.[15] Balaam was warned that if he struck his faithful ass, he would be slain,[16] and the Psalmist praises God who

[13]See Dr. J. S. Raisin's "Humanitarianism of the Laws of Israel", being No. 6 of the valuable pamphlets by the Tract Commission, Cincinnati.

[14]Gen. xxiv. 14.

[15]Gen. xxix. 7; xxxiii. 13.

[16]Num. xxii. 30f.

"*openeth His hand, and satisfieth the desire of every living being*".[17]

God is the Good Shepherd;[18] for this reason were the rulers and leaders of Israel, the patriarchs, prophets and the first two rulers of Israel taken "*from following the sheep*".[19] How deeply those spiritual architects of Judaism felt for all can be seen from the fact that when Isaiah, in a tender moment, speaks of the inexpressible anguish of his people, he pictures Israel as "*a lamb that is led to the slaughter, and as a sheep that before her shearers is dumb*".[20]

The Torah design for life has much to teach a world groping for light and safety and especially to impress upon those in authority that just as God has provided plenty for the needs of all, so should it be their responsibility to see that this plenty is shared by all equally. Our ethical codes insist that the ideal Jew must be distinguished by his mercy (*rahmanut*), even as God is the Father of Mercies (*Av Harahamim*). This quality of mercy Judaism is most authorized to teach mankind.

Our Scriptures weary not in the reminder that His tender mercies are over all His works, and our Talmudic writings insist that nothing created is superfluous. All fit into the divine jig-saw pattern of the universe. "*The Lord hath made everything for His own purpose*",[21] taught the wisest of all men. This teaching our Rabbis have voluminously supplemented and reinforced by lessons derived from their penetrating interpretation of the Torah. Our sages taught that to study the needs of others so as to alleviate them is the best way of worshipping God and walking in His ways.

[17]Ps. cxlv. 16.
[18]Ibid. xxiii. 1.
[19]2 Sam. vii. 8.
[20]Isa. liii. 7.
[21]Prov. xvi. 4.

We have seen above that Moses was chosen as the Lawgiver, because he ran after a stray lamb and helped it slake its thirst.[22] Another teacher draws attention to God's mercy for all creatures that cannot voice their wants in a way understood by all. The dog is able to endure hunger for three days, lest he be not fed. This considerateness gave a short tail to the animal that feeds among the thorns, and a long neck to the one that seeks to pick the high leaves. It gives protection to the young raven against its cruel parents and provides for the hind when it calves.

"How manifold are Thy works, O Lord! In wisdom hast Thou made them all: the earth is full of Thy creatures."[23] Pseudo-piety and scholarship cannot atone for heartlessness, as Rabbi Judah Hannasi found to his cost for pushing aside a lamb pursued by its slayer that ran to him for safety, with the remark: *"Go; it is for this that thou wert made"* (B. Metz. 85[a]). This kindness which permeates their ethical laws Jews must teach humanity. By this advocacy for sympathy unto all, peace will be promoted and stability and happiness will be restored to the world. Jews must be tirelessly consistent in this mission of teaching mankind the art of living together amicably.

Judaism must concern itself more with the social problems of nations. It has always regarded itself as a civilization rather than as a religion, as a programme of right conduct towards one another and as a constitution designed for *"a Kingdom of priests and a holy nation"*. It brooks no class distinction and tolerates no man-made partitions between those who have and those who have not. In the agrarian society of Biblical days, the land belonged not to *one* class but to *everybody; for "Mine is*

[22]Ex. R. iii. 1.
[23]Ps. civ. 24. See Sabb. 155[a] for the consideration shown by God when creating His various creatures.

the whole earth".[24] He is the Father of *all* and, accordingly, all men are His heirs. Temporary disturbances were periodically adjusted by the Jubilee laws,[25] and much of our Biblical legislation shows that man is meant to be a member of an organic community, not an isolated being concerned only with himself.[26]

Though the Torah system allows for private initiative and responsibility, a man's property and wealth are not to be regarded as his exclusively. He is merely the custodian of God's bounty, a bounty which must be shared with those in need. This vital contribution towards the Social Order Judaism must make to-day from its new Commonwealth and wherever its influence is felt. All men are brothers, with equal rights to enjoy the fruits of this *"good earth"*; all must be spurred on by an obligation to co-operate and to help, not to compete and fight for possession and mastery.

Without minimizing the important contributions the *Golah* must make to the establishment of peace and goodwill on earth, it is the State of Israel which is most competent to proclaim the Torah attitude towards life. "This does not mean[27] that all we have to do is to re-introduce the social laws of the Torah exactly as they are written. Since those laws served for an agrarian society, they would not solve all the problems introduced by industry and commerce. A *supplementary* legislation will be necessary, imbued by the Torah spirit which would ensure equality of opportunity and the avoidance of economic inequality and exploitation of class, and one which would guarantee an ideal state which exists in many *Kibbutzim* of Israel."

[24]Lev. xxv. 23.
[25]Ibid.
[26]See an essay by Rabbi H. Heinemann on *"Torah and Social Order"*, a Bachad publication, 1944.
[27]Ibid. p. 13f.

This new supplementary legislation, far from being contrary to our Torah loyalty, is an expression of it. It is *because* we wish to build Jewish life on Torah principles that we seek adjustments and reinterpretations; an evolutionary process, by the way, which has proceeded uninterruptedly throughout Jewish history.

The Mishnah is full of Rabbinic legislation of a religious, social and economic character, motivated by "*Tikkun Ha'olam*", freely translated as "*the promotion of the world's welfare*".[28] When the Jews ceased to be an agricultural people, measures were introduced to safeguard the Torah ideals under the new conditions. Talmudic legislation then adopted laws against the soaring of prices, against speculation and the hoarding of essential commodities[29] and against taking unfair advantage of another's innocence, or ignorance. These measures were a sincere adaptation of Torah principles to changed conditions.[30] This type of *halachic* adjustment will be essential if the Jewish State is to possess a sound social and economic policy of its own. It will also act as a model for the world of nations of the philosophy of statecraft.

The formulation of *new* laws in the *spirit* of the Torah does not necessarily mean rigidity to existing, halachic regulations. It means to be guided by them to higher standards of life, standards not possible at a time when conditions were still primitive.[31] The Torah is not only a code of laws; it was given to us, says an ancient source,[32] "*like wheat, to turn it into fine flour*". The Bible is the material from which we must extract the ideas on which to shape our lives. Heinemann does wisely in stressing that: "We shall not content ourselves with building up a

[28]Gittin iv. *passim.*
[29]Maimonides: Mishneh Torah, Hilchot Mechirah xiv. 1-7.
[30]Ibid. p. 15.
[31]Cf. Luzzatto: *Mesillat Yesharim*, xviii.
[32]Eliahu Zutta II (quoted by Heinemann on p. 17).

Social Order in Israel which does not conflict with the Torah. We shall endeavour to create a society which corresponds to its true intentions as closely as possible. We shall no longer base our social and economic life on *Hetterim*, loop-holes of the law, as the medieval Jew had to do and as we ourselves still cannot avoid doing to a large extent in the countries of the *Galut*. This desire to do away with compromises, with a life guided by the Torah in its private sphere but by other principles in its social sphere is, perhaps, one of the strongest reasons for religious Zionists to turn to Israel for the salvation of Judaism as well as of the Jewish people. For only there shall we be able to lead a life based entirely on the Torah."[33] The contribution made in the past by Judaism was mainly in the religious sphere. Judaism is still potent to establish a new World-Order in which peace of mind and freedom from want will no longer be fleeting glimpses but abiding visions of the large "*families of the earth*" that have at long last succeeded in establishing the Kingdom of God on earth.

IV. CONCLUSION

TWO VIEWS OF JUDAISM: MAIMONIDES AND TOLSTOY

To conclude, we will cite two remarkable utterances, each in its way demonstrating what faultless precision instruments Jewish ethics can be in the chiselling of character and the welfare of society. Tolstoy has been linked here with Maimonides only to show that Judaism can inspire those of other beliefs as well as those of our own. Judaism needs no recommendation apart from the assurance in the Torah that to follow it is to choose life.

[33] Ibid. p. 17.

I. MAIMONIDES

Our first quotation is from the "*Last Will and Testament of Maimonides*", which may be regarded as a summary of Jewish Ethics by a master of condensation. It consists of thirteen paragraphs (a number reminiscent of his "*Thirteen Creeds*"[34]), is addressed to "*My beloved children*" and is signed "*Your father who wishes to see you all happy—Moshe, the son of Maimon Hasefardi*". Here is the text, in its English translation.

1. "The Almighty, in whose hands my life is entrusted and who has blessed me with wisdom and strength of mind, so that I have great love for Him, has inspired me to advise you, my dear children, to follow the dictates of God and to learn His holy Bible, so that you should inherit the same thing as I have inherited from my parents. This message of conduct I wish to implant in you in the last minutes of my life before the Almighty will take me to Him to protect my soul under His wings.

2. "Listen to me, my dear children! May God, who has created the sky and the earth and who sends His blessings to the world and unto all things He created, from the bottom of the deep sea to the sky above, bless you with the best in life. Please resolve to be honest and upright before God and man. Believe in and pray to the God of Abraham, Isaac and Jacob with all your heart and soul because the fear of God will guard you from sin and the love of Him will strengthen your heart to follow his dictates. Always remember that for all your deeds you will have to account before Him.

3. "Conduct yourselves properly. Stay away from bad company, preferring instead to associate with those who are clever, noble and honest. Love and pursue learning as others pursue wealth and pleasures. Sit at the feet of

[34] See Singer's Prayer Book, pp. 89-90.

the learned, drinking in deeply the words of wisdom and
the counsels of perfection that drop from their lips as
honey from the bee-hive.

4. "Study eagerly and assiduously in your youth, before
the ailments of advancing age make themselves incon-
veniently apparent and before your memory is impaired.
Know that a time will come when you will desire to
learn but when you will not be able to do so. Remember,
to be forewarned is to be forearmed.

5. "Should anything in Jewish teachings seem incomprehensible and inexplicable to you, you being unable to
grasp its truth or comprehend its significance, do not be
hasty in condemning your religion. Your difficulties are
the result not of the fallibility of Judaism and its tenets,
but of your own lack of knowledge and limited power of
understanding.

6. "Above all, admire truth and justice, even when
such admiration spells loss of possession. It is far better
to be poor but honest than to be rich but corrupt. Never
seek to possess that which belongs to another; peace of
mind and happiness will not be gained that way.

7. "Strive to unite those whom dissension has separated.
Be a source of comfort and friendship to the sorrowing
and the lonely, treating them always with a smile and a
good deed. Forgive those who have wronged you, but
shun those whose words and actions proclaim them as
vulgar and irresponsible. Let your time be spent in the
company of good people and be polite and considerate to
your women-folk. Know that blessings come to a home
because of the virtuous wife.

8. "Be loyal to your friends, guarding their reputation
and protecting their possessions as you do your own.
Remember, however, that worship belongs only to God;
to trust in men 'In whom there is no salvation' is folly.
That way, frustration lies.

9. "Do avoid even the slightest semblance of quarrels, for life's most bitter moments result from them. It is advisable to part company even from those whom you consider as your dearest friends if you perceive in them a tendency to be cantankerous.

10. "Know that man is beloved by God more than anything else He has created. Hence has He blessed him with the power of speech, so that man should be able to praise God and study the Torah for which purpose only should speech be employed. To speak falsehood and evil, or to utter ribald jests and indulge in abusive language is to abuse this divine gift which is exclusive to man. Since a word once spoken is difficult, if not impossible to recall, do think very hard before you allow the words to proceed from your mouth.

11. "Neither eat nor drink to excess. It is fallacious to imagine that strength of body will come from abundance of food; on the contrary, the less you eat the more energy your system will display in digesting the food and suffusing the whole body with nourishment. When one eats over-abundantly, digestion becomes a difficult process. Thereby, physical energy is lost, the resilience of the mind is weakened and your pocket is considerably lightened. Whatever you do, do not be tempted into ways of drunkenness; that is, if you love your own soul and cherish your good name.

12. "Let your conduct be above reproach. By loving and respecting *others*, *you* will be respected and beloved. The gateway to greatness is humility; pride cometh before a fall. The virtue which made Moses the greatest of prophets was his humility.

13. "Finally, my dear children, I appeal to you to cherish light rather than darkness, to love life rather than brood on death. Do, please, remember that all the good things I have asked you in this Last Will of mine to cherish

will be yours, should you so wish. For unto each of us has been given the choice to prefer the noble and to shun the bad. May God be with you always."

Could Judaism have been presented with greater simplicity, more comprehensively and more sympathetically? Happy the children who have such a wise father to guide them; happier still those who weave into life the advice offered by one of the Titans of the Jewish spirit.

II. TOLSTOY

The second quotation is the answer of Leo Tolstoy to the question: *"What is a Jew?"* It is proof of the power of Judaism to kindle enthusiasm and admiration in the greatest minds, regardless of the faith into which they have been cradled.

"What is a Jew? This question is not at all so odd as it seems. Let us see what kind of peculiar creature the Jew is, whom all the rulers and nations have, together and separately, abused and molested, oppressed and persecuted, trampled and butchered, burned and hanged and, in spite of all this, is yet alive! What is a Jew, who has never allowed himself to be led astray by all the earthly possessions which his oppressors and persecutors constantly offered him in order that he should change his faith and forsake his Judaism?

"The Jew is that sacred being who has brought down from heaven the everlasting fire and has illumined with it the entire world. He is the religious source, spring and fountain out of which all the rest of the peoples have drawn their beliefs and their religions.

"The Jew is the pioneer of liberty. Even in those olden days, when the people were divided into but two distinct classes, slaves and masters, even so long ago had the law

of Moses prohibited the practice of keeping a person in bondage for more than six years.

"*The Jew is the pioneer of civilization.* Ignorance was condemned in ancient Judea more even than it is to-day in civilized Europe. Moreover, in those wild and barbarous days, when neither life nor the death of anyone counted for anything at all, Rabbi Akiba did not refrain from expressing himself openly against capital punishment, a practice which is recognized to-day as a highly civilized way of punishment.

"*The Jew is the emblem of civil and religious toleration.* '*Love the stranger and the sojourner*', Moses commands, '*because you were strangers in the land of Egypt.*' And this was said in those remote and savage times when the principal ambition of the races and nations consisted in crushing and enslaving one another. As concerns a religious toleration, the Jewish faith is not only far from the missionary spirit of converting people of other denominations; on the contrary, the Talmud commands the Rabbis to inform and explain to everyone who willingly comes to accept the Jewish religion all the difficulties involved in its acceptance, and to point out to the would-be proselyte that the righteous of all nations have a share in immortality. Of such a lofty and ideal religious toleration not even the moralists of our present day can boast.

"*The Jew is the emblem of eternity.* He whom neither slaughter nor torture of thousands of years could destroy; he whom neither fire, nor inquisition was able to wipe off from the face of the earth; he who was the first to produce the oracles of God; he who has been for so long the guardian of prophecy and who has transmitted it to the rest of the world—certainly cannot be destroyed. It is everlasting as is eternity itself."

A religion, with its own original design for living, that

can produce such testimony from a noble and enlightened spirit outside its ranks is surely worthy of the study and attention of the whole world to-day. It deservedly commands the unswerving loyalty of its own countless adherents in the *Golah* and in *Medinat Israel*. It is to the increase of this loyalty in the hearts of its faithful masses that this book has been lovingly dedicated.

END

APPENDIX I

THE JEWISH CONCEPTION OF MAN

"Know thou thyself: presume not God to scan:
The proper study of mankind is man."

IF for every man this be sound advice, how much more so for the Jew? Few scholars will disagree with the opinion of the late Kaufmann Kohler that next to the proclamation of a strict monotheism, the doctrine most fundamental and characteristic of Judaism is the doctrine of the place held by man in the scheme of the universe and his relationship with God. Our religion does not regard man as having fallen from grace and an inveterate sinner, but has crowned him as *"the lord of the creation"*, a being in whom the heavenly and the earthly singularly blend.

To undertake a presentation of the salient features of the Jewish view of man in a brief Appendix to a study of Jewish ethical and moral teachings may savour of a task that is as difficult as it is pretentious. Yet it is one which need not deter us. This book has been written not primarily for the scholar eager for comprehensive explanations of subjects which, owing to the scope of the present work, could receive only passing attention. It is intended for the general reader, eager to have before him, in lucid and popular form, the results of the investigations of generations of thinkers and writers on our ethical teachings.

The dignified place in Judaism occupied by man is stressed in the opening lines of our Torah. He is the chief figure in the narrative of the Creation. Everything else forms the background for the guest whom God has invited to partake of the bounties of a wonderful world. This central emphasis on man is elaborated by Israel's prophets and teachers, and is characteristic of Hebrew thought down the ages. By coining man in His own image, God manifested His love for His handiwork, raising him far above the brute creation and promoting him to the rank of "co-partner in the work of Creation".

Everywhere the Bible stresses the loving care of God. Nature yields her forces to supply man's demands, and over all his actions does his Creator shed the benign rays of Providence. In spite of the firm Jewish belief in the divine control of *each* human life, man has never been regarded as a puppet, a helpless toy in the arms of Fate. Judaism does not describe man as a being soiled by guilt, doomed to sorrow, fated to die an ignominious death unless he has received atonement for a sin never committed by him. He is "the Lord of Creation", and is capable, despite many imperfections, to rise to noble heights.

When we turn (as we have done in the thirteen preceding chapters) to our voluminous Rabbinical literature, we find man raised to the apex of the Universe. The views of Talmudic teachers like Hillel, Akiba, Meir and Ben Azzai are characteristic of the Talmudic doctrine of man. Hillel regarded the love of one's fellow-beings as the quintessence of the Torah; the care of the body he deemed a sacred duty. Akiba proved the greatness of man from his bearing the likeness of his Maker. Rabbi Meir and others stressed the marvellous organism that constitutes man and pointed out the equality of all by their descent from the same ancestral pair and from the fact that the body of Adam was moulded from the dust collected from all parts of the earth. Ben Azzai declared the whole world to have been created in man's honour, adding that the image of God must be reverenced in every man, of every creed. He who despises man, *ipso facto*, despises God.

Other sages of Israel taught that he who destroys a soul is not only a *deicide* but is also accounted the slayer of a *whole* world. Did not God fashion only *one* man at the beginning of all things? This keynote of the value and personality of man is struck and reverberates throughout the pages of our medieval literature. It is in Jewish theology, not in Greek philosophy, that man was first regarded as a moral and spiritual being in close dependence on God and clothed with a soul and body that makes the whole world kin. Israel was the first to teach, and will be the last to surrender, the belief of the soul's affinity to God; that all human life is divine; and that the entire family of mankind are loving children of One Father in Heaven above as on earth below.

This claim for Jewish theology is strengthened by a comparison of the views held by Jewish teachers with those held by the ancient Athenian philosophers. The Hebrew interest in human nature is *religious* and *concrete;* the Greek, *abstract* and *philosophical*.[1] Compare, as an illustration, the views of Isaiah or Ezekiel with those of Aristotle and Plato and you will notice that whereas the metaphysics of Greece are chiefly dualistic, contrasting form and matter and making the soul a purely heavenly substance and the body a source of evil, Judaism makes the *whole* of man a perfect Theistic being, *pure* in soul and body.

In Neoplatonism—a school of thought from which men, to cite only two, like Ibn Gabirol and Joseph ibn Zaddik, the author of "*Olam Katon*", graduated—this Greek dualism of form and matter is further developed

[1] As we have shown in Chapter Two of this book.

into the idea of God and the World, the Infinite and the Finite, Good and Evil. Similarly, there is a wide gulf in the conception of moral evil between Hebrew and Greek thought; the latter was intellectualistic, the former volitional. Socrates traces evil to ignorance; Plato to a want of harmony; Aristotle to a deviation from the "*Golden Mean*"; while Judaism traces evil to man's power of Freewill, regarding sin as the *wilful* disobedience by man of the will of God.

This distinction is natural since the Greeks, and especially the Stoics, almost categorically denied Freewill to man, making him the helpless sport of the gods. Among Jewish philosophers, however, the doctrine of Freewill held undisputed sway till its sovereignty was questioned with the rise of Islamic philosophy and its fatalistic theories. Philo strongly maintained the prerogative of man in being a free moral agent and Josephus regards the problem of Freewill and Determinism as one of the main disputes between the Pharisees and the Sadducees.[2] Akiba, in an attempt to reconcile the apparently insoluble problem of Providence and Freewill, declared that "Everything is foreseen by God, yet freedom of choice is given to man" (Ethics of the Fathers, iii. 19).

The genius of our faith is mirrored clearly in this teaching. Man, guided and influenced by divine intervention, nevertheless remains a free individual, responsible for his own actions. This sublime power of man the ancient Greeks almost denied, early Christianity seriously humbled and Mohammedanism painfully reduced to the narrowest margin. Only in Judaism does man come into his own, a glorious co-partner with God in the preservation of the world.

The Jewish conception of man begins to emerge. We

[2] See Chapter Four *supra*.

can now see why scholars err when they speak of a specific *Christian* doctrine of man. Is there such a thing? The New Testament is eclectic, being mainly a composition of early Hebraic thought and the later conclusions of Greek thinkers. It is these conclusions which dwarfed, and finally almost eliminated, the contributions made by our own Bible to the world of thinking men. Any thoughtful student of the New Testament can trace clearly these two schools of thought, side by side. It is, therefore, somewhat surprising to find a scholar[3] expressing the view that "*only in the teachings of Jesus of Nazareth does man become such a great being that he inevitably projects himself into Eternity, and the present world cannot contain him*" (*sic*).

What about the diatribes against all those who refused to subscribe to the new teachings? The Jewish student, familiar with Christian literature, has become quite acclimatized to what was, at first, a strange phenomenon; namely, to witness scholars who write with profound scholarship and common sense on general Biblical problems lose their heads when trying to prove the superiority of the New over the Old Testament. It was the late S. R. Driver, renowned for his Hebrew learning, of whom it was said that he was *Canon* Driver when he wrote on the New Testament but *Doctor* Driver when he discussed the Old Testament.

The supremacy of Judaism as an authoritative guide to life can also be derived from another aspect of its conception of man. Nowhere does it speak of "the fall" of man from Divine grace. The story of man's first disobedience has never been regarded as more than an allegory and as an inspired fragment of the earliest history of civilization. The Church reinterpreted the story and made it into one of the chief planks of its new religious

[3] Bruce in his "Kingdom of God", p. 131.

platform. There are, indeed, some Talmudic passages that attribute the birth of death in a world meant to pulsate with everlasting life to man's first disobedience; but these have been traced to Persian influence having been imported into our mythology during the Babylonian exile. The strong rational sense of our religion rejected this doctrine from the beginning and taught that man was born for abounding life with the possibility of obtaining perfection by means of the two Jewish Saviours—Penitence and Good Deeds.

The Rabbis never viewed man in the light of a corrupt being, certainly not as one born with anything else but a pure soul. They frankly admit that man is inclined to sin, but they urge him to conquer his evil inclination. They never taught, however, that man was *born* a sinner; that would be casting aspersions on the Creator for making something grossly bad and would mean a lapse into heathenism. *Not* Adam was responsible for the sorrows and evils of life, but what the Rabbis called "*the leaven in the dough*", or what Professor S. Schechter describes in "*Some Aspects of Rabbinic Theology*" as "*a certain quasi-external agency; whilst man himself, by his spontaneous nature, is only too anxious to live and act in accordance with the commandments of God*".

Sinlessness is almost inconceivable in Jewish thought, since every infraction of the Divine Word in the Torah is regarded as a "*laesa majestatis*", a denial of God's right to rule our world. Even the righteous err from time to time. The Biblical and Talmudic storied records show that the Homers of Jewish literature have been known to nod. "*There is no man so righteous on earth who does only good and sinneth not.*" "*Behold*", said Job (xv. 15-16), "*He putteth no trust in His holy ones: yea, the heavens are not clean in His sight. How much less one that is abominable and impure, Man, who drinketh iniquity like water.*"

The ideal Jew is not one who shuns the legitimate pleasures of life by seeking refuge in a cloister. There is shrewd philosophy in the Rabbinic utterance that the evil impulse in man is an indispensable factor to the individual and rational life of mankind; for without it, no man would build a house, take a wife and beget children, or engage in a trade. Man can worship God with the Evil Inclination by making it subservient to his will for doing good. Contrast with this the sinless perfection preached by St. Paul and you will understand why the teachings of the Church are subjected to searching doubts in an age of common sense.

It is a mistake, however, to concentrate these batteries of onslaught on Jewish teachings; for Judaism, from the first, avoided these mistakes and has remained to this day the source of admiration of the greatest non-Jewish thinkers. Study the two massive volumes by George Foote Moore on *"Judaism"* and you will come across a striking tribute to the genius of our faith.[4] Our religion has never regarded man as *"a miserable sinner"*—to borrow the phrase of Christian Theology—but as one possessed of a soul that makes him ever strive heavenwards; that urges and enables him to pluck a bit of heaven and plant it in the soil of earthly life. One poetic mind of the Talmud assures us that God formed the soul in the shape of a bird that it might rise aloft on pinions of kindliness and godliness, finally winging its way heavenwards (after life's play on earth has ended) to the celestial throne of the Lord of Life and Death.

We have repeatedly tried to show in the course of this book that the Jewish conception of man takes into consideration his religious aspects, genius, talents and boundless possibilities. Our Bible does not, and in the

---

[4] See also the works of Travers Herford, James Parkes and Doctor (now Professor) Danby on various aspects of Judaism.

nature of things cannot, pronounce the latest theories of modern sciences that were then unborn. It is essentially a book of religious history, not a text-book of cosmology, or a manual on anthropology. It is, therefore, futile to argue that the Bible is wrong because Darwin is right. One need not be branded an obscurantist if one pins one's faith to the verbal inspiration of the Torah. The hypotheses of the Darwinian school may scientifically account for many problems but they leave far greater ones unsolved.

The Jewish view of man tries to account for his greatness, for the genius of the poet, the passion of the prophet and the flights of the scientist. The prevalent scientific view that man descends from an anthropoid ape will never explain why man is often godlike and whence his loftiest thoughts emanate. Nothing is so contrary to the whole spirit of Judaism as the belief that man's first ancestor was "a coarse and filthy savage, repulsive in feature, gross in habits, warring with his fellow-savages, tearing half-cooked flesh and cracking marrow-bones with stone hammers, sheltering himself in damp and smoky caves, with no eyes heavenwards and possessing only the modest beginnings of the most important arts of life". Against this estimation, we put the appraisal of the Psalmist (viii. 6-7): *"Yet Thou hast made him but little lower than the angels, and hast crowned him with glory and honour. Thou hast made him have dominion over the works of Thy hands: Thou hast put all things under his feet."*

We do not intend here, neither are we competent, to discuss the accuracies or the fallacies of the views adumbrated by Darwin in his *"Origin of the Species by Natural Selection"*. The subject, however, is of vital importance to our present study and our temerity in dealing with it may be excused. Discretion is not always the better part of valour, especially when one is fighting the battle of the

Lord. If Science had proved itself infallible it would be like tilting at windmills in a vain effort to stop them from revolving if one were to shut one's eyes to its latest theories on matters dealt with in the Scriptures; but some of the leading opponents of the Evolution theory are scientists themselves. They confess that it has its insurmountable difficulties and are the first to admit that there are territories which are ruled by other laws than those to which the realm of science is subject.

The supremacy of man over all animals is impregnable, both on account of his psychical powers and his amazing intellectual development. All the civilized nations of antiquity regarded man as the direct *fiat* of God. The Chinese tradition of *Pao-hi;* the Babylonian legend of man created from the blood of the gods; and the Egyptian account in the "*Book of the Dead*" that speaks of "*a divine Architect who made the world to be the home of man coined in the image of his Creator*", all corroborate the view promulgated in Genesis.

Zöckler, in his article,[5] cites proof for his statement that the belief in the Divine origin of man was almost universally held until the middle of the eighteenth century when a materialistic philosophy sought to degrade man to the position of an animal or a robot. Eminent scientists like Linnaeus (1707-1778), and Blumenbach (1752-1840) (according to some the real founder of Anthropology as a science) voted, however, for the Biblical conception of man on account of his upright walk, perfectly developed hands, protruding chin and articulate speech. Wallace, the joint author with Darwin of the theory of Natural Selection, maintains that man is a direct work of God. Those who refer to the article of Zöckler[6] will be fortified

[5] See Herzog's "*Real Encyclopaedia*".
[6] Ibid.

with strong arguments in the defence of the Jewish teaching of the origin of man against the onslaughts made by the followers of Darwin.

It is the Sinaitic doctrine of man that gilds life's edges, that spurs man on to write his name on the page of history and that supplies him with a raft with which to float on life's agitated seas. What inspiration can a man have when he is told to regard himself as a one-day insect, placed against infinite Time, or as an imperceptible atom in the spinning realms of space? What incentive can he have to make the most of his precious *"bundle of years"*— if he is assured that his days on earth are mere pulsations before he disappears like a dream, a shadow, or a flash of lightning? They err who speak of life as an empty dream, a vale of tears. How elevating is the Jewish belief that man is infinity bounded in a nutshell; that he is the sovereign of Creation; the golden chain linking up earth to heaven!

Considered merely from his physical aspect, he is but a blade of grass that *"in the morning sprouteth afresh, but in the evening withereth and is cut down"*. Spiritually, with his wonderful consciousness in which the whole universe is reflected; with his tremendous intellect which can search the ocean to its lowest depth and span the heavens above; which can measure and weigh the sun and stars distant from him millions of miles; which can surmount space, and overcome almost every obstacle, man must be pronounced godlike. "Only a religion", says Kohler,[7] "which regards man not as a mere cog in the wheel or as a passing wave in the ocean, but as a beloved child and co-labourer of God; only a theistic system of ethics which teaches man to walk with the frown and the smile of the Eternal, with threats and promises of a divine justice, will be able to guide and save mankind from dashing itself

[7] See his "Jewish Theology".

against the jagged rocks that line the round of daily existence."

In the light of what has been said on this subject in the course of this book, there is no need to re-emphasize man's relationship with God or to point out that the Fatherhood of God, with its implication that all are members of one family, are ideas which form the warp and woof of our faith. Judaism reveals God as a Father, the fountain of virtue, the pattern after which we must weave our own lives. Man is coined in His image, possessing a soul which is a spark of God Himself, which is compared to a lamp in which an undying fire glows; a fire fed on earthly life but radiating God's infinite wisdom, gleaming as a live coal from some empyrean altar. As we have indicated above, the Jewish means of Salvation is not by faith only, or by "*a contritio cordis*" (contrition of the heart) and a "*confessio oris*" (a confession of the mouth); but chiefly by a "*satisfacio operis*", by Repentance and Good Deeds. "*Imitatio Dei*", the conscious attempt made by man to lead the godly life, will prevent him from becoming completely estranged from his Creator.

Another aspect of our subject can only be lightly touched upon here. Is death the last chapter? The baffling nature of this question should not in any way weaken our belief in a life after death. John Fiske voiced the opinion of many when he wrote: "It is not likely that we shall ever succeed in making the immortality of the soul a matter of scientific demonstration; we lack the requisite data. This belief must, therefore, ever remain an affair of religion, rather than of science. In other words, it must remain one of that class of questions upon which I may not expect to convince my neighbour; while at the same time, I may entertain a reasonable conviction of my own upon the subject." Being a practical guide-book to life on earth, the Bible contains no explicit reference but merely veiled hints to a *World to Come*, in which those who have been laid to rest here below will clothe themselves anew with immortal life.

To deny a belief in Immortality is to deny the God of Love and Justice, an essential doctrine of Judaism, as well as to belittle the status occupied by man in Jewish thought. Has God fashioned so marvellous a piece of work as man for no other purpose than that it should be demolished in the end like a worthless vessel of clay? Are we to regard the work of the Creator like that of children who build castles of sand merely for the pleasure of seeing them washed away by the oncoming tides? Are all those "*immortal longings*" of man only a hollow mockery— a chimera that leads to deception?

Neumark[8] explains the remarkable reticence of our Torah in discussing Eschatology by suggesting that Moses had become so vividly impressed with the evil effects which a continual speculation upon death had wrought upon Egyptian life that he deliberately and studiously avoided the subject. The religion of Osiris seemed to have been entirely centred on death. The Egyptian Bible had the morbid name of "*The Book of the Dead*". They excelled in the building of wonderful pyramids, the tombs of their kings and princes, and in splendid mortuary chapels and richly-furnished graves. The spade of the excavator has time and again unearthed buried glories that make us, of this age, hold our gaze.[9] Thousands of lives seem to have been wasted in those ages of antiquity in the service of the dead. It was no doubt in reaction to all this that Judaism preached ideals intended to inspire men to devote their strength and their

[8] In his Hebrew work entitled "*Toledot Hapilosophia B'Israel*", "The History of Philosophy in Israel".

[9] A good example is the discovery of Tutenkhamen's Tomb in Luxor (Egypt), in 1922.

intellect to the amelioration of the sufferings of living human beings and to a continual labouring for righteousness.

The idea of immortality, however, whether in the sense of a physical life after death, or the deathlessness of the soul, has always been one of the basic fundamentals of our faith even before it was developed by Aristotle and Plato. The teaching that man bears the likeness of his Maker betokens immortality. The God *in* us can never crumble into dust. Our prayers are dotted with confessions of this belief. Maimonides made it one of the dogmas of Judaism and every other teacher in Israel has subscribed to this view. One of the most prominent philosophers of the Deistic school, Moses Mendelssohn, in an era of enlightenment and scepticism, revived in his "*Phaedon*" the Platonic doctrine of life after death, emphatically asserting the divine nature of man by presenting new arguments on behalf of the spiritual substance of the soul.

With Immortality, we may well draw this Appendix to a close. We have tried to show that Judaism regards man as the "*gloria mundi*" (glory of the world); who, though confined to a narrow spot on this globe, and though his span of life is reduced to a few courses of the sun he is, nevertheless, possessed of a soul and an imagination which no despotism can crush; which at all times longingly and lovingly reaches out for higher and nobler things. It is only the physical element in him which prevents him from attaining immortality. The body in Judaism is not regarded, as it is by Plato and his disciple Swedenborg, as a prison but as a window opening upon nature by which the soul holds communion with the Universe. Man is a compound being, clod of earth and breath of God; but he is not, as Pascal would have us believe, a bundle of contradictions, a muddle of paradoxes and eternal opposites. The spirit of God unites all these seeming

differences. It makes man, though an inhabitant of earth,
destined for heaven. His soul spans the *hiatus* between
earth and heaven, between spirit and matter. In Judaism,
man has always been regarded as:

"A sacred spark created by God's breath,
The Immortal mind of man His image bears:
A spirit living 'midst forms of death,
Oppressed but not subdued, by mortal cares."

APPENDIX II

I. WHAT IS JUDAISM?

AT the end of a book on Jewish Ethics, one may well look
for a concise answer to the question often asked: *"What
is Judaism?"* Since Judaism covers every aspect of life,
regarding no thought or action outside its scope, it is
easier to answer the question by first stating what Judaism
is not. It is *not* meant to be a burden or a hindrance to
the Jew, but an unfailing source of guidance and inspiration
at all times, sad or gay. Since Jews are essentially in a
minority in all the lands of their adoption, with the
exception of the State of Israel, it became necessary to
make Judaism all-comprehensive, so as to serve as a
reminder that they must be loyal to their ancestral beliefs
and practices even if these run counter to the prevailing
usages and customs around them.

For this reason has a Jewish life been surrounded with
many precepts and the Jewish year been made colourful
by the observance of Sabbath and Festival. The survival
of the Jewish people, a miracle to some and an enigma to
others, is mainly due to the distinguishing nature of
Judaism, which is not merely a creed but a mode of
living. Without these distinctive features in prayer and
in the common acts of daily life; without the control of
his Torah, recalling in every detail his Jewishness, the Jew
might long ago have ceased to exist as a member of a
faith with a special mission to the world and a valuable
contribution to make to civilization.

Mankind would, indeed, have been the poorer had the
Jew been engulfed in the whirlpool of attrition and the
vortex of assimilation. Variety is the spice of life in

spiritual as well as in material matters. All thoughtful people have much to learn from the beliefs and ceremonies of the Jewish people with their unforgettable messages of holy thinking and simple living. If a *simile* may be permitted, the nations of the world could be compared to the component members of a large orchestra, each with his own particular instrument to play; but when guided by the baton of the conductor, all this cacophony and disharmony of sound is melted into a divinely harmonious composition. Similarly, each religion has something unique to offer to the treasury of life and thought. Each contribution, offered in sincerity, is lovingly accepted by our Heavenly Father. "*For have we not all one father? Hath not one God created us? Why do we deal treacherously every man against his brother, profaning the covenant of our fathers?*" (Mal. ii. 10).

Much of the unnecessary prejudice between the Gentile and Jew would disappear if all men of true faith would take Malachi's questions to heart and henceforth determine to make the Golden Rule of "*And thou shalt love thy neighbour as thyself*" our lodestar in life. To be intolerant of another's beliefs; to deny the righteous life to those who worship God on Saturday instead of on Sunday; to bar heaven from those who derive the virtues of self-restraint, discipline and holiness from some of the food they may eat and to regard as *aliens* those who pray in the language in which God spoke to His prophets is to sport with one's faith and reduce religion to a battleground of ideas.

II. HOLINESS—THE IDEAL

It is significant that when God told Moses to teach Israel "*Ye shall be holy, for I the Lord your God am holy*"

(Lev. xix. 2), He asked him to speak those words *"unto all the congregation of the children of Israel"*. Why? As we have repeatedly shown in the course of this book, it was to stress the duty laid upon *each* Jew to be holy and to lead a life without fear and reproach. In Judaism, the honour of *all* is in the keeping of *each*. This ideal of holiness must be enthroned in office and factory; it must reign unrivalled in synagogue and school. To divorce *living* from *believing* is to indulge in a lip-service to God which is as foolish as it is despicable.

The few in our midst who besmirch the fair name of the Jew, by indulging in sharp practice and dishonesty, forfeit the right of calling themselves the adherents of Judaism. Nowadays, Jewish authorities do not possess the power of excommunicating or of inflicting corporal punishment on those blasphemers of God's Name, and must content themselves with the penalties imposed by the civic courts. They would only, in all fairness plead that the faith to which the transgressor *nominally* clings should not be used as an adjective to describe the man when his guilt is recorded in the Press or in the courts of law. One does not read of a *Roman Catholic* black-marketeer, or a *Presbyterian* bankrupt. Is it then more characteristic of the Jewish creed to raise such delinquents? This book on Jewish ethics has been primarily written to reveal the inner beauties of Judaism, in the sincere hope that better understanding may exist between neighbours of different creeds, all bent on serving the same Heavenly Father according to their light.

What does being *holy* mean to the Jew? It means, first of all, worshipping God by praying to him thrice daily—in the early hours of the morning, in the afternoon and in the evening. It means awakening at dawn with a prayer and closing one's eyes in sleep with a blessing on our lips. It means not partaking of any food or drink without reciting an appropriate blessing; not experiencing any physical or intellectual enjoyment without due appreciation of Him who made those pleasurable sensations possible. Looked at in this way, the numerous regulations that govern the life of the Jew do not destroy the spirit of faith; on the contrary, they enrich it and stimulate the Jew towards a life of perfection.[1]

To be *holy* means to *imitate* God—"*Ye shall be Holy, for I the Lord your God am holy*". All the qualities of truth, justice and mercy that are associated with our teachings of the Fatherhood of God must be woven into the daily fabric of our life. "*Just as He is loving and compassionate, so must thou be considerate unto all and bear malice towards none*", says a Rabbinic teacher of the third century. To imitate His goodness means to translate into everyday thought and action that remarkable nineteenth chapter of Leviticus. There we find a brief summary of some of the things required of the loyal Jew; to abstain from all things that defile, physically, mentally and spiritually; to eschew forbidden meats; to look with disfavour on all attempts made to obliterate the beliefs and practices of Judaism; to be charitable and considerate towards all. To be *holy* means to be members of a loving brotherhood in which holiness is not an abstract or mystic idea, but a regulative principle in daily life.

III. THE IDEAL JEW

The ideal Jew must be kind in thought and deed; must observe his Sabbath and festivals in no exclusive spirit; must sanctify his life by daily prayer and hallow his home with piety and ceremony; must honour his parents and teachers; must respect the learned and the aged; must be

[1] See the writer's "Jewish Customs", Shapiro, Vallentine, 1950.

thoughtful of the poor man's need; and must pay, at the close of each day, the labourer his hire. He must have a clean and unendorsed record for clean living, moral thinking and honourable dealing and a reputation for justice, cordiality and general helpfulness. In view of the travesty of the Jew so beloved still of the popular stage and sensational press the description of the ideal Jew given by an Anglo-Jewish preacher[2] should serve as a corrective.

"To be a Jew is to be a faithful and fearless witness for God and to feel oneself a member of a great brotherhood in which the safety, welfare and honour of all are in the keeping of each. It is to stand firm against temptation and corrupt example from far and near, and to make sacrifices of time, toil, treasure and comfort for our faith. It is to answer all detractors by a blameless life. It is to be in sympathy with and, as far as may be, to bear a part in all endeavours for the betterment of the world. It is to glory in our heaven-directed history and to bear in mind that he who cares not for Israel's past is not likely to do much that will be worth remembering in Israel's future. It is to cherish our inheritance in the Word of God and diligently and lovingly to study it. It is to unite with all who are willing to help according to their opportunities and to roll away the reproach of religious apathy from a people in whom such a reproach is least pardonable. To realize these holy truths and to translate them into life and action is to be the ideal Jew."

To make this sublime ideal attainable, the Jew is reminded at every turn to make all his thoughts and deeds conform to a certain divine pattern. By placing the *Mezuzah* on the door-post of his house, he is exhorted not to allow any impurity to find even a temporary resting-place in his midst. The phylacteries and the fringes he

[2] "Lectures and Addresses" of S. Singer, edited by Dr. Israel Abrahams.

dons when engaged in prayer are silent yet eloquent pleas
to link himself unto God, to approach whom no intermediary is required. The Sabbaths and the Festivals,
with their enforced respite from labour, are opportunities
for additional worship and study, serving as further
reminders to the Jew that the purpose of our existence on
earth is to acquire those virtues of justice and kindness,
selflessness and self-discipline which are the passport to
heaven when earth's race is run.

The Dietary Laws he observes are aids to self-restraint
and reminders that the purpose of life is not solely *"to eat,
drink and be merry, for tomorrow we die"*; but *"to do good,
love justice and walk humbly with the Lord thy God"*.
These laws of food may have been originally intended to
teach the duty of being kind to animals and to encourage
the Jew to be a vegetarian; for the slaughtering of animals
for food is hedged round by so many meticulous laws as
to make the eating of meat difficult. It is important that
the Jewish ritual slaughterer be a God-fearing man and
of good repute; that the slaughtering-knife must be keen-
edged and absolutely notch-less; and that the cut must be
made on the jugular veins so as to promote an almost
instantaneous death.[3] To consecrate the act, a blessing
must be recited. Laws regarding moderation in drink have
helped to keep the Jew sober, protecting his home from
the want caused by money spent on alcoholic stimulants.
The laws governing marriage and the married life aim
at the target of holiness, and at self-analysis and self-under-
standing. A Talmudic Rabbi stated that man grows in
holiness the more he aspires to be pure. *"When one tries
to lead a holy life, one receives every encouragement from
Divine sources."*

From a careful reading of the chapters which have

---

[3] See the writer's article on *"Shehitah"* in Vallentine's *"Jewish
Encyclopædia"*.

preceded, it will have been seen how much we have to learn from Judaism, with its incessant reminders in every aspect of life and thought, how men and nations can make this world a safer and happier place to live in, and how a spiritual revival in our midst can be ushered in. To quote Lord Samuel: "The world does, indeed, urgently need religion. Men will not live like the beasts of the field, intent only on material things and earthly satisfactions. A spiritual striving is innate. We have been asked to believe many incredible things; but that there is nothing to be believed, would be the most incredible of all. Religion has been, all through the ages, a chief bulwark of morals. It is a discipline as well as a faith. Were religion to disappear as a factor in the life of mankind, the whole structure of morality would tremble and sway."[4]

The pious and thoughtful Jew raises his eyebrows in amazement when he is told that he is tied to a faith whose requirements are obsolete and out-of-joint with the times. To him, ceremonies and observances are so many reminders that God rules our waking thoughts. The desires of frail, petulant men can never be fully satisfied, often proving as unending a torture as that imposed on Sisyphus.[5] Without religion, man hungers though he eats; thirsts though he drinks; seeks and never finds. This is the bitter core of modern man, a being never satisfied. It is because Judaism has grasped this fundamental truth, namely, that outward calm as well as inner contentment will come only by removing the line of demarcation between religion and life, that it has impinged on all man's beliefs and actions.

[4] See his thought-provoking book "Belief and Action", p. 51.
[5] Greek mythology tells of Sisyphus, a crafty and avaricious King of Corinth, condemned in Hades to roll up a hill a huge stone, which constantly rolled back.

Far from being an outworn creed, discredited by events and refuted by the march of time, the religion of the observant Jew is unsurpassed for its lofty conception of God and man; for its emphasis on social justice; for its examples of noble character moulded by faith and for its message well adapted to the intellectual, moral, social and spiritual needs of to-day. Lord Snell, the leader in his day of the Ethical Movement in England, wrote: "There has been gathered during the centuries a great treasure, through the teachings and lives of the founders of faiths, prophets and poets, saints and sages, which is a precious heritage of this modern world. It would be a disaster for mankind were the treasure to be dissipated."

IV. SOME PREJUDICES REMOVED

When one recalls the stress laid by Judaism on cleanliness, whereby the Jew must wash his hands before praying and eating, after attending to the needs of the body, after a bath or contact with the dead; and in view of the intricate system of ablutions for the purpose of family and individual purity, it is clear that the opprobrious term "*dirty Jew*" should become as mythical as the "*Wandering Jew*" now that we have a Jewish State of our own.

One need but cite the example of Hillel who was especially careful to teach cleanliness. The ancient Roman sage who remarked that "*unless a vessel is clean, whatever you pour into it will turn sour*", was epigrammatically stating one of the basic principles of the Jewish faith. The besetting sin of those who ridicule the Jew is that they judge Judaism by its *worst* adherents, and not by its *best*. No nation consists entirely of saints or sinners, and no people on earth has monopolized all the good and the virtuous men and women within its own folds.[6]

Enough has been cited to show how unfair it is to class Jews as unclean, or as given over to vice and morbidity. The Jewish religion is a faith of light and joy and has looked askance at gloomy manifestations of obedience to the will of God. Our heroes and saints have never been ascetics or recluses; nor have our Synagogues been made to resemble prison-houses of the soul by their gloom and austerity. To borrow the words of Judah Ha'levi, a teacher of the twelfth century: "The essence of our whole law is contained in these three things—reverence, love and joy. They are the way to bring us near to God. Thy contrition on the day of fasting is in no wise more pleasing to Him than thy joy on the Sabbath or festival, if so be that thy delight comes from a full and devout heart. For just as prayer requires reflection and devotion, so does joy in God's commandments and the study of His revelation."

Another popular misconception is the statement that the Jewish God is a *tribal* deity and that the world had to wait for Christianity to be taught that "*God is love*". Prophets like Isaiah and Micah, Amos and Malachi, breathed the last word in international fellowship and had glorious visions of a community of nations living in concord and peace with swords beaten into ploughshares and spears into pruning-hooks. Throughout the Bible, God is depicted as a loving Father; clothing the naked (Adam and Eve); visiting the sick (Abraham); comforting the lonely (Jacob); and burying the dead (Moses). The very fact that the Jew in his approach to God needs no intermediary shows how accessible He is to all His children.

Central to Judaism is the idea of a *personal* God. It is

[6] Dr. W. R. Inge's "Outspoken Essays" on this subject has been quoted in an earlier chapter.

comforting to be assured that man is not alone in a universe apparently friendless. God is not an absentee landlord, but a gracious benefactor who cares for all and is deeply concerned for their destiny. A modern Jewish teacher writes: "What mars the relationship between man and God is the doing of injustice, or any act leading thereto. Divine reconciliation can be effected by the doing of justice. For this restoration of Divine harmony, the need of a mediator is not desired."[7]

The Jewish rejection of Jesus as the Messiah is not due to blind bigotry. The person of the Messiah is not an integral part of the Jewish conception of the Messianic Age. The Jewish belief is that this "Golden Age" will be ushered in by a descendant of the Kingdom of David only when justice and truth shall greet each other and Social Justice becomes the universal life among nations. The Messiah, in the light of Jewish opinion, has not yet appeared in the world for the simple reason that at no time yet in the history of mankind has the idyllic description of those "*latter days*" been a reality for long. Judaism teaches man to look *forward* to better times in the future, rather than sigh for days already gone by.

Nor is it because Jews are "*a stiff-necked people*" that they observe the Sabbath not on the first day of the week but on the seventh, the day which God Himself proclaimed to His people to be holy for all times. It is important to bear in mind that only at the Council of Nicea, in 325 C.E., did Pope Innocent III decide to break away from the dates of Jewish observance. Before that time, Christians kept the Jewish holy days at the same times as the Jews did. This continuity Israel has preserved to this day, still loyally observing the historic events which Passover, Pentecost and Tabernacles, Purim and Hanukkah commemorate. Those days still recall emotion-

[7] See "Judaism", by Rabbi Dr. I. Epstein.

ally the past national greatness; still suffuse the Jew with historic consciousness and arouse his sympathy in all suffering.

V. MORE FALLACIES EXPOSED

To claim that Christianity first taught the existence of a life after death is to brand oneself ignorant of what Judaism stands for.[8] Apart from many implied references in the Bible to the immortality of the soul, the doctrine has become the core of Rabbinic teaching. It is a common error among non-Jews that the development of the Jewish genius for religion ceased with the close of the Biblical age. In fact, a Jew of the time of Ezra the Scribe, whom tradition has appointed as the editor of the scriptures, would not recognize the Judaism of to-day. In the Talmud it is explicitly stated that life does *not* end with the grave. Would God have created such a wonderful piece of work as man only to destroy him at the end of an uncertain tenure of life? Immortality is an integral part of Jewish belief, and no teaching was held more tenaciously from the earliest days than that of the existence of another life. Recall the incidents of Enoch and Elijah who soared to heaven, and turn to the Bible and the Talmud for implicit and explicit views on this subject.

Why should immortality be an impossible belief? Just as God makes possible the miracle of birth, so can He endow those who have died with a new lease of life. Why should resurrection be more mysterious and impossible than the phenomenon of Nature on earth? If the seed placed in the soil during winter can be kissed into life at the approach of spring, why is it impossible that all those "*who sleep in the dust*" be awakened to eternal life by the trumpet-blast of the Messiah? To qualify for immortality,

[8] This subject has been discussed in Appendix I.

man must lead the godly life, not only *doing* good, but *being* good. Sin and injustice estrange one from God; justice and charity bring Him nearer.

Ignorance of the true facts is also responsible for the current belief that the Jew likes to evade manual labour, choosing instead the easier occupations that help him to get rich quickly. It is unfair to brand a whole people as parasites because of alleged faults on the part of a few. The vast majority of Jews are hard-working, regarding it as a religious command to add to the knowledge, comfort and wealth of the world by the work of their hands and brains. The treatment meted out to Jews by the nations in whose midst they dwelt is mainly responsible for the transformation of an essentially agricultural nation into a people mainly engaged in trades and professions.[9] Had it not been for the tireless industry and superhuman courage of the Jew, the greatest miracle of modern times—the creation of a Jewish State—would have been impossible.

The importance of the Jew's following a manual occupation is stressed throughout Rabbinic literature. The Rabbis *practised* what they *preached*, as we have shown extensively in these pages. Most of them were labourers in field or workshop, refusing to use their learning to earn their living. *"Great is work; it honours the workman"*, they taught. They believed that even *"if there should be seven years of famine, the craftsman would never want"*. Adam cried out when his punishment for disobeying God's first command was that henceforth he would eat thorns and thistles—the fare of the beast of the field. Only when he was told that he would *"in the sweat of thy face"* eat his food, did he become reconciled to his fate.

Another prejudice is the accusation that Judaism does

---

[9] One has only to visit *Medinat Israel* in order to realize that, given the occasion, no labour is too menial or too back-breaking for the Jew who yields to none in zeal for sheer work.

not encourage the Jew to share the full responsibilities of citizenship. At every synagogue, he says a special prayer for the welfare of the nation of which he is a part; and throughout his legal codes he is exhorted to respect the laws of the country in which he lives and to obey its authorities. The prophet Jeremiah, already in the sixth century B.C.E., commended his co-religionists, in the name of God, to pray for the well-being of the countries in which Jews would find themselves.

We have also seen how unjust it is to accuse the Jews of exclusiveness, when it is their non-Jewish fellow-citizens who erect these barriers. Apart from the demands of his faith, which it is his solemn duty to obey in order to help to preserve the continuity of his great traditions, the Jew has much in common with others. He is only too eager to redress social wrongs; to remove slums and unemployment; to ensure for all a good education and decent living; to ameliorate the ills to which human beings are heir. Of course, there are cases of Jews who have flagrantly thrown overboard the teachings of their faith, just as there have been criminals of every other faith. But to visit the sins of the few upon a whole nation is more than unjust—it is a crime. "*Shall* one *man sin and Thou shalt be angry with* all *the congregation?*"

Similarly, to attack the Jew for being too clever is childish. First, it is not true. With some notable exceptions, the greatest scientists and literary men to-day are not Jews. What *is* true is, that the Jew has been taught to respect the learned man and to love learning for its own sake. It was the "*Tree of Knowledge*" that tempted Adam to sin, and one of the first blessings recited by the Jew each morning expresses thanks to God for graciously bestowing knowledge on man and for the opportunity given him to study the Torah. If some Jewish children are particularly bright at school, two causes are mainly responsible. They come from homes in which culture and learning are encouraged and respected, besides being the offspring of a people that has tended the lamp of learning throughout the Dark Ages of history. Also the fact that many are bi-lingual almost from the start (in that they are taught Hebrew outside school hours), tends to sharpen the brain and stimulate the intellect. Intellectual resourcefulness and nimbleness of wit are part of the spiritual capital inherited by Jews to-day from ancestors for whom most of the gates of the world were closed.

Jews are sometimes chided for being vulgar in manner, loud in talk and ostentatious in dress. Never have so many been blamed for the vices of so few. The ideal Jew is the very negation of this censure. The particular belief of an individual has no *direct* association with his lack of manners; there are vulgar people of all creeds and races. One of the primary aims of Judaism is to produce the godly man, who should bear the imprint of goodness and the heavenly image in his character and in his bearing. That some Jews, on the whole, are more emotional and excitable than their non-Jewish fellow-citizens may be traced to the fact that their immediate forebears, if not they themselves, have come from oriental countries, where the pulse of life seems to beat more quickly. Natural instincts are less repressed and emotions, in general, felt at an accelerated tempo. Those Jews, whose forebears have lived in the same country for many generations, possess few external differences from their neighbours. In speech, dress, external appearance and even temperament, it would be very difficult to single them out from their neighbours, either for praise or derisive comment.

VI. SALVATION BY DEEDS

Many answers can be vouchsafed to the question *"What is Judaism?"* Here is one given by a writer quoted more than once in these pages: "Judaism is a scheme communicated by God to mankind for the establishment of a Divine order. In this task, all nations are invited to co-operate, each one making its own specific contribution, with the seven laws, said to have been given to Noah, as a common basis. The highest contribution must be made by Israel, through its loyalty to God and His revealed Torah. Round this idea—the essence of the Jewish religion—there has grown the Jewish nation, with its own history, language, literature, culture and civilization. The Jewish conception of a nation, in all its varied manifestations is, however, only secondary to its world-wide mission. It is only a *means* to an end, rather than an *end* in itself. The end is the establishment of the Kingdom of God and the fulfilment of the prophetic vision of the coming of the day when 'the Lord shall be King over all the earth. In that day shall the Lord be One and His name One' (Zech. xiv.)."[10]

"What is Judaism?" It differs from other faiths in that it lays stress on action, as well as on faith. *"Ye shall, therefore, keep My statutes and Mine ordinances, which if a man do he shall live by them."* The man who *practises* them, *lives* by their help and their spirit, and finds in them the purpose of life. Only when religion is made the *way of life*, will man be lifted above his cares and sorrows and brought into fellowship with higher powers. Jethro advised Moses: *"And thou shalt teach them the statutes and the laws, and shalt show them wherein they must walk and the work they must do"* (Ex. xviii. 20). In Judaism,

[10] See "Judaism", by Dr. I. Epstein.

there is no cleavage between secular and holy, between thought and deed. *"Great is learning"*, says a Rabbi, *"for it leads to action."* While in Judaism there are many *"duties of the heart"*, there are duties also allotted to head and foot, to brain and brawn.

Judaism stresses not so much the theoretical doctrines and mystical ideas associated with other religions, but concerns itself with showing man *"the way wherein man must walk and the work he must do"*. The Jew is, by nature, practical and realistic. Take the Decalogue as an example. After God had proclaimed that He it was who brought Israel out of Egypt, and that no idols may be worshipped, He pronounced on the importance of Sabbath observance and the respect due to parents, concluding with solemn warnings against the sin of murder, adultery, stealing, perjury and covetousness. Significant is also the fact that the Decalogue is immediately followed by practical laws on human relationships; on the humane treatment of those who work for us; on injunctions concerning the rights of person and property; and the treatment to be meted out to the stranger. No less than *thirty-six* times in the Bible are we told to *"love the stranger"*.

What guidance to the nations in their treatment of aliens in their midst! Had this precept been adopted by the nations during the Hitler war, thousands of innocent men, women and children, sailing the seven seas in cockleshells of boats, in an attempt to escape the fury of the oppressor, would not have found a watery grave even while they were in sight of the Promised Land, awaiting anxiously to receive them.[11] Wars come because the moral law is violated. Nations, like individuals, cannot sin, and

---

[11] A painful echo of the fate that met the *Athlit, Struma, Patria,* and other vessels that carried Hitler's victims to the beckoning safety of *Eretz Israel.*

sin again and then expect to escape. There is a divine Nemesis which follows a "*Lex Talionis*", a law which punishes the offender in a manner not unlike the hurt he has done to others.

What is Judaism? It is *not* a religion that claims supremacy on account of miracles performed by those who preach in its name. Since miracles may be quoted in support of *every* creed, they cannot, therefore, afford conclusive proof for *any*. Neither is it a religion that insists on the *letter* of observance, and not on its *spirit*. Judaism prescribes for every phase of life because it is fully aware that there is a right and wrong way of doing everything. Its sole aim is to direct those who conform with its teachings to do the *right* things in the *right* way.

The early teachers of Israel realized that the largest portion of our lives, whether we will it or otherwise, is regulated from *without*, not only by the Bible and by the organized rites of religion but also by the laws of the land and the imposed rules of accepted guides as well as by the social conventions, current fashions and popular maxims of the age. To be effective, a religion must be all-embracing in character, colouring and impinging upon all man's actions and thoughts. When people speak slightingly of the ceremonial nature of Judaism, let them remember that however much mankind may advance in the liberal sciences and paths of virtue, the fact will for ever remain that men will need tangible expression of the abstract ideas held out before them. To seek to make a religion acceptable to *all* by reducing it to a minimum of faith, is to end up by making it dear to *none*. To borrow the words of Morris Joseph, author of "*Judaism as Creed and Life*": "The Jew must be a *particularist* in order to be a *universalist*. He must live as a true Israelite and not as a religious cosmopolitan. His religion must be Judaism, not a vague theism."

What is Judaism? Those who have carefully read the foregoing pages will be in a better position to answer this question. They will realize that all honour is due to the faithful Jew who sacrificed so much to preserve the continuity of the legacy of idealism handed down to him by ancestors who performed unforgettable deeds of heroism. When people learn to respect the views and beliefs of others, they will have made considerable advance towards the ushering in of the Messianic Age for which all their great prophets, seers and sages have thought of and fought for throughout the ages. One can only hope that prejudice and hatred, bias and anti-Semitism will be banished for ever, and justice for the Jew, and love and goodwill between all men will in future be the characteristic features of the New World Order for which so many sacrifices have been made in our own generation. Towards this new world, the civilian at home, turning the wheels of industry and following his peaceful pursuits, has as important a contribution to make as the soldier jeopardizing his life in the contest of battle. This contribution consists, to a large extent, in the removal of the bias and hatred so frequently accorded to the Jews in their midst.

INDEX

(Note: Biblical and Talmudical references are not included in this index. These are easily found in the text of this book.

A

Abba Umana	283
Abelson, J.	148
Abot d'R. Nathan	297, 304
Abrahams, I.	353
Agunah	182
Ahad Ha'am	137
Akkum	223
Albo, J.	113, 213
Alexandra, Queen	281
Am Ha'aretz	223
Amidah	296
Aquinas, S. Thomas	96
Aristotle	84, 93, 112, 148, 227, 337, 338, 347
Arnold, M.	112
Asceticism	289
Aurelius, Marcus	220

B

Bahyah Ibn Pakuda	89–92, 108, 118–119, 213
—logic of Mitzvot	166
Bal tashhit	74
Bar-Cochba	204, 215
Bar Mitzvah	80
Bernfeld, S.	171
Beruriah	275
Besht	105, 106, 150
Beth Din	182, 186
—and Proselytes	219

Bikkurim, *see* First-fruits

Binnah 272

Brotherhood of Man 42

Brown, L. 87, 97, 103

Buber, M. 104, 105, 106, 135–136, 179

Buddha 24, 235

Buddhism 23

C

Cabbalah 101–102

Cain and Abel 210

Chosen People 174, 204

Cohen, A. 96, 98, 262

Cohen, Hermann 134–135

Confucius 21–23

Crescas, Hasdai 112

D

Darwin, C. and Bible 341–343

Demosthenes 216

Derech Eretz 300

Derech Eretz Zuta 279, 304

Determinism 20

Diaspora 212

Dietary Laws, and Holiness 73

—and Hygiene 285

—and Self-restraint 354

Divorce and Judaism (Get) 244–246

Do ut das 47

E

Eddington (Sir), A. 166

Emerson, R. W. 101

Epstein, I. 55, 95, 134, 358, 363

Erubin 81
Eruv Hatzerot 81
Eruv Tavshillin 81
Evil Inclination, *see* Yetzer Ha'ra
Ezra and Nehemiah 214

F

Fallacies 359–362
Falsehood 265–268
Family Life 246–254
Fatherhood of God 42
Finkelstein, L. 242
First-fruits 269
Fiske, J.—on Immortality 345
Forgotten Sheaf 211
Freewill 155
   —and Providence . . . 84, 87, 158, 301, 338
   —and Original Sin 157
   —and Providence (in prayer) . . . 273
Friedlander, G. 273
Fustel de Coulange 216

G

Gabirol, Solomon Ibn . . . 87–91, 134, 337
Galut 328, 334
Gaon of Wilna 104, 109, 150
Geiger, A. 118
Gemillut Hasadim 206
Gersonides 111–112
Ginzberg, Prof. L. 62
Goethe, W. 192, 321
Gordon, A. D. 137–138
Gordon, J. L. 116
Gore, C. 25
Goy 223
Grätz, H. 107
Gregory VII, Pope 252

H

Hadlakah, Lag B'omer 75
Hafetz Hayyim 52, 127–134
Halachah 53
—Charity 54
—Ethics 57
—Profits 59
—Perfect Life 62
—Dignity of Man 75
—Business Morality 78–80
—Progress 81
—Modern Times 323–328
—Ethical Background 315–631
Halevi, Yehudah . . . 52, 92–93, 112, 149, 178
Hallot 64
Hasidism 105–106, 135
Haskalah 120
Hatam Sopher 124–127
Hegel, G. W. F. 27
Heine, H. 298
Heineman, H. . . . . . . 234ff.
Hellenism 27, 84
Herford, Travers 223, 338
Hertz, J. H. 315
Higher Critics 179
Hillul Ha'shem . . . 12, 13, 57, 99, 150, 162, 200, 203
Hirsch, S. R. 116–118
Holiness, see Kadosh
Homer 252
Honi Ha'meagel 291
Humility 255–261
Huxley, T. H. 29
Hygiene 285–293

I

Idleness 300
Idumeans 219

Ikkarim 113–114, 214
Imitatio Dei 5, 40, 84, 147, 345
Immortality 346–348
Inge, Dr. W. R. 357
Innocent III, Pope 358
Isaac of Antioch 34

J

Jabneh 259
Jannaeus, King 281
Joseph, M. 99, 365
Jubilee Year 211, 235, 267, 326
Judaism—and Current Problems . . . 187–190
—and Social Ethics 196–199
Justice 261–265

K

Kaddish 201
Kadosh 163–169, 280
Kant, I. 19, 27, 116
Karo, Joseph . . 104, 107, 130, 184, 189, 242
Kavanah 7, 270
Keriah 74, 201
Ketubah 242
Khazan 220
Kiddush Ha'shem 8, 16, 40
—and Ideal Life 57
Kiddushin, see Marriage
Kohler, K. 225, 228, 335
—on Man 344
Kook, Rabbi A. I. 128, 131, 190
Korban Todah 61
Kosher 79, 247
Krochmal, N. 136

L

Labour and Judaism 228–236
Lashon Ha'ra 129
Lauterbach, Prof. J. Z. 53, 59, 60
Lazarus, M. 138
Lecky, W. E. H. 35, 323
Levy, S. 20, 69
Lex Talionis 182, 365
Lichtigfeld, A. 111, 134
Lipkin, Israel (Salanter) 119, 124
Lishmah 19
Logos 84
Luzzatto, M. H. 107–110, 213

M

Maimonides 52, 93–98, 167, 308
　—Charity 55
　—and Aristotle 149
　—Mishneh Torah 184, 189
　—Guide 214
　—Last Will and Testament . . . 324–332
Man in Judaism 335–348
Manna 64
Marriage 239–244, 246–254
Marx, K. 234
Mendelssohn 114–116
　—Phaedon 347
Mezuzah 184, 353
Mitzvah-mitzvot 38, 48, 268, 317–318
　—Daily Life 53
　—Godliness 63
　—Joy 130
　—Reward 169
Mohel 64
Montefiore, C. G. 192
Moore, G. F. 341

Morris, N. 307
Musar 9, 121–122

N

Nahmanides 104
Nevelah 67
Neo-Hasidism 106
Neoplatonism 337
Neshamah Yeterah 156
Neumark, Prof. D. 346
Nietzsche, F. 21
Nirvana 24
Noahide Laws 47, 217

O

Omer 69
Onkelos 45, 220
Original Sin 20, 158
Original Virtue 20
Osiris 346

P

Parents as Teachers 310–314
Pascal, B. 347
Peah 212
Pesikta 174
Pharisees—and Heathens 223
    —and Sadducees 338
Philo 83–85, 338
Pilpul 125
Plato . . . 27, 84, 85, 95, 148, 337, 338, 347
    —Phaedo 321
Plutarch 252
Polygamy 241

Prayer 268–275
Proselytes 214–224

R

Rahmana 62
Raisin, J. S. 323
Rashi 52
Renan 44
Repentance, *see* Teshuvah
Reward and Punishment 172–173
Rokeah 14, 98–101
Roth, L. 135
Ruah Ha'kodesh 148

S

St. Francis of Assisi 34
St. Jerome 34
Saadiah 86
Samuel, Lord H. 355
Sanhedrin 181, 287
Schechter, Prof. S. 58, 110, 147, 340
Schopenhauer 21
Sha'atnez 66
Shaddai 152
Shakespeare 274
Shechinah 8, 148, 217, 257, 264, 304
Shehitah 64, 180, 295, 354
Shema 8, 294
Sheva Berachot 254
Shohat 64
Shivah 151, 201
Shylock 274
Sifra 66
Sifre 67
Silverstone, Rabbi A. E. 220

Simon (Sir), L. 137
Singer, S. 16, 275
Siphre Emet 45
Sisyphus 355
Slander 281–282
Slave, in Judaism 77, 231
Snell, H. (Lord) 356
Social Justice 54
Socialism and Judaism 234–236
Socrates 252
Sotah 183
Spinoza Baruch 35, 112
Study 301–306, 319–323
Suicide 288
Swedenborg, E. von 347

T

Taharat Ha'mishpacha 237
Takkanot 242
Tallit 147
Tanhuma 63, 263
Ten Commandments 32, 177
   —Belief and Action 18
   —Labour 52
   —Honour to Parents 238, 310
   —Sabbath 310, 364
Tephillah Betzibbur 272
Tephillin 64, 147, 184, 195, 237
Tertullian 253
Terumah 205
Teshuvah 298–300
Theucydides 247
Tikkun Ha'olam 327
Tolstoy, Leo 332–334
Trefah 79
Truth (Emet) 45, 265–268
Tsaddikim 106

Tsedakah 21, 54, 204–214
   —Justice 263
Tsitsit 237

V

Vidui 299
Vulgate 34

W

Weiss, H. 185
Wilna, Gaon of 104, 109, 150
   —Ethical Will 150
Woman 237–254

X

Xenophon 252

Y

Yahrzeit 201
Yalkut 308
Yashar, M. M. 132
Yetzer Ha'ra 188, 298
Yetzer Tov 300
Yir'at Ha'shem 188
Yizkor 201
Yovel, see Jubilee Year

Z

Zarathustra 25
Zohar 101, 103
Zunz, L. 99, 136